Barrio Ballots

Barrio Ballots

Latino Politics
in the 1990 Elections

EDITED BY
Rodolfo O. de la Garza,
Martha Menchaca,
and Louis DeSipio

WITH A FOREWORD BY
Sidney Verba

Westview Press
BOULDER • SAN FRANCISCO • OXFORD

Copyright © 1994 by Westview Press, Inc.

Published in 1994 in the United States of America by Westview Press, Inc., 5500 Central Avenue, Boulder, Colorado 80301-2877, and in the United Kingdom by Westview Press, 36 Lonsdale Road, Summertown, Oxford OX2 7EW

Library of Congress Cataloging-in-Publication Data
Barrio ballots : Latino politics in the 1990 elections / edited by
    Rodolfo O. de la Garza, Martha Menchaca, and Louis DeSipio.
        p. cm.
    Includes bibliographical references and index.
    ISBN 0-8133-8573-3
    1. Hispanic Americans—Politics and government. 2. United States—
Politics and government—1989–1993. 3. Elections—United States—
History—20th century. I. De la Garza, Rodolfo O. II. Menchaca,
Martha. III. DeSipio, Louis.
E184.S75B37 1994
323.1'168—dc20   93-29239
                                                                         CIP

Printed and bound in the United States of America

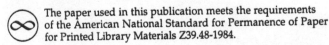
10   9   8   7   6   5   4   3   2

To La Raza Unida and the Young Lords
They Helped Democratize America

Contents

Tables

Foreword

A major natural experiment has been taking place in the United States in recent decades. New waves of immigration have brought in large populations and thrown them, usually with little preparation, into American life. In the classic agricultural experiment, one holds everything constant—for instance, the soil, the weather, the water, the fertilizer—and varies one thing, such as the seeds. The constant in this case is American society; the seeds are the immigrants coming from different cultures. The situation cries out for comparative study of the different immigrant groups. And for the political scientist the natural subject matter is the incorporation of these groups into American political and civic life.

The American polity has traditionally been fairly open to new groups coming from other countries. A competitive electoral system provides a major incentive for political elites to convert immigrants into voters and, hence, into constituents. Indeed, throughout much of American history, the major legal and quasi-legal barriers to political participation have been raised against African Americans, not against the foreign-born. This openness has not applied to Latinos, either, whether immigrants or U.S.-born. In many places, particularly in the Southwest, various barriers, including linguistic ones, have in the past kept Latinos out of the voting booth and out of politics more generally. But since the voting rights acts of the 1960s and the 1970s, these barriers to African Americans and to Latinos have fallen as well.

New immigrants to the United States face no insurmountable legal impediments to joining the political system—to becoming citizens, to becoming voters, and to going beyond voting to become participants in the political process in all the myriad ways in which citizens take part. And whatever legal difficulties there are in becoming a citizen or joining the ranks of the electorate, they are difficulties placed with relative equality before all groups.

But the absence of legal barriers to full political participation is just the beginning of the story. The other factors that enhance or impede civic involvement make the story much richer and the experiment much more interesting. To become a participant one needs resources, one needs motivation, and one needs to be connected to networks that give access to the political process. Immigrants come to America with differing economic resources, and differing levels of linguistic and civic skills. They also come with a different understanding of and commitment to democratic norms. They bring different networks with them. And once here, they are exposed to new resource development opportunities through the economy and through education as well as to new group interests and group norms. In addition—and of crucial importance—they find a political process more or less open and welcoming, depending on the political and social conditions of the places where they settle.

The natural experiment cries out for close social science study. How do different groups fare? And what makes some do better than others? The Latino National Political Survey (LNPS) and the associated Latino Political Ethnography Project (LPEP), the latter the subject of this book, represent a major attempt to answer these questions for three Latino groups: those of Cuban, Mexican, and Puerto Rican origin.

Of course, the real world never delivers to us neat experiments. We do not have different seeds placed in the same soil and treated the same way so that we can isolate the effects of the nature of the seeds from all else. Indeed, a close look at Latinos in American politics makes clear how complex is the experiment. The three groups differ in their place of origin, which might form the basis for our experimental comparison of the three kinds of seeds being planted in American political soil; however, the three groups differ in many and complex ways. One is class: Cubans are more likely to be middle class in origin than are Puerto Ricans or Mexican Americans. Another is citizenship: Puerto Ricans have the advantage here. And one of the most important differences based on place of origin is the relationship of the group in America to the homeland. Cuban American politics is dominated by the considerations of the homeland in a way not evident in the other two groups.

The three groups differ from each other, but that does not mean that they are homogeneous internally. Occupation, educational attainment, length of residence in the United States, and English capability all divide each of the three Latino groups, just as they divide most other population groups. Thus, we plant a complex set of experimental seeds.

In addition, our varied experimental seeds are not all planted in the same soil: Los Angeles is not Chicago, Miami not New York, and Houston something else again. The nature of the preexisting political system and how it responds to the new groups are important. As the various ethnographies show, the nature of the party system and the system of elections has a significant effect on the way in which Latinos enter into and act within the political process. The variety of settings, from the decaying but still significant Chicago machine to the highly decentralized politics of New York, structures the issues facing the Latino community as well as the opportunities to become politically active that are open to them.

The Latino National Political Survey and the Latino Political Ethnography Project thus faced a task as formidable as it was important. How does one approach such a topic? The controlled experiment provides a useful logic, not because we can come even close to approximating it, but because it tells us how we might begin designing research to provide reliable and valid description and explanation. The notion of an experiment suggests that we ought to make careful comparisons and that they ought to be systematic. The two projects did this, one in the framework of a national sample survey and the other in the framework of parallel ethnographies across five Latino communities. The combination allows one to grapple in a reasonable manner with the analysis of the complex social experiment going on in America.

Surveys are the optimal approach for characterizing populations in a systematic way. No other technique allows us to describe the social characteristics, the behavior, and the attitudes of large populations so accurately and reliably while allowing us to try to explain the relationship among characteristics, attitudes, and behaviors. Surveys tell us a good deal about the central tendencies of groups, but they also enable us to deal with the variations within populations. Thus the LNPS allows multivariate comparison among the three Latino groups by focusing on place of origin as well as distinctions of class, culture, and language ability that cut across the groups. It also allows a focus on such crucial variables as length of time in the United States. The study does not focus on immigrants but on Latinos, a focus that tells us more about the role of Latino ethnicity and immigration than could a study with a narrower scope.

Surveys are strong on providing reliable descriptive estimates of group characteristics and reliable estimates of causal connections, but they are often weak in validity. We can only ask standard questions; we are never certain that we are getting to the heart of the matter about what politics really means to people and how the political world appears from the perspective of citizens rooted in their community. Nor can surveys—at least not with the finite resources available to researchers—deal effectively with context. Political involvement depends on the characteristics of individuals, but it also depends on the opportunities afforded to them in their local communities.

This is where the Ethnography Project, reported in this volume, comes in. These studies provide a close look at particular locations at particular times (during the election campaigns of 1990). These studies observe political activity up close and in context, activity that responds to stimuli and opportunities provided in the community. Often what they observe is the lack of activity. In a survey study, the explanation of inactivity would be found in the characteristics of the individuals. Here one can see the effect of political neglect on the part of the larger political system.

Almost all social scientists interested in systematic empirical work have been faced with the dilemma: surveys versus ethnographies. Most of us, faced with such a choice, have said we really ought to do both—if only there were world enough and time (and also money)—and have then gone off to pursue one of these approaches. These studies have done it both ways. In so doing, they have provided a model of multimethod social research. And they have illuminated, as other studies cannot, some important developments in American politics.

Sidney Verba
Cambridge, Massachusetts

Acknowledgments

We would like to thank the Latino Political Ethnography Project's advisory board for assistance in developing the research questions that guided the research. The board consisted of Robert Brischetto, Southwest Voter Research Institute; Thomas Cavanagh, Yale University; Angelo Falcón, the Institute for Puerto Rican Policy; Douglas Massey, the University of Chicago; Henry Selby, the University of Texas at Austin; Carole Uhlaner, the University of California at Irvine; and Sidney Verba, Harvard University.

We would also like to express our appreciation to several individuals and institutions who helped publicize the study's findings. In New York, the Centro de Estudios Puertorriqueños and the Institute for Puerto Rican Policy hosted a symposium on the project coordinated by Ana Lobiondo. In Chicago, the Latino Institute hosted a similar forum. The Institute's Rob Paral served as Chicago coordinator. The University of Houston's Center for Mexican American Studies hosted a symposium organized by the Center's deputy director, Lorenzo Cano. Bernice García and Fernando Guerra of Loyola Marymount University coordinated a forum to report on the Los Angeles findings. Finally, in Miami, Florida International University's Cuban Research Institute hosted a meeting on the Project's findings. Linda Salup coordinated the event and offered excellent assistance under a tight deadline.

Finally, we would like to acknowledge the support of the Ford Foundation and the Project's program officer, Dr. William A. Díaz, for both financial support and continued interest in enhancing our understanding of the dynamics of Latino political activity.

Rodolfo O. de la Garza
Martha Menchaca
Louis DeSipio

1

Overview: The Link Between Individuals and Electoral Institutions in Five Latino Neighborhoods

Rodolfo O. de la Garza and Louis DeSipio

As Latinos[1] have become an increasingly significant segment of the nation's population during the past two decades, scholars and political analysts have steadily increased their expectations for the role Latinos will play in the nation's political life. To date, however, this attention has only begun to generate research that significantly advances our understanding of Latino political participation. This volume reports on the findings of the Latino Political Ethnography Project, one of two interrelated studies intended to contribute to this developing corpus of information.

The LPEP examined political activities in the key Latino barrio of five of the nation's principal cities during the 1990 elections: El Barrio of New York; Magnolia of Houston; Chicago's Pilsen; Boyle Heights in Los Angeles; and Calle Ocho in Miami. We selected these sites because they are the most established barrios in these cities and are at the core of the cities' Latino communities. The project used ethnographic methods to assess grass-roots political participation in conventional electoral politics. The results of these case studies complement the findings of the Latino National Political Survey, the first nationally representative survey of Mexican, Puerto Rican, and Cuban political values, attitudes, and behaviors.

This chapter begins by suggesting how the results of the LPEP and the LNPS will contribute to the existing literature on Latino political participation. Then it offers an overview of the political environments of the five cities included in the LPEP and some baseline data from the LNPS regarding electoral and community participation and policy concerns of Latinos in these cities. Finally, we synthesize the findings from the five sites and analyze the interaction between the Latino community and the electoral process.

Review of the Literature

The contemporary literature on Latino political life suffers from several major shortcomings.[2] It is disproportionately about Mexicans and has little to say about the Cubans, Puerto Ricans, or other Hispanic national-origin groups.[3] There are no comparative studies of the several Latino populations that explicitly examine political values, attitudes, and behaviors and that focus on more than one site. Virtually without exception, existing studies focus on one city or state, or on one national-origin population, or on numerous national-origin populations that are grouped under a generic label such as Hispanic (García, de la Garza, and Torres 1985; García et al. 1992).

The last type of study confuses rather than clarifies our understanding because of the characteristics that distinguish the national-origin groups thus subsumed (Bean and Tienda 1987; de la Garza, Fraga, and Pachon 1988; Pachon and DeSipio 1988; Fuchs 1990). This approach fails to assess differences in political culture associated with distinct socialization experiences within the United States and the countries of origin and neglects the link between those differences and political behavior.

Until the development of the LNPS, there were no national data sets like those for the general or African American populations that provide reliable baselines from which to begin analyses. Thus, it has been impossible confidently to answer questions about changes in the rates of Latino electoral participation, partisanship, or any other aspect of Latino political life (de la Garza 1986; García, García, Falcón, and de la Garza 1989; Uhlaner, Cain, and Kiewiet 1989).

Another void in the literature is analyses that incorporate the unique factors that might affect Latino political involvement. There is only a fledgling analytical literature on the significance of "culture" (or ethnicity) to Latino political attitudes and behaviors (Nelson 1979; Polinard, Wrinkle, and de la Garza 1984; de la Garza and Weaver 1985), and it suffers from the limitations previously noted. By contrast, the salience of race and ideology in explaining black political behavior has been well established (Verba and Nie 1972; Gurin, Hatchett, and Jackson 1989; Jackson 1991). Until recently, scholarship on Latino politics has also neglected the impact that high levels of noncitizenship have on Latino political participation (Pachon 1991; de la Garza and DeSipio 1992; de la Garza and DeSipio 1993).

There is a similar paucity of literature on the effects of ethnicity on routine Latino electoral mobilization, for example, during the regularly held elections that are the foundation of the nation's political life. There are virtually no studies documenting the effects on Latinos of voter registration drives, of grass-roots responses to appeals for support by Latino and non-Latino candidates, of the correspondence between the issues that are salient to Latinos and those discussed by the candidates, or of the relative saliency of local, state, or national elections to the Hispanic electorate.

The literature that begins to address these questions concerns the effects of electoral arrangements on Latino (almost exclusively Mexican American) representation (Browning, Marshall, and Tabb 1984; LBJ School 1984; Fleischmann and Stein 1987; MacManus and Bullock 1987; Welch 1989; Bullock and MacManus 1990; Avila 1990; Middleton 1991). Except for Browning, Marshall, and Tabb's work, however, these are aggregate data analyses lacking contextual information. That is, they do not inform us about the processes and activities associated with electoral participation and, therefore, provide a useful but limited insight into Latino political life.

The Latino National Political Survey begins to address some of these gaps. It provides individual-level baseline data regarding almost every major dimension of individual political involvement and ideological orientation for the Mexican- , Puerto Rican- , and Cuban-origin populations of the nation (de la Garza et al. 1992). The LNPS also allows analysis of the relative impact that socioeconomic and ethnic variables have on political values, attitudes, and behaviors.

Despite this richness, the LNPS cannot capture a community's dynamics. The LNPS documents how Latinos view and act in the political world, but it cannot provide the context within which those attitudes and behaviors become manifest, nor can it indicate what factors in that environment have the greatest impact on the individual. The LNPS will report how many and what types of individuals participate in distinct political and electoral activities. It cannot, though, identify the kinds of opportunities that are available to individuals during a campaign, nor how they respond to these opportunities.

These are the kinds of questions that the LPEP attempts to answer. The research teams observed the extent to which candidates and campaigns reached out to Latinos during the 1990 elections. They assessed the extent to which campaigns sought to mobilize Latinos, the themes and strategies candidates used when they tried to mobilize voters, and whether these differed between Latino and non-Latino candidates. The LPEP also sought to determine whether the issues

that were salient to Latinos in the several barrios matched the issues
that were salient to the campaign.

Together, then, the LNPS and the LPEP add substantially to our understanding of Latino political participation. Overall, we found the
LPEP's ethnographic descriptions of attitudes and behaviors of barrio
residents to be compatible with LNPS survey findings. As an added
benefit, the local case studies provide a rich context for those attitudes
and analyze whether barrio residents consider elections to be opportunities for acting on those concerns. By examining the efforts of parties
and candidates to penetrate the barrio in search of voters, the case
studies describe the extent to which elections constitute meaningful occasions for electoral participation. Integrating the results of the two
studies therefore helps us answer the question: Is Latino political participation a function of individual attributes, group characteristics, or
institutional practices and environmental characteristics?

The Political Environments of
New York, Chicago, Miami, Houston, and Los Angeles

As we will show, the interactions between communities and campaigns varied widely from barrio to barrio. Some of this variation is
due to the diverse political opportunities offered by the electoral environments in each of the cities and states under study—cities whose
politics are as different as their weather. We can only briefly discuss
the political and electoral environments of the five sites and can make
no conclusive remarks about how these environments affect Latinos in
the respective sites. Yet, it is important to keep these factors in mind
when analyzing the summaries presented in this chapter and the more
detailed project site reports in the next section.

With the possible exception of Chicago, all of these cities have
experienced the effects of seven major structural changes that the
American political system is undergoing:[4]

1. The decline of political parties and, at the community level,
   local partisan ethnic clubs or organizations;
2. The decline of partisan competition in many races, which reduces partisan mobilization efforts. The consequences of this
   decline are particularly felt by those less familiar with the
   American electoral system, such as the naturalized immigrant
   and the traditionally marginalized native-born citizen;
3. The rise of candidate-centered campaigns run by consultants independent of the parties;
4. The increase in safe, uncompetitive, and ethnically homogeneous

districts produced by the Voting Rights Act (VRA). These districts usually produce intense competition only when they are initially established or when they become vacant;

5. The increasing reliance on campaign technology that allows candidates to target their message so that it reaches only those registered voters most likely to vote and reduces outreach to communities that have not voted at high rates in the past;

6. The use of direct-democracy ballot strategies such as initiatives, referenda, constitutional amendments, and bond authority. Combined with the increase in the number of elective offices, particularly for ambiguously titled special districts, these measures make the vote increasingly complex; and

7. The increasing diversification of the electorate, accompanied by extending ethnic-specific voting protections such as bilingual electoral information and districting guarantees to traditionally excluded groups such as Asian Americans, Native Americans, and Latinos.

While these changes affect the electorate as a whole, we are convinced that their impact is particularly felt by new electorates, for instance, by naturalized immigrants, and by traditionally marginalized electorates, such as native-born Mexican Americans and Puerto Ricans. Moreover, only the seventh of these enhances minority participation. This positive effect is surely overwhelmed by the dampening impact on electoral participation of the other six, which together may account for much of the decline in electoral turnout the nation has experienced in recent decades. Furthermore, except as noted in the overviews of the political environments of the five cities and states under study, these seven conditions apply in each of our sites.

New York

New York's Puerto Ricans have not enjoyed the political success of the city's European ethnics. Instead, they have been politically marginalized in local and state politics. Historically and with a few notable exceptions, Puerto Ricans prior to the 1960s did not engage in New York politics. In part this is because Spanish-dominant Puerto Ricans were disenfranchised by New York's English literacy requirement (*Torres v. Sachs* 1974; Santiago 1984). Many Puerto Ricans were also born in Puerto Rico and thus were more interested in Puerto Rican issues than in New York ones. Moreover, representatives of the Commonwealth of Puerto Rico in New York successfully endeavored to prolong this orientation (Jennings 1977).

Puerto Ricans shifted their focus to New York in the 1970s, when the English literacy requirement was declared unconstitutional and community leaders began directing their demands to city and state officials (Baver 1984). By then, however, the Democratic party, with which most Puerto Ricans identify, was no longer a viable vehicle for mobilizing voters or communities (Arian et al. 1990: chapter 1).

Another factor contributing to Puerto Rican political marginalization is the highly decentralized character of New York City politics. The mayor is strong relative to the city council, yet much of the power that traditionally rests with mayors is held by other bodies in New York. Throughout the city's history, the mayor's role has been balanced by that of the presidents of New York's five boroughs. Until 1989, one body—the Board of Estimate—attempted to unite the diverse interests of the mayor, the city council, and the borough leaders. After the board was found unconstitutional for giving boroughs with unequal populations equal footing, the newest city charter increased the powers and the size of the city council. It is too early to evaluate the success of this restructuring (Viteritti 1990).

In addition to the mayor, there are two other major citywide elective offices—comptroller and president of the city council. The mayor is also constrained by the Municipal Assistance Corporation, a nonelective body established to supervise New York's finances after the collapse of the mid-1970s. Finally, the state legislature often intervenes in city matters. Hence, successful mayors must build coalitions to govern.

The power of other principal municipal offices is also highly decentralized. Thirty-two community-school districts jointly govern the public school system with a centralized administrative bureaucracy. The boards have authority over curriculum, staff, maintenance, repairs, and food services. While some boards have implemented innovative and successful education programs, others are used for political advancement and patronage opportunities. None have been able successfully to challenge the power of the Central Board of Education.

Governmental responsibility is also decentralized through fifty-nine appointed community boards and thirty-four appointed public authorities. These authorities, such as the Port Authority of New York and New Jersey and the Triborough Bridge and Tunnel Authority, are also appointed. Each board, however, has different rules for appointment of members (Rogers 1990; Walsh 1990). Further weakening the mayor has been the decline of the New York Democratic party and the city's old political machine.

With so many decision points, it is essential to be a part of the city's governing coalition in order to effect major policies. This requires control over resources that have citywide impact. Language-based disenfranchisement, geographical concentration, poverty, and the historical focus on Puerto Rico combined with the absence of a party or machine to overcome these obstacles have resulted in Puerto Ricans' inability to develop the necessary resources to become part of the city's governing coalition.

Non-Puerto Rican candidates have on occasion included Puerto Ricans and other Latinos as part of their winning coalitions. Still, there is no regular pattern at either the city or the state level of incorporating Latinos into winning electoral strategies.

Nonetheless, Puerto Ricans have opportunities that many other Latinos do not have. Regardless of whether they are born in Puerto Rico or New York, Puerto Ricans are U.S. citizens by birth. Hence, they can vote in any New York election after just thirty days of residence. Latino immigrants, on the other hand, must wait three to five years to naturalize before they may vote, and many wait much longer. Second, as Democrats, Puerto Ricans are members of the majority party within the city and in the state assembly. This allows the possibility for Puerto Ricans to attain citywide office or leadership roles in the state assembly. Yet, in recent years, Puerto Ricans have been distant from the ruling Koch coalition in New York's Democratic party. So, in races for citywide office, they usually run as outsiders (Wade 1990: 292; Arian et al. 1990). Indeed, Herman Badillo's unsuccessful mayoral campaign in 1973 is the only instance of a Puerto Rican running a competitive race for any of the city's principal offices.

Finally, New York is a competitive state during statewide and presidential elections. For Democrats to carry the state in close races, they must receive the majority of the Puerto Rican vote.[5]

Houston

Despite rapid urbanization, Texas politics often manifests a small-town quality. In part this may be because of the design of governmental institutions. In 1987, Texas had 254 counties, 1,156 municipalities, 1,111 school districts, and 1,891 special districts (Kraemer and Newell 1992: 52). This gives it the third-highest number of governments and elected officials, behind Illinois and Pennsylvania (U.S. Bureau of the Census [hereafter Census] 1990). It has the most school board members in the country, the second-highest number of members of county councils, and the third-highest number of elected members of boards of special districts.

Mexican Americans, who are 91 percent of the state's Latinos, are increasingly being elected to these posts in Texas. In 1991, they held 1,969 elective offices across the state (NALEO Educational Fund [hereafter NALEO] 1992). Although this represents just 7.3 percent of all elective offices in Texas,[6] the number of Texas Latino officeholders has grown by approximately 14 percent per year for the past eighteen years. While concentrated in municipal, county, and school board offices, Latinos also constitute a significant share of the state legislature. In 1990, 5 of the 31 senators and 20 of the 150 representatives were Mexican American. In 1990, the state also elected Dan Morales as attorney general, making him the first Mexican American elected to a nonjudicial statewide office. In 1991, Governor Ann Richards appointed state representative Lena Guerrero to the Texas Railroad Commission (Rodríguez 1991), making her the first Mexican American to serve on what has been characterized as one of the nation's most powerful regulatory agencies (Prindle 1981).[7]

Unlike the other states in this study, Texas has moved closer to active two-party competition in recent decades. This has generated battles among Democrats for ideological control of the party. Although this struggle continues, the progressive faction is currently in control, and it actively solicits Mexican American support and is responsive, albeit grudgingly, to their demands (Davidson 1990).

Texas's Republican party has only recently begun courting Mexican American support, and its efforts suggest a schizophrenic interest in this community. In 1986, it ran Roy Barrera, a Mexican American, for attorney general, a year when a former Republican governor sought reelection in a bitterly contested race. When it appeared that Mr. Barrera's candidacy might mobilize Mexican American voters, who would vote for him *and* the Democratic slate, the party appears to have denied him access to its resources. Mr. Barrera lost in a surprisingly close race while the Republican governor won. In 1990, Clayton Williams, the unsuccessful Republican gubernatorial candidate, emphasized his knowledge of Spanish and familiarity with Mexican ranch culture in the hope that this would generate Mexican support. Despite this personal outreach to Mexican American voters by candidate Williams, Republican state legislators introduced legislation to have English declared the official state language, a position strongly opposed by Mexican Americans.

The active and unfettered role Mexican Americans now play in Texas politics is a relatively recent phenomenon (de la Garza and DeSipio 1993). While some areas in South Texas have historically allowed Mexican Americans to vote, their vote was usually controlled by Anglo landowners (Anders 1982). In other regions, the vote was often denied to Mexican Americans. The urban Mexican American vote was controlled and delivered to the highest bidder. In cities without a large enough Mexican American vote to auction, districting strategies were devised to reduce the effectiveness of the Mexican American vote. Until the early 1970s, Houston fell into this final category. As we have suggested, this older system has been replaced by an unde-terred and even sought-after Mexican American vote (de la Garza 1992; Morris 1992).

The political environment in Houston continues to show vestiges of the older system. Just one of the city's fourteen city council members is Mexican American, and he attained his post during the 1980s thanks to redistricting (Kaplan 1983). Current efforts to rearrange the council to create a Latino second seat are stymied. Only recently has one of the county judgeships gone to a Latino. While two other large Texas cities (San Antonio and El Paso) have elected Mexican Americans as mayor, Houston has elected only one Mexican American to a citywide office (comptroller), and that was in the early 1970s.

Even the creation of seats with a strong likelihood of electing a Latino offers no guarantee of success. In 1992, the Texas legislature created two seats in greater Houston to represent areas with large con-centrations of Latinos—one for the Texas Senate and one for Congress. The congressional seat represents an area that is 60 percent Latino, but just 35 percent of the registered voters are Hispanic. Despite the dis-trict's elaborate design, looking, according to one pundit, like a "scared Mayan bird," it failed to elect a Latino in the 1992 Democratic primary (Burka 1992). The Texas Senate district, larger than the U.S. congressional district and slightly lower in percentage Latino, also failed to elect a Latino (Rodríguez 1992).

Thus, Mexican Americans in Texas are responding to many new electoral opportunities. The formal barriers to participation no longer exist. To the contrary, Texas now has one of the most voter-friendly registration and voting systems in the nation. Combined with VRA-created districts, these openings are a major reason why Mexican Americans are succeeding at electing co-ethnics to local and state of-fices. Yet, Mexican Americans continue to maintain low levels of electoral participation. The politics of Houston offers an insight into this dynamic.

Chicago

Politics in Chicago has avoided the candidate-driven campaigns and partisan dealignment that characterize the four other cities. Instead, shifting alliances with the "machine" shape most Chicago campaigns, candidates, and electorates. The city has few elections and, depending on the strength of the machine, they are often not contested. District-based elected officials include aldermen (members of the city council), state representatives and senators, and a party official—the committee person—who may be the most powerful of the four.[8] While Democrats control most of the wards, factional disputes have divided Chicago Democrats since Hispanics have become active players in Chicago politics.[9]

Chicago's Hispanics achieved political recognition with the redistricting that followed the 1980 census. The initial efforts at redistricting by the remnants of the Daley machine sought to continue the disenfranchisement of Chicago's Latinos. "Pilsen and Little Village Mexican communities on the Near Southwest side were split among four wards. West Town, Humboldt Park and Logan Square, predominantly Puerto Rican neighborhoods on the Near Northwest Side, were split into six wards" (Fremon 1988: 9). These gerrymandering efforts gave way to judicial intervention, which succeeded in creating four aldermanic districts likely to elect Latinos (*Ketchum v. Byrne* 1984).

Ethnicity and machine politics combined to determine the results of the 1986 aldermanic election, the first after redistricting. The four successful candidates were all Latino. Alliances with the two factions of the Democratic party also shaped these races, however, and brought added attention to the Latino districts. Two of the Latino aldermen were ultimately allied with Mayor Washington and two were allied with the opposition. For Mayor Washington to have a veto-proof majority, however, he had to carry one Latino district that was rated a toss-up. In a runoff, the Washington-allied Latino won, making Latinos a crucial component of the governing bloc.

The four Latino aldermen presented a united front in the struggle to succeed Mayor Washington after his death; however, they all sided with the losing candidate. Perhaps more interesting, in the initial confusion after Mayor Washington's demise, one of the Latino aldermen was briefly discussed as a possible interim mayor.

State races in Illinois more closely follow the models of other states under study. They are centered more around candidates than parties or the machine and they rely more extensively on campaign technology and media campaigns than on the traditional get-out-the-vote efforts of local races in Chicago. Depending on the level of factionalism in the Chicago Democratic party, the city vote can, but does not always, help the statewide ticket.

Although there was no pattern of statewide campaign outreach to Chicago's Latinos evident prior to 1990, the Republican candidate for governor in 1990 did target some advertising toward Latinos. It is interesting that this outreach was sensitive to differences between Puerto Ricans and Mexican Americans.

Unlike many states, Illinois is competitive in presidential races. Since either party can carry the state in the electoral college, Illinois is not dismissed by either party in national campaigns (Fraga 1992).

Thus, while the machine has decayed in Chicago since the death of the first Mayor Daley, the intensity of machine politics has remained stable. At the local level, Latinos have not always been unified and, when they have been, they have been on the losing side. Nonetheless, the vestigial power of the machine, the recognition of ethnically driven political coalitions, and the competitiveness of statewide elections offer opportunities for Chicago's Latinos to play an electorally decisive role that is unavailable to Latinos in the other sites. As they increasingly are recognized as one of the politically significant blocs in Chicago's ethnic mosaic, they will have the opportunity to play Chicago's politics. They may well lose, as they did on the death of Mayor Washington, yet, they also have the opportunity to win; winning opportunities were denied to Chicago's Latinos prior to 1985.

Los Angeles

At the beginning of this section, we highlighted a series of factors that discourage the political mobilization of new electorates and more marginalized electorates. California is a leader in each category and adds more. Both parties are in decay. Nonpartisanship is mandated in all but statewide and legislative races. Although they are partisan, statewide and legislative races are centered around candidates, driven by money, run by consultants, and dominated by technology. The majority of Latino-held seats are noncompetitive. California not only is racially and ethnically diverse, but also is characterized by intrastate regionalism and urban divisions. The state's electorate also experiences constant change because of the continuous addition of new migrants from across the nation.

The state's political rules further complicate its electoral life. Both the primary and the general election ballots for statewide races contain initiatives and referenda on an increasing variety of subjects (more than 475 between 1879 and 1990). On occasion, there have been several referenda addressing the same topic on the same ballot. Sometimes measures are added to the ballot for the sole purpose of mobilizing a specific electorate that otherwise might not turn out in the hope that it will vote a certain way on the other issues and candidates on the ballot. The campaigns for many of these measures are often organized by professional consulting firms and may only tangentially protect the public sentiment that such initiatives and referenda were designed to guarantee.

While these forms of direct democracy formally offer citizen input into governance, the structure of governments in California serves to reduce democratic control. The state boasts 58 counties, 435 incorporated cities, and over 6,000 special districts. Counties and cities often have overlapping jurisdictions. Los Angeles County, where the majority of California's Latinos reside, has a similarly complex system of government, with 86 municipalities, 95 school districts, and 275 special districts.

Mexican Americans, who make up 80 percent of the state's Latinos, have not had a major role in governing California. Although several served in the state's first constitutional convention and one served as governor in the 1870s, none have held statewide office in the twentieth century. Most of the major "firsts" for Mexican American office-holding have occurred in the last decade. The major exception is Edward Roybal, who served on the Los Angeles city council from 1949 to 1962. Roybal's first two efforts to move to higher office, to lieutenant governor in 1954 and to Los Angeles County Board of Supervisors in 1958, failed. In the redistricting that followed the 1960 census, however, he was able to win a seat to the U.S. Congress. No Mexican American again served on the Los Angeles city council until 1985 (Guerra 1991). The first Mexican American in the twentieth century to serve on the Los Angeles county council was not elected until 1991, after the Justice Department intervened under the Voting Rights Act to create a majority Hispanic district. Similarly, to be elected to the state Assembly and Senate, the most common path for Latinos is to run for open majority-Latino seats created through redistricting.[10]

The pattern that appears in each of these levels of elective office is that Latinos are usually elected only by Latinos. Bruce Cain sees that pattern among African Americans as well. He notes, "California's minority candidates can expect little help from the state party organization and relatively high levels of voter disloyalty from the white Democratic party identifiers" (1991: 20).

Thus, while Mexican Americans and other Latinos have won three congressional seats, seven legislative seats, and over six hundred local offices in California, the political system of the state and in Los Angeles is not welcoming to Latinos.

Miami

The political environments of Miami and Florida offered a ripe opportunity for the post-1959 Cuban immigrants to influence the political process. The Cubans seized it.

From the end of the Civil War through the early 1960s, Florida remained solidly Democratic in presidential voting.[11] In terms of party affiliation, it remains solidly Democratic today (Craig 1991: 89). Like the South in general, however, Florida's one-party rule has been characterized by a weak and highly factionalized Democratic party that was unprepared to adapt to the challenge posed by the large post-World War II migration from other states (Key 1949). Initially, many of these migrants were Democrats, but over time more independents and Republicans joined the ranks of new Floridians. Nonetheless, Democrats remained dominant in the 1960s, when large-scale Cuban immigration to South Florida began. Democratic party leaders may therefore have assumed Cubans would follow the path of other newcomers and native Floridians and join their party. This may explain why the party did little to incorporate Cubans. The assumption proved true for a time; as late as 1978, Dade County Cubans were more likely to favor Democrats over Republicans by a margin of 50 to 39 percent (DeCew 1980).

Beginning in the mid-1960s, however, national political and ideological considerations began the steady move of Cubans to the Republican party. The single-most-important event in this shift was the Kennedy administration's refusal to provide U.S. military support to the Bay of Pigs invasion forces. Given Kennedy's verbal support of Miami Cubans' desire to overthrow Fidel Castro, many in the community, particularly exiled leaders who had been active in planning and implementing the invasion, treated Kennedy's refusal as treachery. While the national Republican party could do little to aid Cubans through the 1960s, its strong ideological opposition to communism appealed to many Cubans who felt betrayed.

Although this perceived treachery lost the Democratic party much Cuban support, political opportunity also drew many Cubans to the Republican banner. South Florida had few Republicans in the 1960s. Hence, the Republican party offered Cuban leaders quick opportunities for advancement within the party. As an example of this partisan opportunism, several Cubans initially ran for office as Democrats; after losing in the primaries to other Democrats, they switched to the Republican party and won the same office in the subsequent election.

This combination of ideological compatibility and political opportunity solidified Republican partisanship among Miami Cubans. A

1986 poll found that 79 percent of Miami Cubans identified themselves
as Republicans while just 17 percent considered themselves Democrats.
By contrast, non-Cuban Hispanics, who make up the majority of
Florida's Latinos (Census 1991), are slightly more likely to identify as
Democrats (49 percent) than as Republicans (47 percent) (Craig 1991:
103).

Governmental arrangements in Miami/Dade County also offer
Cubans many opportunities. The county includes a large number of political jurisdictions; the county charter is very specific and does not
create overlapping responsibilities between county and municipal
government. It contains twenty-seven incorporated municipalities, including Miami, each with a city council. The county is governed by a
nine-member council. County government is responsible for a wide
variety of services, including transportation, mass transit, parks and
recreation, and environment, as well as for all services in unincorpo-
rated areas. Education is a county responsibility and is governed by an
elected school board. Municipalities are responsible for fire and police
protection, regulation of taxes, and alcoholic beverage sales.
Municipalities may also exceed county-set zoning standards.

Over the past decade, Miami Cubans have been very successful
within this environment. In 1974, they held fourteen offices in all of
Florida. By 1991, the number had increased to sixty, with forty-seven
in the Miami/Dade County area. Unlike in other states, a high proportion of these are state legislative and congressional seats. Of the
forty-seven Miami/Dade County Cuban elected officials in early 1992,
one was a member of Congress, three were state senators, and seven
were state representatives (NALEO 1992). In part, this success is due to
Miami Cubans, who vote at higher rates than whites or African
Americans (Mohl 1983). Miami appears to be the only city in the
nation where Latinos outvote Anglos.

During the 1980s, a Latino served as Florida's governor. As the
chapter on Miami explains, Governor Martínez was not part of the
post-1959 Cuban migration to the United States. Although he relied on
Cuban support in both his 1986 victory and his 1990 defeat, he is not a
product of Cuban political mobilization in Miami. Indeed, no Cuban
has won or been a serious candidate for statewide office. Republican
statewide candidates must have Cuban support to win office.

Furthermore, the growth rate of Cuban elected officials is not likely
to continue. The opportunities generated by the growth and concentration of the Cuban population in Miami/Dade County have now been
substantially exhausted. Future increases in the area will be incremental and more difficult. Elsewhere in Florida, the Cuban population is
more sparse, making statewide growth equally incremental. Further,

since Cubans are members of Florida's minority party, they will not have the opportunity to elect co-ethnics to statewide office on a regular basis unless they make extensive alliances with other groups in the Florida electorate.

Political Perspectives of Barrio Residents: Insights from the Latino National Political Survey

Prior to reviewing the results of the political ethnography project, we examine data from the Latino National Political Survey. We focus on three questions that relate to the political ethnography project: To what extent do residents of barrios participate in electoral politics? Do they participate in nonelectoral civic and educational activities? What national and city issues concern them?

While these data offer useful insights, we offer two methodological caveats.[12] First, the LNPS respondents we are about to describe do not necessarily reside in the neighborhoods studied in the LPEP. Instead, we report on LNPS respondents who reside in barrios in each of the five Standard Metropolitan Statistical Areas (SMSAs) in which the LPEP sites are located. We define barrios as neighborhoods with 50 percent or more Mexicans, Puerto Ricans, or Cubans. In all of the five sites, the barrios in the SMSA include the project site as well as other majority Latino neighborhoods.

The second limitation on these data is that they are not intended to be representative of each city or of the barrios in those cities. Instead, these data are a subsample of a nationally representative sample. Thus, these data should be seen as suggestive of the perceptions and behaviors of barrio residents. In the case of Miami (n=360) and Los Angeles (n=174), cities where the barrio samples were substantial, however, the barrio respondents described here may be representative of barrio residents in those cities generally.

Electoral, Political, and School Participation in the Five Barrios

To get a snapshot of the level of electoral involvement of barrio residents in 1988, we begin with an examination of voters' partisan preferences and participation in the 1988 presidential election in these five cities (see Table 1.1). The data were gathered in 1989 and 1990.

Although national voter turnout has been declining for decades, the highest rates of voting occur in presidential elections. Voter turnout varies markedly from city to city. Just 13 percent of Los Angeles respondents reported voting. At the other extreme, 61 percent of New

TABLE 1.1 Voting Preferences of the Mexican, Puerto Rican, and Cuban Populations in the Five Project Cities

	NY	CHI	MIA	HOU	LA
Voted					
Dukakis	22	4	8	1	16
	(39.3%)	(10.5%)	(2.2%)	(8.3%)	(9.2%)
Bush	12	10	99	2	6
	(21.4%)	(26.3%)	(27.5%)	(16.7%)	(3.4%)
Another					
candidate	0	1	1	0	0
	(0.0%)	(2.6%)	(0.3%)	(0.0%)	(0.0%)
Eligible, did not vote					
Not registered	14	2	35	2	15
	(25.0%)	(5.3%)	(9.7%)	(16.7%)	(8.6%)
Did not vote '88	7	7	17	2	17
	(12.5%)	(18.4%)	(4.7%)	(16.7%)	(9.8%)
Not eligible					
Not a U.S. citizen	1	14	200	5	120
	(1.7%)	(36.8%)	(55.5%)	(41.7%)	(69.0%)
Sample size	56	38	360	12	174

Source: The Latino National Political Survey.

Notes: These data were collected as part of a nationally representative sample of Mexican-, Puerto Rican-, and Cuban-origin adults in the United States (excluding Puerto Rico). To meet the needs for the national sample, Puerto Rican and Cubans were oversampled relative to Mexican Americans. The sample population for each city was drawn to meet the needs of the national sample. As a result, the data on Chicago (*n* = 38) and Houston (*n* = 12) should be viewed as descriptive and not representative. For a more extensive discussion of the methodology of the LNPS, see de la Garza et al. 1992: Appendix 2.

The data presented here are not solely from the research site for the project on Latinos and the 1990 elections. Instead, they are highly homogeneous neighborhoods (exceeding 50 percent Mexican, Puerto Rican, or Cuban origin). We would hypothesize that, with the exception of the Chicago site, these areas of the LNPS are largely contiguous and similar in political attitudes and behaviors to the research sites. In Chicago, the highly homogeneous areas include the research site as well as the area with high Puerto Rican concentration.

York respondents say they turned out. Non-U.S. citizenship explains much of the nonvoting. More than two-thirds of Los Angeles respondents and half of Miami respondents were not U.S. citizens in 1988.

Political participation extends beyond voting, especially for noncitizens. Therefore, we examine a broad range of possible participatory activities. Table 1.2 indicates that political activities that go beyond voting involve no more than one-quarter of barrio residents. Overall, residents in New York and Chicago tend to be more politically active than do residents in the other three sites.

Respondents were more likely to get involved in education-related activities than in either elections or nonelectoral political activity. Between 38 percent (in Houston) and 87 percent (in New York) of

TABLE 1.2 Civic/Electoral and Educational Participation Among Mexican Americans, Puerto Ricans, and Cubans in the Project Sites

	NY	CHI	MIA	HOU	LA
Civic/Electoral					
Has signed	13	7	33	1	15
a petition	(23.2%)	(18.4%)	(9.2%)	(9.1%)	(8.8%)
Has written	7	2	22	0	9
to press	(12.5%)	(5.3%)	(6.1%)	(0.0%)	(5.3%)
Has attended a	10	8	13	0	10
public meeting	(17.9%)	(21.1%)	(3.6%)	(0.0%)	(5.9%)
Has worn a	10	6	32	1	6
campaign button	(17.9%)	(15.8%)	(8.9%)	(9.1%)	(3.5%)
Has attended	5	4	14	1	6
rallies	(8.9%)	(10.5%)	(3.9%)	(9.1%)	(3.5%)
Has volunteered for a	2	4	7	1	3
political party	(3.6%)	(10.5%)	(1.9%)	(9.1%)	(1.8%)
Has made a political	2	1	12	0	7
contribution	(3.6%)	(2.6%)	(3.3%)	(0.0%)	(4.1%)
Sample size	56	38	360	11	170
Educational[a]					
Has met with	32	15	112	3	79
teacher	(86.5%)	(55.6%)	(64.4%)	(37.5%)	(66.4%)
Has attended	23	11	90	2	59
a PTA meeting	(62.2%)	(40.7%)	(51.7%)	(25.0%)	(49.6%)
Has met with	25	6	77	2	60
principal	(67.6%)	(22.2%)	(44.3%)	(25.0%)	(50.4%)
Has attended a school	10	3	21	0	26
board meeting	(27.0%)	(11.1%)	(12.1%)	(0.0%)	(21.8%)
Has voted in a school	10	4	18	1	16
board election	(27.0%)	(14.8%)	(10.3%)	(12.5%)	(13.4%)
Sample size	37	27	174	8	119

[a]The denominator for educational participation is parents in the high-density neighborhoods in each of these cities.
Source: The Latino National Political Survey.
Notes: See Table 1.1.

parents have met with a teacher. Significant percentages have also attended PTA meetings and met with school principals.

These three gauges of participation indicate that these barrios have low levels of electoral and civic involvement; however, these neighborhoods are not completely detached from civil society. On school issues, people get involved. It is also important to remember the high rates of non-U.S. citizenship in four of these communities. Lack of citizenship serves to exclude participation in electoral activities and can make involvement in nonelectoral political activities even less likely. The overall impact of high rates of noncitizenship is suggested by the fact that New York barrios, made up principally of U.S. citizens of Puerto Rican origin, report higher participation than do barrios elsewhere, where many noncitizens live. This suggests that it is essential that the effects of noncitizenship on Latino political mobilization be kept in mind throughout the discussion of project findings in this chapter and in the site reports that follow.

Issues of Concern in Barrios

Across all sites, respondents identified drugs as the most serious issue facing the nation (see Table 1.3). Respondents also mentioned drugs as the most serious issue facing their cities in four of the five cities. Other issues mentioned as national problems in two or more sites were poverty, gangs, and unemployment. At the city level, gangs, crime, and lack of housing appear on two or more top-five lists.

Thus, the issues concerning barrio residents in these cities have some commonality. Perhaps as important, almost all issues that people mentioned reflect concerns at the neighborhood level. They mentioned only a few issues that could be solved only at the national level (such as immigration and the economy). As we examine the findings from the LPEP, we will examine the degree to which the candidates and the campaigns addressed the residents' concerns.

The Latino Political Ethnography Project

The Latino Political Ethnography Project complements the LNPS and seeks to overcome some weaknesses in the literature on Latino politics. The design of the project sought to minimize the problems that have characterized research on Latino political behaviors, attitudes, and values. It did this in two ways: first, by selecting a broad range of sites; and second, by developing a set of common research questions for each site.

TABLE 1.3   Top Five Issues Facing the Nation and the Respondent's City, by SMSA, 1989

	NY	CHI	MIA	HOU	LA
Top five national issues[a] (Number of respondents)					
1.	Drugs (37)	Drugs (25)	Drugs (201)	Drugs (4)	Drugs (78)
2.	Poverty (7)	Gangs (4)	Unemployment (23)	-	Unemployment (16)
3.	-	-	Crime (12)	-	Poverty (9)
4.	-	-	Communism (11)	-	Homelessness (8)
5.	-	-	Economy (10)	-	Gangs (tie) (5)
					Prejudice (5)
Total respondents	56	37	342	9	163
Top five city issues[a]					
1.	Drugs (31)	Drugs (18)	Drugs (169)	-	Drugs (37)
2	Lack of housing (8)	Gangs (6)	Crime (47)	-	Gangs (34)
3.	-	-	Unemployment (21)	-	Lack of housing (7)
4.	-	-	Immigration (14)	-	Crime (tie) (6)
5.	-	-	Gangs (10)	-	Overdevelopment (6)
Total respondents	54	38	335	8	130

[a]Issues listed only if mentioned by four or more respondents.
Source: The Latino National Political Survey.
Note: See Table 1.1.

The study is comparative in approach. It examines communities with significant Cuban, Puerto Rican, and Mexican American population as well as Latinos from other parts of the Americas. It includes sites in the five cities with the largest Latino populations. These cities include all regions of the country with sizable Latino populations. This dispersion assures that characteristics of Latino electoral and political participation will not be confounded with differences in political culture and political opportunities. Finally, each of the three major Latino populations is represented in an attempt to control for inter-Latino differences.

The design of the project and the cross-site coordination assure that findings may be generalized across the sites. A senior ethnographer or political scientist with experience in the community directed the research at each site. Each site used three to ten undergraduate and graduate students as ethnographers to monitor campaign activities in the community and to interview community residents. The project directors met with each site's principal investigator (PI) to discuss the project before its inception, and one of the project directors visited each site at least twice during the fieldwork period.

To assure further that results could be compared across sites, the project directors, the advisory board, and the PIs developed thirteen research questions that guided each site's research (see Table 1.4). These focused on forms of campaign activity, the importance of these activities to residents, issues of importance to the residents and to the campaigns, and the presence or absence of uniquely Latino issues and mobilization strategies. These questions sought to capture both top-down political mobilization and bottom-up demand making and participation.

Each site used participant observation, elite and mass interviewing, daily community observations, and exit polling to elicit answers to the questions. The period of field study lasted from September 1, 1991, to November 15, 1991. A more complete discussion of the project's methodology can be found in chapter two.

The focus of the study, the 1990 elections, featured competitive races in which the Latino electorate could play a decisive role. Although 1990 was an off-year election, each of the five states under study had a gubernatorial race as well as congressional and legislative races. In three states, the gubernatorial seat was open, suggesting the possibility of a competitive race. Further, 1990 offered the last major elections before redistricting. Party leaders, therefore, had reason to be particularly concerned about winning governorships and maximizing their victories in the state legislature, since these offices would play crucial roles in shaping their prospects for the 1990s (Butler and Cain

TABLE 1.4 LPEP Core Questions

1. What is the level of electoral activity in the neighborhood?
2. Do established neighborhood organizations (churches, clubs, union locals) participate in these activities?
3. Who organizes these activities (activists, recognized neighborhood leaders, "normal" residents, or outsiders)?
4. Who attends activities such as rallies and meetings? What is the level of neighborhood involvement?
5. How salient is the election to the neighborhood in September? In October? On election day?
6. Are the issues discussed in the neighborhood the same ones discussed by the candidates? Does this relationship change between September and November? If so, how?
7. How do candidates attempt to get their message to the neighborhood?
8. Are there specific Latino issues at stake in any of the elections? Any Latino candidates?
9. What significance does the neighborhood have to the elections as a whole?
10. What is the role of the media in the election?
11. Overall, what, if any, message is being sent to Latinos as to why they should be active in the election as Latinos? Are there attempts to mobilize Latinos based on ethnic appeals, class appeals, or issue appeals? Which candidates (parties) use which appeal and when?
12. What role do women and women's issues play in the campaign?
13. How did the campaigns under study end? More than simply who won and who lost, what issues and positions won and lost? How did the Latino community do in the November 1990 elections?

1992: 94). Latinos in general and these communities in particular stood to benefit from the redistricting (de la Garza and DeSipio 1989). Whether they will benefit commensurately with their numbers is in part a function of the level to which they have supported candidates and parties and established debts to be repaid at redistricting time.

Individual-Electoral Linkages in Five Barrios

The LPEP examines two facets of the linkage between individual demand-making and electoral institutions, that is, parties, campaigns, and candidates. We examine what residents of the barrios and community organizations do to make their needs known to these institutions. Second, we examine how these institutions try to reach the residents of the barrios. Chapter two presents an additional analysis of the field data that explores nonelectorally focused political activity in these barrios.

Demographic characteristics that diminish political participation among Latinos and other characteristics such as high rates of noncitizenship, lower incomes, lower rates of formal education, and youth

(Wolfinger and Rosenstone 1980; Pachon and DeSipio 1988) can be overcome in two ways: through community mobilization, or through active outreach by electoral institutions. For example, the contemporary African American community votes at rates disproportionate to its socioeconomic status. The most widely accepted explanation for the black community's ability to transcend class limitations on voting is the legacy of the civil rights movement (Gurin, Hatchett, and Jackson 1989; Jackson 1991). Mexican Americans in New Mexico offer a similar exception. Despite economic disadvantage, they tend to vote at rates comparable to those of non-Hispanic whites (Hain and García 1981: 224). In both of these cases, the primary source for mobilization comes from the groups themselves.

Examples of electoral institutions that mobilize particular communities are harder to find in the contemporary political environment; however, historical examples include machine outreach in the late nineteenth and early twentieth centuries and populist efforts at the state-level around the turn of the century and into the 1920s and the 1930s in California. Machines, it should be noted, not only mobilized and politically educated the poor, but they also helped naturalize immigrants.

How and to what extent did the barrios in our study mobilize? We ask this question because of the recognition that, if left to act individually, barrio residents will vote at the low rates predicted by their class and education. Conversely, if Latinos are to have an impact on the political process, special efforts will have to be made to connect them and their communities to the political process.

The five sites in our study manifest three models of linkage between barrios and electoral institutions. At one extreme, the community is uninterested in electoral politics, distrustful of politicians, and unwilling to engage the political system; the electoral institutions match this disinterest and make little effort to reach out to the barrio. In this model, which appears in the New York field site and to a lesser extent in the Houston site, there is no mobilization. The second model features the community, or at least elements within it, actively trying to use the political system to meet public policy needs, but failing to catch the interest of electoral institutions, which do not respond to barrio-specific interests. This was the case in Los Angeles and Chicago, where electoral institutions did not specifically try to reach out to the barrio in a manner significantly different from the city- and statewide campaign. In these cases, mobilization was generated by barrio initiatives. In the third model, popular interest in the election is high and electoral institutions reach out to the barrio. Of the five sites under study, this pattern appeared only in Miami. By examining the commonalities and differences during the electoral campaigns in these communities, we elaborate on these models in greater detail.

Besides being almost universally Latino in population, the sites share several characteristics that influence political participation as well as political attitudes and behaviors. Each of these communities is poor. Four may be characterized as working-class, and New York's El Barrio as a community in poverty. None of the sites are, however, economically homogeneous. Also, a strip of small businesses, some locally owned, is present in each site.

The barrios are also ethnically heterogeneous. They increasingly include diverse national-origin groups. Mexicans and Dominicans are the newest residents of El Barrio. Central Americans are slowly replacing Cubans in Calle Ocho and Mexican Americans in Boyle Heights. Each site also has a large population of native-born Americans and recent immigrants, and there is division within the recent immigrants between the legal permanent resident and the undocumented immigrant. Each site reports some tension between old and new residents. Except for the Puerto Rican migrants, these new residents are noncitizens and excluded from voting in the elections under study here.

The Campaign from the Perspective of the Barrio

Despite the varying demographic and citizen/resident compositions of these neighborhoods, a series of common policy issues emerge in four of the sites, excluding Miami. The core issues in these four sites—education, housing, drugs/gangs, and the unresponsiveness of government and elected officials—overlap, but are somewhat broader than, the issues identified in the LNPS. Together they may be grouped as an urban poverty agenda. Each barrio also voiced particular concerns reflecting its distinct situation: prisons in East Los Angeles, housing in New York, or redistricting in Chicago and Houston.

Calle Ocho residents articulated a different set of issues. Most important was "Cubanness." Protean and nebulously defined, this issue manifested itself in several ways. It played a key role in a race between a foreign-born and a U.S.-born Cuban American for the same office. The low point in this debate had the American-born candidate's mother going on the radio to say that it was not her son's fault that he had been born in the United States. Business leaders in the Calle Ocho area battled efforts to rename the area the Latin Quarter out of concern that it would devalue the Cuban role in shaping the area. Discussions of candidates related to their Cubanness; in the right circumstances, this attribute could be extended on an honorary basis to non-Cubans whom a Cuban community leader presented as supporting the community's agenda.

Although Cubanness was the driving force in Calle Ocho's electoral activities, residents articulated a series of other issues—poverty, homelessness as it affected Caribbean and Central American immigrants, the needs of the elderly, taxes, transportation and, to a more limited extent, abortion.

These nonethnic issues, however, did not emerge as significant to the conduct of the campaign in Calle Ocho. That candidates did not systematically address these nonethnic issues raises an interesting question that cannot yet be answered. This neglect may represent the beginning of inattention to barrio concerns, which may lead to the alienation from electoral politics that characterizes other communities. Or Calle Ocho residents may trust electoral institutions sufficiently to assume that elected officials will ultimately address these issues.

To examine how the barrios communicate their concerns to electoral institutions, we looked at mass and elite behavior. At the mass level, Miami again proves the exception. While residents of Calle Ocho were active participants in the process, residents of the other four sites were not mobilized and exhibited high levels of apathy and political alienation. The Los Angeles report noted two reasons for this. First, respondents reported being overwhelmed by other responsibilities and not having time to prepare for the vote. Second, many respondents reported that they felt that voting had little impact. Findings from Houston echoed these interpretations. Respondents reported that voting would not accomplish anything. In Chicago, the machine (or the image of the machine) added to the sense of the futility of voting.

In the New York site, there was no evidence of any efforts by either party or by candidates to mobilize voters. Many respondents were not even aware of the election; those who were aware felt that they had few options, since most races were noncompetitive. In view of these findings and given that turnout in presidential elections is always higher than it is in off-year elections, it is not surprising that turnout in 1990 was significantly lower than the pattern of turnout reported in the LNPS for the 1988 presidential election. Although we have no evidence to support this, it is reasonable to assume that there was more party- and candidate-initiated activity in the barrio in 1988. That would explain some of the difference in turnout between 1988 and 1990. The minimal turnout in 1990 in the face of no party- or candidate-driven activities, however, strongly suggests that, left to themselves, barrios in New York will not mobilize to engage the electoral system.

Calle Ocho offers a very different picture. The campaign permeated the community. Three elections (two primaries and the general election) occurred within three months. The Spanish-language radio stations carried ads and talk shows preceding each election. Shop owners and campaigns placed campaign posters throughout the neighborhood. Candidates, from the gubernatorial candidates on down, visited the neighborhood.

The articulation of community interest took a somewhat different form among barrio elites. In Los Angeles, Chicago, and, to a lesser extent, Houston, residents sought solutions to barrio problems through community organizations. In New York, on the other hand, there were lower expectations and higher apathy among neighborhood elites. Miami, again, offered an anomalous pattern.

Each site, including Miami, saw neglect of many community issues by electoral institutions. In three sites, this neglect was, in some ways, compensated for by the existence of community-based organizations of widely varying strength. Although these groups have different structures and focus on different problems in each city, they share a common function: they aggregate community demands and seek to present a common front to governmental officials. A pattern that emerges in four of the five sites (Houston is the exception) is that women from the community created and continue to lead these organizations.

The community organizations differed from site to site. In Boyle Heights, the most important community organization mobilized to prevent the construction of a new prison in East Los Angeles. It expanded its focus, however, to address issues such as health, environmental safety, and the physical environment.

Chicago's political machine shapes the community organization structure in Pilsen. Whether in support or opposition, the community organizations operate in an environment shaped by the machine. In this environment, there is no dominant community organization, and several compete to speak for the community on key issues such as housing, education, drugs, and gangs. These organizations started at least three competing voter registration drives during the 1990 election cycle, none of which were particularly successful. The range of organizations and their constant infighting contributed to some respondents' frustration with the political system and diminished, to some extent, the attention paid to the electoral campaign.

The final site where community organizations attempted to articulate popular needs is Houston. At least in Magnolia, the level and focus of community organizations are qualitatively different from Los Angeles or Chicago. First, their mobilization is much less pronounced. Second, the focus is not only on community issues, but also on voter reg-

istration and turnout. The major organization is a church-based affili-
ate of a Saul Alinsky-type community organization. Its major focus
during the campaign was not issues, but registering and educating
voters. It also coordinated efforts to take voters to meetings and
rallies.

For different reasons, community organizations did not play such an
important role in either Miami or New York. As indicated earlier,
Cuban American politics in Miami revolves around questions of ethnicity. In the 1990 campaign, candidates and campaigns spoke directly to
voters about ethnicity. The electorate seemed to accept this as sufficient. Although foreign policy did not play a role in the 1990 election,
community and elite organizations in Miami embrace foreign policy
issues. Moreover, these organizations invoke ethnicity to express
themselves politically. That is, they make it clear that to be Cuban
means to be anti-Castro *and* anticommunist. Although it did not happen during the period of fieldwork, organizations have formed sponta-
neously in Miami over specific issues, such as the Latin Quarter issue or
enforcement of English-only legislation. To date, however, no ongoing
politically oriented community organization plays a role in Miami
politics.

The absence of community organizations in El Barrio in New York is
not a function of a highly articulated interaction between voters and
candidates, of the form that is evident in Miami. Instead, their
absence underscores a general finding of apathy in both voters and
candidates. The research found that elites within the community saw
a role for themselves, but there was no mass organization. In fact, the
campaign had little salience for the community. People on the street
did not talk about the election and on the day of the primary, many
were unaware an election was being held.

These varying levels of community interest in the campaign and in
the perceived ability of community members to articulate interests,
either directly to candidates or through community organizations,
manifest themselves in differing electoral turnouts. In New York and
Houston, the areas of lowest electoral interest and community-group
mobilization, approximately one-quarter of eligible voters turned
out.[13] In Los Angeles and Chicago, areas with somewhat higher community interest and group activity, these turn-out rates increased to
approximately 40 percent. Sixty percent of the registered voters in the
Calle Ocho neighborhood voted.

These numbers illustrate a pattern that distinguishes Latinos,
especially barrio residents, from the national population. Nationally,
approximately 80 percent of registered voters turn out on election day
(Census 1989). In these five barrios, between 25 and 60 percent of regis-

tered voters voted in 1990. These figures exceed the turnout rate in some years for registered voters in Texas barrios (Brischetto 1988: 6).

The reasons for this low turnout are unclear. As was true in 1990, however, registration drives often target barrios such as these. That turnout rates remain so low despite such efforts suggests the limited value of registration drives. This may be because, as traditionally conducted, registration drives expand the rolls but do not necessarily link individuals who are otherwise disengaged from the political system to the electoral process. That relationship was developed historically by parties or organizations associated with candidates. As we have stated, neither of these institutions was active in the four barrios with the lowest turnout. This combined neglect may account for much of the low participation rates and widespread apathy we found in four of the five sites.

There is, then, little to connect barrio residents to the election. In general, parties and candidates are not visible; when they are present, candidates and campaigns neglect many or all of the issues of concern to the barrios. In two of these communities, however, community-based organizations filled some of the void.

Although less clear, two other notable patterns emerge. First, Latino voters are willing to support female candidates. Stereotypes of machismo among Latinos might suggest otherwise, but in four of the five sites, the people voted for women for state and national office. Second, activists in each community had their eyes on the future. Rather than focus on mobilizing for this election, they emphasized laying the foundation for future elections, when, after redistricting, the chances for electoral impact presumably would be greater.

The Campaigns in the Latino Barrios

The 1990 campaign in two of these communities lacked even the minimal gesture that has historically characterized campaigning in barrios—what the literature on Latino politics characterizes as "taco" or "fiesta" politics (DeSipio and Rocha 1992), which consist of symbolic outreach to Mexican American (and, by extension, Latino) voters at rallies where candidates praise Mexican culture and serve tacos and beer. The candidate, usually an Anglo Democrat, uses the event to demonstrate an attachment to Mexican American voters. At its extreme, this rally would take place just before the election and be the only contact between the campaign and the Mexican American community. Even this token gesture to a controlled and manipulated Mexican American vote was not present in New York and Houston during the

1990 elections analyzed here, and it is unclear if anything has replaced it.

Campaign strategies ranged from virtual noncampaigns in New York and Houston to active door-to-door outreach in Miami. In between, Chicago and Los Angeles saw limited, but targeted, outreach to community residents. With almost no campaign, New York and Houston are below taco politics. In the other three sites, targeted efforts spoke to Latinos, if not to Latino issues. We examine this by looking at three general aspects of the campaign: (1) visible signs of the campaign in the communities; (2) targeted ethnic outreach and voter registration; and (3) get-out-the-vote efforts.

At one extreme, New York and Houston did not really feature campaigns. In New York, there were no rallies, no street signs, no campaign offices, no visits by candidates, and only a few fliers and newsletters. The governor's race was effectively uncontested, all candidates for statewide office were non-Latino, and the barrio's legislative representatives—both Puerto Ricans—were unopposed. The low intensity of the campaign is perhaps reflected in the decision of an incumbent state legislative candidate from the area to take a vacation around election day (see chapter three).

Since there was no campaigning, there was obviously no ethnic campaigning. One legislator indicated that she felt that she owed her election to the Puerto Rican community, but that she represented her entire district, that is, Puerto Ricans and others. She felt no need to campaign, since the voters knew her record. There was some frustration with her performance and attitude, but voters and community leaders were reluctant to express it because they did not want to jeopardize the position of "one of our own."

The high level of community and candidate apathy makes it difficult to evaluate the importance of ethnicity to this election. At a minimum, with regard to the legislative races, the prevailing apathy seems to have prevented anti-incumbent mobilization while also contributing to community and candidate apathy.

The campaign activity level in Houston was not as low as in New York. There were rallies and some candidates reached out to the neighborhood. While all campaign events took place outside the barrio under study, there was a major rally nearby and a breakfast for interested residents with Dan Morales, candidate for attorney general. A victorious candidate for the state legislature resided in the barrio, though his campaign did not focus its efforts there (see chapter four).

There were several local voter registration efforts coordinated by Mexican American organizations. These supplemented a Houston-wide effort coordinated by the Southwest Voter Registration and Education

Project. These, too, suffered rather than benefited from competition with at least three drives that occurred simultaneously.

Again, ethnicity did not seem to play a major role in the campaign. Ethnic themes were not raised, and candidates (including Dan Morales) did not make ethnic appeals to voters. Two Anglo candidates distributed campaign materials in the barrio, but they did not campaign there. Although there was an undercurrent of conflict with Houston's African American community regarding representation on the city council, this did not manifest itself electorally in 1990. One theme in the voter registration effort, however, was preparing for postredistricting elections.

Evaluating the level of campaign activity in Los Angeles and Chicago is somewhat more difficult. On the surface, although more active than Houston's, the campaigns in these two cities did not target the barrio. Yet, the researchers in both sites suggest that more was going on than met the untrained eye.

In Los Angeles, there was little formal campaign activity focused on the barrio. Despite the contested nature of the gubernatorial race and the strongly Democratic bias of Mexican Americans, Democratic candidate Dianne Feinstein did not open her East Los Angeles office until late September, one week before the deadline for registering for the November election. She also did not dedicate campaign resources to voter registration. The Democratic party did coordinate several rallies on the east side, one of which took place in the research site.

Beginning in October, more visible signs of the campaign began to appear. Posters, yard placards, and Spanish television ads promoted candidates and initiatives. One initiative in particular, an attempt to raise the alcohol tax, received particular attention from area merchants; they opposed the initiative. Only a few bilingual placards promoting the Feinstein campaign appeared. Community residents who had voted in recent elections received mailings for a variety of offices and initiatives. The tenor of the campaign did not pick up considerably around election day. The Democratic party ran get-out-the-vote telephone banking.

The role of ethnicity is again clouded in the case of Los Angeles. The state representative and state senator as well as the member of congress from Boyle Heights are all Mexican American, and each ran for re-election with only token opposition in 1990. The statewide offices contested in the 1990 election did not have major party Latino candidates. These statewide candidates and the initiatives ran some ads on Spanish television and produced some bilingual placards. Overall, however, there was no distinctive barrio campaign; instead, the same message that was sent out statewide was delivered to Boyle Heights, but even this attained little visibility.

The analysis of the Los Angeles elections emphasizes two aspects of the campaign in California—incumbency and new campaign technologies—that diminish campaign visibility (see chapter six). It is axiomatic that incumbents seek to assure victory. Rather than mobilize new voters with unknown preferences who could block an otherwise nearly assured victory, they increasingly use technology to target particular voters.[14] For example, campaign technologies now have the precision to distinguish individuals who voted in four of the last four elections from those who voted in three of four. This type of targeting is the preferred strategy in campaigns with high numbers of incumbents seeking reelection. This may also be why, as part of this otherwise low-key campaign period, there were no significant voter registration or get-out-the-vote efforts.

These patterns resemble the results of the project in Chicago. The political machine has traditionally mobilized or demobilized the vote based on its needs. Since the machine has never included the Mexican American community among its core constituencies, the barrios often see competition between machine candidates and insurgents. Although the machine was gearing up for aldermanic races in the spring of 1991, the November races focused on state and county offices. Project respondents were most aware of two statewide races—the senatorial and the gubernatorial—although they reported that these races were less important than the aldermanic races that would follow.

Campaign activities to attract the voters of Pilsen were not directed just at Pilsen, but instead at all Latino areas. The Chicago Latino community is divided roughly evenly between Mexican Americans and Puerto Ricans. In the tradition of Chicago politics, this focus on all Latinos instead of just those living in Pilsen would suggest that ethnicity was of greater importance than in Los Angeles, Houston, or New York. In the tradition of taco politics, politicians attended several festivals and parades in the Latino community, including three parades that passed through the research site. Two of these, coordinated by the Democrats, occurred during the last two weeks of the campaign. The Democrats, however, did not run Spanish-language television ads.

Unlike in traditional taco politics, Republicans sought Latino votes (see chapter five). Their outreach strategy made subtle intraethnic distinctions. The Republican gubernatorial candidate, Jim Edgar, had two Spanish-language television ads. The first used as a backdrop a park in the Puerto Rican area of Chicago with Puerto Rican flags in the background. The second showed the candidate in front of an elementary school in the project site. This active Republican outreach to Latinos did not mention that Edgar was a Republican. Although the exit polling is inexact, some sources suggest that Edgar garnered as much as 40 percent of the Latino vote. Since his overall victory margin was 51 percent to 48 percent, this higher-than-average Latino support for the Republican may have been essential to his victory.

Voter registration efforts coordinated by community-based organizations aimed not at the November elections, but at voter education and at the 1991 aldermanic races. As a result, there was little noticeable effort and few new registrants in 1990.

Candidates and campaigns in Miami operate on a different level than do those in any of the other four sites. Races from the governor on down took place in front of the voters of Calle Ocho. Campaigns filled the streets and store windows with placards. Spanish-language radio covered every intricacy of the campaign. Candidates walked the streets.

Several candidates for office in this race were incumbents, but this did not seem to diminish the intensity of the race in Calle Ocho. Each incumbent faced more than token opposition. Again, Cubanness separated candidates more than issues.[15]

As was indicated earlier, ethnicity served as a key link between Cuban American voters and Cuban American candidates. Other types of connections also linked Calle Ocho voters to the electoral process, however. Anglo and African American candidates actively sought and received Cuban American votes. An Anglo candidate for the state legislature and an African American running for the county commission both won because of high levels of Cuban support. Cuban support is not sufficient, however, to guarantee victory at the county (or state, for that matter) level. The Cuban-born candidate for the Dade County Commission carried the Cuban vote, but lost to his U.S.-born Cuban American rival, who carried the Anglo and African American vote.

Neither voter registration nor voter mobilization played a significant role in this campaign. The high intensity of electoral activity and popular awareness may have made these unnecessary.

Conclusion: Individual-Electoral Linkages in Five Barrios

Before evaluating the significance of these results, it is important to keep in mind several aspects of the design of the project that limit our ability to generalize about the findings. The sites are not representative of all Latino neighborhoods, and the Latinos in these barrios are not representative of all Latinos who live in more heterogeneous neighborhoods. The time period for the project did not include the full campaign period and in some cases excluded primaries, which often generate great interest. The research focused on district and statewide elections and did not spotlight local and national elections, both of which may be of greater salience to these barrios.

Each site is a port-of-entry community. The high concentrations of aliens who legalized under the Immigration Reform and Control Act (IRCA) of 1986 and the steady inflow of permanent residents and undocumented immigrants suggests a permanent, if continuously changing, mix of new and old residents. These are working-class areas surrounded by more middle-class Latino neighborhoods. If socioeconomic status affects Latino political participation as much as it does the non-Hispanic white community (Wolfinger and Rosenstone 1980), then these barrios may be examples of the baseline of Latino electoral participation. Reinforcing this hypothesis is the fact that our results are very similar to those produced by residents of comparable neighborhoods with the Latino National Political Survey. In more affluent areas, with higher concentrations of U.S. citizens, we would expect different patterns both in how individuals relate to the electoral system and in the efforts electoral institutions make to reach those individuals.

Furthermore, these sites are among the densest in terms of concentrations of Latinos in the cities included in the study. To the extent that the salience of ethnic issues depends on the density of co-ethnics in the barrio, these areas offer fertile ground for political candidates making ethnic appeals. It is therefore noteworthy that only Miami saw this phenomenon in the 1990 elections. Outside the barrio, ethnic campaigns may backfire. Thus, even though these results cannot be used to explain how all Latinos behave politically, they should offer insights into some of the more significant and unexplored aspects of barrio political life.

A second limitation on the data stems from the period of data collection. Project funds allowed only three months of field research. As a result, the field study missed the primaries in Texas, California, and Illinois. It is not possible to know how this affects our findings. As we noted, the races observed in three of the sites were uncontested. Primaries, however, often feature the apex of competition. This is particularly true for Latinos, who have strong partisan ties. The Miami primaries proved to be as interesting to observe and as important to the community as the November general election. Thus, our results may not characterize the full extent of barrio electoral engagement. This does not diminish the validity of the descriptions of electoral activities in the general elections; it does require caution in using those results to characterize all barrio electoral life.

Another limitation results from the decision to focus on the 1990 general election. Although there were a few local elections (county offices in Miami, Los Angeles, and Chicago) in November 1990, in three of these sites, the major contests were for state office, statewide referenda, and Congress. Elections for city office in all sites are separate from the general election. As we have indicated, we hypothesized that the 1990 elections would generate interest in the barrio because of the effect they could have on the impending redistricting and because of the gubernatorial races in each state.

Nonetheless, the results described here may not characterize barrio electoral participation per se. To see barrio political activity at its strongest, it may be necessary to study local or national campaigns. The principal investigators in each site developed the impression that local elections generate the most community interest. While this is in line with Tip O'Neill's axiom that all politics is local, local elections may be especially important to individuals with less information about public policy issues and to neighborhoods that are less regularly attended to by governing institutions. To the extent that this impression is accurate, local elections that are usually contested would be particularly useful events for generating insight into autonomous mobilization within the barrio. National elections, especially if highly contested, should illustrate the effects of institutional penetration on barrio mobilization.

Finally, it is necessary to discuss the validity and reliability of the data; that is, to what extent do the variations in the findings reflect actual differences among the sites rather than differences in the research strategies of the respective teams? There is no absolute answer to this. To some degree, each team used techniques appropriate to its specific site and expertise that may have produced results that were in some ways distinctive. All the teams also relied on a common methodology, however, and were guided by one set of core questions. Further, the project directors in Austin regularly communicated with each site and each site was visited twice. These visits were used to ensure that the fieldwork was being conducted as had been designed. Additionally, Martha Menchaca, the project's ethnographic director, carefully reviewed all field notes to ensure their reliability. Finally, at a seminar that brought together the principal investigators of each site and the project directors, each field report was carefully reviewed, with particular attention given to how the fieldwork was conducted.

Together, these procedures make us confident of our results. Reinforcing this conclusion are the findings themselves. As we noted, they are supported by results from the Latino National Political

Survey and other research. Equally significant is that they illuminate what might be called a previously dark corner of research on Latino electoral behavior rather than offer startlingly new or contradictory information. With this, they help us understand more fully the reasons for the existence of a well-established pattern—that is, why Latinos do not vote.

A final factor that we must remember when we consider these data is the disparate political environments of the five cities under study. At the one extreme, Chicago's machine shapes urban politics. It assures incorporation for many Latinos who would be passive in other cities. At the other, Los Angeles's formally nonpartisan political environment and California's confusing money-driven politics have the opposite effect. Latinos and non-Latinos alike are discouraged from political participation. Since Los Angeles Latinos are more likely to have the demographic characteristics associated with nonparticipation, however, they are more likely to be among the discouraged. The political environments of the other three cities place Latinos in the barrios under study between these extremes.

What do we conclude from all this, then? Most significant, it is clear that formal obstacles such as language requirements and residency requirements no longer affect Latinos disproportionately. Indeed, in none of our sites was there evidence of voter discrimination or intimidation (although this was reported in other parts of Texas and California) (Pachon et al. 1992). Thus, with the passage and enforcement of the Voting Rights Act, formal openness has come to characterize the American political system.

Our findings clearly point out, however, that the system's formal openness is not matched by institutional efforts to incorporate barrio residents. *This is why Latinos do not vote.* When socioeconomic characteristics are controlled, Latinos vote at rates comparable to Anglos (Wolfinger and Rosenstone 1980). Most Latinos, however, are substantially poorer and less educated than Anglos, and almost half are also noncitizens. The majority of lower-income Latinos live in highly homogeneous neighborhoods. The effects of these factors can be overcome through outreach by political parties or other organizations or by a candidate's own efforts. It is ironic that this outreach occurs on a wide scale only in Calle Ocho; as the most economically successful and ideologically oriented site in the study, it is the barrio that least needs such initiatives.

Equally ironic is that the creation of VRA-required districts in barrios may also be contributing to the decreased efforts parties are making to mobilize barrio residents. VRA-mandated districts produce homogeneous local, state legislative, and congressional districts, which, with few exceptions, are contested only when they are created or when there is a vacancy. Thus, in these districts, incumbents have few electoral incentives to mobilize new voters; moreover, they are not indebted to their party for their office, and they have no reason to seek party support to win re-election. These districts are also safe seats for the incumbent's party. Thus, neither the incumbent nor the party is likely to try to mobilize voters in these districts. The design of these districts, therefore, may effectively eliminate the party's need to mobilize the grass roots.

To the extent that these findings reflect the electoral activities in other barrios, it is clear that parties and candidates generally neglect the voters in these areas. This is particularly unfortunate, not just because of the neglect of potential voters, but, more important, because potential new voters—the newly naturalized and the children of the electorally inactive—do not get socialized into electoral politics. Sadly, this lack of institutional outreach contributes to the reproduction of political apathy and alienation.

Having said that, we should add that there is no single model for electoral activity in Latino barrios. Where the stereotype of taco politics may once have represented the experience of many Mexican Americans, the current situation for Latinos is no longer so clear. The alienation of voters from candidates and candidates from voters in New York and Houston bears little resemblance to the intensity of Miami's campaigns. The behind-the-scenes campaign of Los Angeles and the machine-shaped political environment of Chicago offer some Latinos involvement while passively excluding others.

In order for Latinos to match their growing numbers with political clout, they must overcome political environments that do not formally exclude them, but that do not actively include them, either. By designing campaigns around traditional class-based assumptions of nonparticipation, the system serves informally to exclude new Latino electorates. New voters and old in these communities are apathetic and alienated, in part for the reasons shared by the rest of the electorate. In part, however, a community with many new members needs more outreach and more information if it is to become electorally engaged.

Thus, if candidates, campaigns, and parties are going to neglect the barrio, the impetus for Latino participation will have to come from within the barrio. One ongoing solution—voter registration—does not seem to have had the desired effect. Many barrio residents sign up during registration drives, but they are not personally motivated to vote, and there are no institutionalized efforts motivating them to do so. In addition to registering voters, then, community leaders and interested electoral institutions should undertake a new strategy to socialize potential voters into the electoral process. Although this socialization should include all native- and foreign-born citizens, it should particularly focus on the large potential client base of legal resident, non-U.S. citizens who could be encouraged to naturalize as a step to promote increasing Latino community political clout. Should barrio electoral participation rates begin to increase through this strategy, electoral institutions could no longer neglect the barrio as they did in four of the five sites in 1990.

Notes

1. We would like to thank Sidney Verba and Luis Fraga for helpful comments on an earlier draft of this chapter.

Throughout this volume, the authors use the terms "Latino" and "Hispanic" interchangeably to refer to persons in the United States who can trace their ancestry to the Spanish-speaking regions of Latin America and the Caribbean.

The authors also use two sets of racial/ethnic identification terms interchangeably—black or African American and white, Anglo, or non-Hispanic white.

2. This chapter does not review ethnographic anthropological literature from the 1960s that explained low Mexican American electoral participation rates. For this discussion, see chapter 2.

3. Except for Puerto Ricans, each of these groups includes native-born citizens, naturalized citizens, permanent-resident aliens, and undocumented immigrants who may or may not become permanent residents. Although there are important political differences among these groups, unless otherwise indicated, we use labels such as "Mexicans" to include all people who trace their ancestry to Mexico, regardless of their nativity, current citizenship, or immigration status.

4. These seven characteristics of the modern electoral system emerged during a postproject meeting in May 1991. Bruce Cain (1991) has developed a similar typology.

5. DeSipio and Rocha (1992) find that the margin of Democratic victory in the 1988 presidential race was great enough that one-third of Latinos who voted for Dukakis would have had to vote for Bush to throw the state's electoral votes to the Republicans, an unlikely event at best. Nevertheless, for the Democrats to win at the state level, they must count on current levels of Latino turnout in close races.

6. California, which, like Texas, is about 25 percent Latino, has just 3.2 percent of its public offices filled by Latinos (NALEO 1992: viii).

7. After it was revealed that she had not graduated from college and had misrepresented her educational credentials, Guerrero resigned her office two months prior to the election. She then lost election to the post.

8. In the late 1980s, Chicago began an experiment with school-based school

boards. They open an as-yet unstudied opportunity for mobilizing local communities around educational issues.

9. Chicago's first "Latino" alderman, William Emilio Rodríguez, served from 1915 to 1918. This example suggests, at a superficial level, that Chicago's Latino politics is not a new phenomenon. Despite his surname, Rodríguez was the exception. He associated more with his mother's German ancestry than with his father's Mexican origins.

10. Again, there is an exception. Riverside County Supervisor Miguel Estudillo served in the assembly from 1905 to 1908 and in the senate from 1909 to 1912. The next Latino to be elected to the assembly was Richard Alatorre in 1972.

11. An exception appeared in 1928, when Florida supported Herbert Hoover over Al Smith, a Catholic Democrat who opposed Prohibition.

12. For a more extensive discussion of the LNPS methodology, see de la Garza et al. 1992: Appendix 2.

13. Several of the reports did not provide estimates of the U.S. citizen voting age population. As a result, the data here on turnout are calculated as a percentage of registration.

14. A court-mandated election to fill a vacant seat on the Los Angeles County Council tested this hypothesis. In a race without incumbents between two well-known Latino elected officials, the candidate who ran a grass-roots campaign won in an upset.

15. An interesting question for further research relates to the degree to which "Cubanness" cloaks ideological differences. While it is clear that Cubanness includes opposition to Fidel Castro and communism, it is not clear what Cubanness says about positions on domestic economic and social issues. As the Cuban American community evolves as an electorate, this question will increase in importance.

References

Anders, Evan. 1982. *Boss Rule in South Texas: The Progressive Era*. Austin: University of Texas Press.

Arian, Asher; Arthur S. Goldberg; John H. Mollenkopf; and Edward T. Rogowsky. 1990. *Changing New York City Politics*. New York and London: Routledge.

Avila, Joaquín G. 1990. "Latino Political Empowerment: A Perspective." Unpublished manuscript.

Baver, Sherrie. 1984. "Puerto Rican Politics in New York City: The Post-World War II Period." In James Jennings and Monte Rivera, eds., *Puerto Rican Politics in Urban America*, pp. 43–60. Westport, Conn: Greenwood Press.

Bean, Frank, and Marta Tienda. 1987. *The Hispanic Population of the United States*. New York: Russell Sage Foundation.

Brischetto, Robert. 1988. *The Political Empowerment of Texas Mexicans, 1974–1988*. San Antonio, Tex.: Southwest Voter Research Institute.

Browning, Rufus P.; Dale Rogers Marshall; and David H. Tabb. 1984. *Protest Is Not Enough: The Struggle of Blacks and Hispanics for Equality in Urban Politics*. Berkeley and Los Angeles: University of California Press.

Bullock, Charles S., and Susan A. MacManus. 1990. "Structural Features of Municipalities and the Incidence of Hispanic Councilmembers." *Social Science Quarterly* 71 (4) (December): 665–681.

Burka, Paul. 1992. "Battle Lines." *Texas Monthly* (March): 50–56.

Butler, David, and Bruce Cain. 1992. *Congressional Redistricting: Comparative and Theoretical Perspectives*. New York: Macmillan.

Cain, Bruce E. 1991. "The Contemporary Context of Ethnic and Racial Politics in California." In Byran O. Jackson and Michael B. Preston, eds., *Racial and Ethnic Politics in California*, pp. 9–24. Berkeley: Institute for Governmental Studies Press.

Craig, Steven C. 1991. "Politics and Elections." In Robert J. Huckshorn, ed., *Government and Politics in Florida*, pp. 77–110. Gainesville: University of Florida Press.

Davidson, Chandler. 1990. *Race and Class in Texas Politics*. Princeton, N.J.: Princeton University Press.

DeCew, Judson M., Jr. 1980. "Hispanics." In Manning J. Dauer, ed., *Florida's Politics and Government*, pp. 321–330. Gainesville: University Presses of Florida.

de la Garza, Rodolfo O., ed. 1986. *Ignored Voices: Public Opinion Polls and the Latino Community*. Austin: University of Texas Press.

———, 1992. "From Rhetoric to Reality: Latinos in the 1988 Election in Review." In Rodolfo O. de la Garza and Louis DeSipio, eds., *From Rhetoric to Reality: Latino Politics in the 1988 Elections*, pp. 171–180. Boulder, Colo.: Westview Press.

de la Garza, Rodolfo O., and Louis DeSipio. 1989. "The Changing Hispanic Political Landscape." In William P. O'Hare, ed., *Redistricting in the 1990s: A Guide for Minority Groups*, pp. 43–54. Washington, D.C.: Population Reference Bureau.

———, eds. 1992. *From Rhetoric to Reality: Latino Politics in the 1988 Elections*. Boulder, Colo.: Westview Press.

———. 1993. "Save the Baby, Change the Bathwater, and Clean the Tub: Latino Electoral Participation after Seventeen Years of Voting Rights Act Coverage." *University of Texas Law Review* (June).

de la Garza, Rodolfo O.; Louis DeSipio; F. Chris García; John A. García; and Angelo Falcón. 1992. *Latino Voices: Mexican, Puerto Rican, and Cuban Perspectives on American Politics*. Boulder, Colo.: Westview Press.

de la Garza, Rodolfo O.; Luis Fraga; and Harry Pachon. 1988. "Toward a Shared Agenda." *Journal of State Government* 61 (2) (March/April): 77–80.

de la Garza, Rodolfo O., and Janet Weaver. 1985. "Does Ethnicity Make a Difference: Chicano-Anglo Public Policy Perspectives in San Antonio." *Social Science Quarterly* 66 (4) (December).

DeSipio, Louis, and Gregory Rocha. 1992. "Latino Influence on National Elections: The Case of 1988." In Rodolfo O. de la Garza and Louis DeSipio, eds., *From Rhetoric to Reality: Latino Politics in the 1988 Elections*, pp. 3–22. Boulder, Colo.: Westview Press.

Fleischmann, Arnold, and Laura Stein. 1987. "Minority and Female Success in Municipal Runoff Elections." *Social Science Quarterly* 68 (June): 378–385.

Fraga, Luis. 1992. "Prototype from the Midwest: Latinos in Illinois." In Rodolfo O. de la Garza and Louis DeSipio, eds., *From Rhetoric to Reality: Latino Politics in the 1988 Elections*, pp. 111–126. Boulder, Colo.: Westview Press.

Fremon, David K. 1988. *Chicago Politics Ward by Ward*. Bloomington and Indianapolis: Indiana University Press.

Fuchs, Lawrence. 1990. *The American Kaleidoscope: Race, Ethnicity, and the Civic Culture*. Hanover, N.H.: Wesleyan University Press.

García, F. Chris; Rodolfo O. de la Garza; and Donald Torres. 1985. "Introduction: Mexican American Political Participation" (Bibliographic Essay). In Rodolfo O. de la Garza et al., eds., *The Mexican American Experience: An Interdisciplinary Analysis*, pp. 185–200. Austin: University of Texas Press.

García, F. Chris; John García; Rodolfo O. de la Garza; Angelo Falcón; and Cara Abeyta. 1992. *Latinos and Politics: A Select Research Bibliography*. Austin: University of Texas Press.

García, F. Chris; John García; Angelo Falcón; and Rodolfo O. de la Garza. 1989. "Studying Latino Politics: The Development of the Latino National Political Survey." *PS: Political Science and Politics* 22 (4) (December): 848–852.

Guerra, Fernando. 1991. "The Emergence of Ethnic Officeholders in California." In Byran O. Jackson and Michael Preston, eds., *Racial and Ethnic Politics in California*, pp. 117–132. Berkeley: Institute for Governmental Studies Press.

Gurin, Patricia; Shirley Hatchett; and James S. Jackson. 1989. *Hope and Independence: Blacks' Response to Electoral and Party Politics*. New York: Russell Sage Foundation.

Hain, Paul, and José C. García. 1981. "Voting, Elections and Parties." In F. Chris García and Paul L. Hain, eds., *New Mexico Government*, rev. ed., pp. 218–239. Albuquerque: University of New Mexico Press.

Jackson, James S., ed., 1991. *Life in Black America*. Newbury Park, Calif.: Sage Publications.

Jennings, James. 1977. *Puerto Rican Politics in New York City*. Washington, D.C.: University Press of America.

Kaplan, Barry J. 1983. "Houston: The Golden Buckle of the Sunbelt." In Richard M. Bernard and Bradley J. Rice, eds., *Sunbelt Cities: Politics and Growth since World War II*, pp. 196–212. Austin: University of Texas Press.

Ketchum v. Byrne. 1984. 740 F.2d 1398 (7th Cir. IL).

Key, V. O. 1949. *Southern Politics in State and Nation*. New York: Vintage.

Kraemer, Richard, and Charldean Newell. 1992. *Essentials of Texas Politics*. St. Paul, Minn.: West Publishing.

Lyndon Baines Johnson (LBJ) School of Public Affairs. 1984. *Local Government Election Systems*. Austin, Tex.

MacManus, Susan, and Charles S. Bullock III. 1987. "The Influence of Race,

Ethnicity and Electoral System Structure on Municipal Electoral Outcomes." Paper presented at the Conference on Ethnic and Racial Minorities in Advanced Industrial Democracies. South Bend, Ind.

Middleton, William J. 1991. "The Impact of Party Reform in California on Minority Political Empowerment." In Byran O. Jackson and Michael B. Preston, eds., *Racial and Ethnic Politics in California*. Berkeley: Institute for Governmental Studies Press.

Mohl, Raymond A. 1983. "Miami: The Ethnic Cauldron." In Richard M. Bernard and Bradley R. Rice, eds., *Sunbelt Cities: Politics and Growth since World War II*, pp. 58–99. Austin: University of Texas Press.

Morris, Celia. 1992. *Storming the Statehouse: Running for Governor with Ann Richards and Dianne Feinstein*. New York: Scribner's.

NALEO Educational Fund. 1992. *1991 National Roster of Hispanic Elected Officials*. Washington, D.C.: NALEO Educational Fund.

Nelson, Dale C. 1979. "Ethnicity and Socioeconomic Status as Sources of Participation: The Case for Ethnic Political Culture." *American Political Science Review* 73 (December): 1024–1038.

Pachon, Harry. 1991. "U.S. Citizenship and Latino Participation in California Politics." In Byran O. Jackson and Michael B. Preston, eds., *Racial and Ethnic Politics in California*, pp. 71–88. Berkeley: Institute for Governmental Studies Press.

Pachon, Harry, and Louis DeSipio. 1988. *The Latino Vote in 1988*. NALEO Background Paper #7. Washington, D.C.: NALEO Educational Fund.

Pachon, Harry; Louis DeSipio; Juan-Carlos Alegre; and Mark Magaña. 1992. *The Latino Vote in 1992*. Washington D.C.: NALEO Educational Fund.

Polinard, Jerry; Robert Wrinkle; and Rodolfo O. de la Garza. 1984. "Mexican American Attitudes toward Undocumented Workers." *International Migration Review* 18 (3) (Fall): 782–799.

Prindle, David F. 1981. *Petroleum Politics and the Texas Railroad Commission*. Austin: University of Texas Press.

Rodríguez, Lori. 1991. "Lena Guerrero." *Texas (Houston Chronicle* Sunday Magazine) (November 24).

———. 1992. "Whitmire Takes Lead in State Senate Race." *Houston Chronicle* (April 15): 1A.

Rogers, David. 1990. "Community Control and Decentralization." In Jewel Bellush and Dick Netzer, eds., *Urban Politics New York Style*, pp. 188–222. Armonk, N.Y.: M. E. Sharpe.

Santiago, I. S. 1984. "Language Policy and Education in Puerto Rico and the Continent." *International Education Journal* 1 (1): 61–90.

Torres v. Sachs. 1974. 381 F. Supp. 309 (S.D. N.Y.).

Uhlaner, Carole; Bruce Cain; and D. Roderick Kiewiet. 1989. "The Political Participation of Ethnic Minorities in the 1980s." *Political Behavior* 11 (September): 195–231.

U.S. Bureau of the Census. 1989. *Voting and Registration in the Election of November 1988*. Current Population Reports. Population Characteristics. Series P–20 #440. October.

————. 1990. "Government Organization: Popularly Elected Officials." *1987 Census of Governments*. Washington, D.C.: U.S. Government Printing Office.

————. 1991. "Census Bureau Releases 1990 Census Counts on Hispanic Population Groups." Press Release. Washington, D.C. (June 18): Table 3A.

Verba, Sidney, and Norman Nie. 1972. *Participation in America: Political Democracy and Social Equality*. New York: Harper and Row.

Viteritti, Joseph P. 1990. "The New Charter: Will It Make a Difference?" In Jewel Bellush and Dick Netzer, eds., *Urban Politics New York Style*, pp. 413–428. Armonk, N.Y.: M. E. Sharpe.

Wade, Richard C. 1990. "The Withering Away of the Party System." In Jewel Bellush and Dick Netzer, eds., *Urban Politics New York Style*, pp. 271–295. Armonk, N.Y.: M. E. Sharpe.

Walsh, Annmarie Hauck. 1990. "Public Authorities and the Shape of Decision Making." In Jewel Bellush and Dick Netzer, eds., *Urban Politics New York Style*, pp. 143–187. Armonk, N.Y.: M. E. Sharpe.

Welch, Susan. 1989. "The Impact of At-Large Elections on the Representation of Blacks and Hispanics." Unpublished manuscript.

Wolfinger, Raymond, and Steven Rosenstone. 1980. *Who Votes?* New Haven: Yale University Press.

2

Latino Political Attitudes and Behaviors in Five Neighborhoods

Martha Menchaca

The Latino Political Ethnography Project is the first study to use an ethnographic approach in exploring the political attitudes and behavior of Latinos in diverse U.S. communities. Previous ethnographic studies on Latino political behavior have been limited to an analysis of Mexican Americans and have not examined other Latino groups. This chapter, therefore, will provide an extended discussion of the research methods used to conduct this ethnographic study and will offer a comparative analysis of the perspectives Latinos in five communities hold regarding electoral politics. The overview of the 1990 electoral campaign results are discussed by de la Garza and DeSipio in chapter one.

Prior to discussing the project's methodology, I will briefly review the anthropological literature on Latino political behavior in order to expand de la Garza and DeSipio's review of the literature on this topic. As they note, in general, the literature on Latino politics suffers from several major shortcomings, and anthropological writings are not an exception. Anthropologists, like other social scientists, have overwhelmingly focused on Mexican Americans and have not offered any comparative analysis of Latino political values, attitudes, and behaviors. In studying Mexican American political behavior, some anthropologists have also advanced questionable ethnographic observations on the relationship between culture and politics by depicting Mexican Americans in derogatory and unrealistic ways. On the latter point, anthropologists are divided on the issue of how culture influences political behavior. The central point of contention is have American political institutions been historically inclusive or exclusive of ethnic groups that are not Anglo American? We now turn to this issue and review the anthropological writings on Mexican American political behavior and attitudes.

Ethnicity and Political Behavior: An Anthropological Debate

Ethnographic literature on the political behavior and attitudes of Mexican Americans reflects a long-standing debate among anthropologists. One position proposes that the political powerlessness of the Mexican Americans must be attributed to cultural dysfunctions (Edmonson 1957; Rubel 1960, 1966; Kluckhohn and Strodtbeck 1961; Knowlton 1962; Madsen 1964; Rubel and Kupferer 1968). This perspective alleges that Mexican American culture has traditionally contributed to the Mexican Americans' disinterest in American politics. The underlying assumption is that their political underrepresentation is a result of cultural problems rather than of institutionalized exclusionist policies practiced by the Republican and Democratic parties. The competing perspective challenges that view and argues that racism and discrimination have produced the social, economic, and political structures that obstruct the full political participation of Mexican Americans (Leonard 1970; Spicer 1972, 1975; Van Ness 1976; Foley 1977, 1988; Paredes 1978; Geilhufe 1979; Kutsche 1979; Kutsche and Van Ness 1981; Menchaca 1988, 1989; Takash-Cruz 1990).

The advocates of the cultural dysfunction thesis advanced ethnographic studies that were widely circulated in academia and came to be used as authoritative sources on the social, economic, and political status of Mexican Americans (Hernández 1970; Rosaldo 1985). These studies proposed that Mexican Americans exhibited a constellation of behavioral cultural traits that produced factionalism, present-time orientation, suspicion, fatalism, invidiousness, and peasantlike apolitical attitudes. The authors argued that, as a consequence of these negative attitudes, Mexican Americans were unable to develop formal organizations that could be used on behalf of their political advocacy. The most widely circulated studies were Florence Kluckhohn and Fred Strodtbeck's (1961) research in New Mexico and Arthur Rubel's (1966) and William Madsen's (1964) ethnographies of two South Texas communities.

Kluckhohn and Strodtbeck (1961) argued in their study that the Mexican Americans' most severe cultural problems were their peasantlike apolitical beliefs and time-orientation concepts. Basing their analysis on Atrisco, a small New Mexican community, Kluckhohn and Strodtbeck proposed that Mexican Americans were a highly emotional people who placed excessive value on maintaining past traditions and seldom planned for the future. They suggested that this type of behavior was politically dysfunctional because Mexican Americans found little value in joining formal organizations. They preferred not to form organizations because they were past-oriented and never thought about the future. Kluckhohn and Strodtbeck also proposed that these problems were associated with the maintenance of an informal peasantlike political practice in which Mexican Americans preferred to delegate their decision making to others, preferably their employers. This type of attitude has been labeled by anthropologists as "patron-peon dependency" and has been identified as originating in Mexican peasant communities. In sum, Kluckhohn and Strodtbeck concluded that Mexican Americans chose not to be active participants within electoral politics. Furthermore, they suggested that, if their political status was to change in the United States, Mexican Americans must learn to emulate the culture and political practices of Anglo Americans and must also shed their peasant culture. In their assessment, however, Kluckhohn and Strodtbeck did not offer any analysis of the impact of Anglo American racism on Mexican Americans, nor did they offer a historical analysis of how Mexican Americans have been treated by American political institutions.

Madsen (1964) examined the impact of Mexican American culture on the community's social, economic, and political behavior. He presented some of the same cultural observations advanced by Kluckhohn and Strodtbeck and concluded that Mexican Americans were past-oriented and practiced a dysfunctional, peasantlike culture that inhibited success in all domains of social life. Madsen, however, added a few observations of his own. He concluded that Mexican Americans were politically powerless because they were fatalistic, envious, and suspicious of each other. Madsen also found that machismo obstructed any type of organization among men because it was their natural tendency to be jealous and suspicious of one other. He proposed that machismo obstructed the formation of leadership behavior among males because they preferred not to call attention to themselves. When a male attempted to assume a leadership role, the community allegedly used witchcraft and gossip to obstruct his success. Madsen also concluded that Mexican Americans preferred not to assume leadership roles because they expected to fail.

The most controversial analysis about Mexican American political behavior and attitudes was advanced by Arthur Rubel in 1966. Also selecting a South Texas community as the research site, Rubel attempted to advance a macrotheory to explain why Mexican Americans were a politically powerless people. Unlike Madsen and Kluckhohn and Strodtbeck—who were careful to state that their findings could only be generalized to other communities with similar social structures—Rubel advanced a grand macrotheory applicable to all Mexican-origin people. He proposed that the Mexican Americans' failure to have an impact on American political institutions was a result of their inability to form enduring formal and informal organizations. He attributed this dysfunction to the Mexican kinship structure.

Rubel argued that Mexican parents encouraged atomistic behavior among their children by socializing them to be uncooperative and suspicious of nonfamily. This type of behavior was allegedly a residual cultural trait rooted within Mexican peasant society and reproduced in the United States. Thus, Rubel asserted, the Mexican Americans' political problems stemmed from their inability to shed their peasant culture and their failure to adopt Anglo American values and practices. He left the impression that Mexican Americans voluntarily chose not to participate in American politics because they behaved like peasants and were jealous and suspicious of nonfamily.

In an earlier study of Mexican Americans, Rubel (1960) presented an abbreviated version of his theory on atomistic behavior and added a biological deterministic component to his argument. Though the purpose of the article was to explain how Mexican American cultural practices produced health and mental problems, Rubel stated that the same constellation of cultural attributes obstructed political organization. He concluded that cultural change was improbable among Mexican Americans because peasant traditions were strongly rooted within their culture and Anglicization could not occur. In other words, "You can take a *ranchero* from the *rancho*, but you cannot take the *rancho* from the *ranchero*" (p. 797). In sum, Rubel felt that Mexican Americans would always behave like peasants because it was in their blood. Thus, he postulated that genetics was the basis of the Mexican Americans' social, economic, and political problems.

In the late 1960s, a Chicano scholarly journal titled *El Grito* (Voices) published numerous articles challenging the observations and conclusions made by anthropologists who alleged that Mexican Americans' political, economic, and social problems were caused by their peasant culture (Rosaldo 1985). Chicano scholars angrily accused anthropologists of institutional racism and of perpetuating stereotypes and unsubstantiated half-truths. They argued that the analyses offered by many anthropologists were racist because Mexican Americans were depicted ahistorically. Anthropologists had failed, the critics agreed, to examine how a history of discrimination and racism had affected Mexican Americans. The simple fact that anthropologists did not examine the impact on Mexican Americans of the aftermath of the

Mexican American War and a long history of social segregation reflected intentional academic racism.

Approximately ten years later, renowned folklorist Américo Paredes (1978) offered a more devastating critique of the anthropological research on Mexican Americans. By this time, many Anglo American anthropologists concurred with Chicano scholars and offered similar critical analyses of the anthropological writings (Spicer 1972, 1975; Van Ness 1976; Geilhufe 1979; Kutsche 1979). Paredes posited that Madsen's, Rubel's, and Kluckhohn and Strodtbeck's research revealed serious methodological and theoretical errors. Their ethnographies were full of mistranslations, scenes were taken out of context, drunk people were often interviewed, witticisms were reported literally rather than figuratively, stories were reported as fact, and field researchers often failed to understand when their informants were telling jokes. Moreover, a more significant methodological error was that anthropologists often failed to report how many people participated in their studies; therefore, the reader did not know if the ethnographies were based on two or one hundred interviews.

In Paredes's review of the methodological problems, he noted that, although the Chicano movement was in full bloom in the community Rubel was studying, Rubel failed to observe the political activism that was taking place. Paredes concluded that, because Rubel was determined to validate his theses at any cost, he preferred to ignore the political mobilization that was taking place. In an ironic tone Paredes stated, "a perceptive anthropologist like Arthur Rubel could spend months in New Lots and never suspect that a political revolution [the birth of the Chicano movement] was taking place before his eyes, concluding on the contrary that Mexican-Americans just were not interested in political issues" (1978: 19).

Anglo American anthropologists also harshly criticized their colleagues' writings. They concurred with the Chicano scholars' criticisms and strongly disagreed that the Mexican Americans' social, economic, and political problems were a result of their allegedly dysfunctional culture. They concentrated their criticisms on issues of interpretation, however, rather than questioning their colleagues' observations. For example, Kutsche (1979; Kutsche and Van Ness 1981) proposed that the lack of political organization in Mexican American communities was simply a result of Anglo American racism. He wrote that, because Mexican Americans had been treated in this country as foreigners and not as true Americans for generations, they had been subtly discouraged from participating in American institutions. He further stated that the fact that Mexican Americans were also discriminated against because of their predominantly working-class status compounded this problem. In sum, Kutsche proposed that Mexican Americans were discouraged and excluded from participating in Anglo American society. Other anthropologists offered similar interpretations and proposed that oppression, discrimination, and political neglect were the sources of Mexican Americans' social, economic, and political problems (Levy 1968; Spicer 1972, 1975; Van Ness 1976; Foley 1977, 1988; Geilhufe 1979).

More recent ethnographic research on the political behavior of Mexican Americans has attempted to move away from the cultural-deficit approach. Instead, these studies offer detailed information on electoral politics and no longer attempt to draw cause-and-effect analyses between the role of culture and the political status of the Mexican Americans. That is, rather than limiting their analysis to Mexican American culture, the authors also examine the impact of Anglo American institutions such as schools, city hall, elected officials, and the labor market on the political behavior of Mexican Americans. Recent scholarship has looked inward at Mexican American culture and outward toward the institutions of the dominant culture. For example, in ethnographic studies based on rural communities, Menchaca (1988, 1989) and Takash-Cruz (1990) found that Anglo American elites manipulated local laws and often used blatant and subtle intimidation to discourage Mexican Americans from participating in local politics. Anglo Americans were able to dominate their communities politically by taking control of city councils. Takash-Cruz and Menchaca observed that, in the ethnically biracial communities they studied, Anglo Americans used the at-large electoral system to preserve their monopoly over city government. Both authors found that the Mexican Americans' ethnic representation in local government was not the outcome of the absence of political organizations. On the contrary, in both communities, Mexican Americans had organized long-standing political interest groups and individuals were actively involved in running for local government positions. The main obstacles to their success were (1) majority-minority voting patterns and (2) the at-large electoral system. Because Anglo Americans constituted the majority population in both towns, by the sheer power of their numbers they were able to elect whomever they preferred. As a consequence, Mexican Americans who ran for office were unable to receive enough votes to be elected. Mexican Americans were aware of the demographic problem and repeatedly attempted to work for single-member districts that would allow Mexican American neighborhoods to be represented by elected officials living in the area. The at-large electoral system allowed the districts to be represented by elected officials who lived anyplace in town. By changing to a single-member district system, Anglo Americans would be unable to run for positions that represented the Mexican American neighborhoods.

In the case of Watsonville, California, where Takash-Cruz conducted her ethnography, the Mexican Americans were eventually able to change the electoral structure to single-member districts. This change occurred after long and bitter litigation between Anglo Americans and Mexican Americans. The attorneys for the Mexican American community were able to prove that the city government of Watsonville had historically used intentional and illegal methods to ensure that Mexican American candidates could not be elected to office. Following the political changes in Watsonville, several Mexican Americans were elected to the city council. In assessing the sources of the Mexican Americans' political successes, Takash-Cruz further observed that, after Watsonville changed to a single-member district system, the political participation of the Mexican American community increased. The community's political spirit was lifted when people realized that they could now elect Mexican Americans to office. Once the political spirit improved, the number of Mexican Americans running for office increased.

Foley (1977, 1988) observed similar events in his study of Mexican American political participation. In a rural community in South Texas, Foley observed that, when Mexican Americans believed that they could elect candidates of their choice, their political spirit was lifted and political mobilization increased. Foley also found that Anglo American elected officials became responsive to the social needs of their Mexican-origin constituents only when Mexican American candidates became a threat. When Mexican Americans ran for office, Anglo Americans found it necessary to compete for the Mexican American vote and in turn responded to the needs of their Mexican-origin constituents.

In sum, the ethnographic studies reviewed here indicate that the political behavior of Mexican Americans is complex and cannot be understood by focusing only on cultural issues. It is also necessary to examine how Anglo American institutions affect the political spirit of minority groups. I shall now turn to the field research gathered in the LPEP and examine the responses of our Latino informants. As we shall see, most of our respondents offer a critical analysis of American politics, and their perspectives parallel the findings offered by anthropologists who propose that Mexican Americans have been discouraged by Anglo American elites from participating in American electoral politics.

Methodology and Description of the Ethnographic Sites

Our ethnographic study is based on the responses of 394 informants who resided in five urban Latino communities and on participant observations conducted by five teams of researchers from September 1 to November 15, 1990. With the exception of 29 of the interviews conducted in Houston, the findings in the study reflect the responses of Latinos. The Latino national-origin groups studied were Mexican-origin,[1] Puerto Rican, and Cuban. The ethnographic data on the Mexican-origin population were gathered in Chicago, Houston, and Los Angeles. The data on Puerto Ricans were obtained in New York, and data on the Cubans in Miami. The barrios where the research was conducted are predominantly working-class. These communities also include residential pockets of poverty. Based on 1980 census data the median incomes of the five communities ranged from $6,574 to $15,686. The median income of the Mexican Americans and the Cubans was similar, with Cubans earning slightly more. The median income of the Puerto Ricans was the lowest of the three Latino groups.

Methodology

The LPEP is a product of a team effort, as thirty-four people were involved in the research project. Five research teams collected the ethnographic data. Political scientist Rodolfo de la Garza directed the project and, with Louis DeSipio and me, conceptualized the main research questions. The methodology for the study was designed by de la Garza and me. I am an anthropologist and acted as field director of the data gathering. I also analyzed the ethnographic data from the five sites to ensure that the reports accurately summarized the field researchers' observations and interview data. DeSipio managed the project, designed an election-day exit poll questionnaire, and analyzed the electoral data.

Each team was headed by a principal investigator. Although the principal investigators were not anthropologists, they had previously conducted ethnographic field research and were experienced in gathering participant observation data. Two of the principal investigators were sociologists, two were political scientists, and one was a sociolinguist. Prior to the commencement of the project, the five principal investigators, de la Garza, DeSipio, and I met for three days to discuss the coordination and implementation of the field methods. At that time, we met with the project's advisory board, which helped to identify issues to be examined and offered advice on the methodology to be used.

When collecting the data, the principal investigators were assisted by twenty-one undergraduate and three graduate students. In addition, two site coordinators assisted the principal investigators in El Barrio and Boyle Heights. Both site coordinators were university professors. Excluding the principal investigators, the number of individuals collecting the data consisted of six in Magnolia, five in El Barrio, three in Calle Ocho, three in Pilsen, and nine in Boyle Heights. The data collection began on September 1 and ended on November 15, 1990.[2] The field researchers were asked to employ participant observation techniques. On a daily basis they were to observe the behavior of barrio residents and identify any political activities. They were also asked to attend community meetings and rallies where political issues were discussed. Formal and informal interviews were also conducted. The field researchers maintained a journal of their daily observations and transcribed their interviews in detail. They also collected newspaper articles and newsletters dealing with the election and listened to radio and television for relevant Latino political issues. During the first two weeks of the project, I visited each site and gave the field researchers a workshop on conducting formal and informal interviews. I also reviewed their field journals to see that proper notes were taken.

During the period of the field research, I maintained close contact with the principal investigators in order to ensure that each field site was at the same stage of data collection. In turn, the principal investigators met with their field researchers on a weekly basis to ensure that they were gathering the data as scheduled. Each week, the principal investigators reviewed their field researchers' notes. Every three weeks the principal investigators sent me the field notes for review.

During the first two weeks of the project, the field researchers walked through the Latino neighborhoods and observed the type of political activity taking place (e.g., posters, billboards, banners). Toward the end of the second week, they continued their observations and began conducting formal and informal interviews. From the beginning of the project, the field researchers were expected to attend community meetings where political issues were discussed.

The collection of the formal and informal interviews continued until November 15. Project researchers collected 429 interviews: 124 in Magnolia, 90 in Pilsen, 122 in Boyle Heights, 47 in El Barrio, and 46 in Calle Ocho. Of these interviews, 150 were formal: 32 in Magnolia, 30 in Pilsen, 42 in Boyle Heights, 35 in El Barrio, and 11 in Calle Ocho.[3] The formal interviews lasted approximately one hour. De la Garza, DeSipio, and I designed a set of twelve core questions that were asked during the formal interviews (see chapter one).

The informal interviews consisted of a modified version of the twelve core questions. In the informal interviews, project researchers asked informants to provide their perspectives on the political activities and structure of the barrios, their views of the Democratic and Republican parties, and their assessment of the political spirit of the community. A total of 279 informal interviews were conducted in the five sites: 92 in Magnolia, 60 in Pilsen, 80 in Boyle Heights, 12 in El Barrio, and 35 in Calle Ocho. The length of the informal interviews ranged from 20 minutes to 1.5 hours. These interviews were conducted in a conversational form.

In addition to the formal and informal interviews, each site used an exit poll questionnaire to assess some of the motivating factors that led people to vote. A total of 383 exit polls were conducted.[4] The general comment was that the respondents voted because it was their duty as American citizens.

When the data collection ended on November 15, 1990, all of the field notes were analyzed. Each principal investigator was responsible for analyzing the site data and writing a report. De la Garza and DeSipio analyzed and summarized the electoral campaign data from the five sites. I summarized the ethnographic information dealing with attitudes and behavior. I also read all the field notes to determine if the reports written by the principal investigators adequately summarized the field researchers' ethnographic observations and interview data. We conducted a final meeting after the reports were completed to review the project findings.

Description of the Sites

Each research site in the LPEP constituted a cultural community that contained residential neighborhoods and a commercial business strip. Because the advisory board decided that it would be impractical to study entire cities, we selected only one barrio in each site. The advisory board also decided to select the number of research sites to be studied based on the national population sizes of Mexican Americans, Puerto Ricans, and Cubans (e.g., Mexican Americans, 63.0 percent; Puerto Ricans, 11.6 percent; 5.3 percent Cuban) (Miranda and Quiroz 1989). In selecting the sites to be studied, we avoided dividing the communities into sectors that did not constitute meaningful cultural communities. The five communities were selected because they are part of the oldest Latino neighborhoods in each of the cities. We did realize, however, that this would pose a limitation to our study because these are primarily working- and lower-class areas. Moreover, within these barrios there are several pockets of residential poverty. El Barrio (Puerto Rican) and Pilsen (Mexican) contain the highest concentration of people living in poverty in comparison with the other sites, while Calle Ocho (Cuban) contains the lowest. The 1980 median income of households in the research sites was as follows: Magnolia, $14,380; Pilsen, $13,633; Boyle Heights, $10,251; El Barrio, $6,574; and Calle Ocho, $15,686.

Excluding Magnolia, the research sites were densely populated. The population sizes of the research sites were as follows: Pilsen, 47,623; Calle Ocho, 13,785; El Barrio, 10,002; Boyle Heights, 10,572; and Magnolia, 6,279. The ethnic composition of the research sites indicates that 82 to 92 percent of the residents were Latinos. In spatial size, each community ranged from approximately three-fourths of a mile to 2.5 miles long.

General physical characteristics of the five communities indicate that the sites are surrounded by freeways, shipyards, dumps, railroad tracks, or cemeteries. The communities are not located near middle-class neighborhoods, parks, or recreational zones. In physical appearance, the neighborhoods in Calle Ocho and Boyle Heights share a strong resemblance. Community pride in these residential tracts is apparent. Though these neighborhoods are economically depressed, the residents maintain the outside of their homes and the yards are well kept. Even the housing project in the Boyle Heights research site is kept clean in its exterior appearance. The physical appearance of the Magnolia barrio is mixed. Some of the housing blocks are economically depressed and resemble junkyards. These residents' yards are full of trash, tires, and abandoned cars. On the other hand, a few houses appear to be similar to those found in middle-class neighborhoods. The houses are larger, the paint on the exterior walls is new, the fences are aesthetically pleasant, and the lawns are manicured.

The barrios in Pilsen and in El Barrio appear to be significantly more economically depressed in comparison with the three other Latino barrios studied. Instead of single-family housing, the residential structures are four- to five-story buildings, close together, and lacking front yards. The streets in the barrios do not appear to be maintained by the city, and it is common to see broken windows throughout the neighborhoods. Unlike in the barrios of the Southwest and Florida, it is common to see homeless people sitting on the sidewalks. Although both El Barrio and the Pilsen barrios are blighted residential zones, most of the residents attempt to maintain clean neighborhoods. That is, although the streets are filled with trash, many women sweep the streets and the sidewalks in front of their buildings. Gentrification also appears to be taking place in both Pilsen and El Barrio. A few buildings have been refurbished and restored for, primarily, office space.

The local community structure of the five Latino research sites differs. Their only common attribute is that each barrio has a business strip where small-scale Latino businesses provide services to the local population. The business strips comprise restaurants, mom and pop grocery stores, and small department stores that sell inexpensive clothing and household goods. In El Barrio and Pilsen, several of the stores are owned by Middle Easterners.

The main difference among the sites is the number of social service and community organizations located in the barrios. Pilsen has twenty-three social service agencies and two Mexican American community organizations (United Neighborhood Organization [UNO] and Pilsen Neighbors). Magnolia barrio has one social service agency—the YMCA—and three community organizations (League of United Latin American Citizens—LULAC, Veterans' Post 472, and the Metropolitan Organization). The Calle Ocho research site has only one social service agency, a senior center, and no community organizations. Members of the senior center, however, appear to use the center as an ethnic-political club. The El Barrio site has no social service agencies or community organizations. The Boyle Heights research site has two community organizations (UNO and Mothers of East Los Angeles), no social service agencies, and one nonpartisan political organization (the National Association of Latino Elected Officials).

In the Mexican research sites, Catholic churches also serve important social service roles. Besides providing spiritual guidance to parishioners, the priests assist people in forming political and community organizations. No churches were located in the Cuban or Puerto Rican sites.

The Political Voices of Five Latino Communities

The findings summarized in this section are only part of the LPEP's data about political attitudes and behavior. The results of the electoral campaigns are discussed in chapter one. Our interview data indicate that the political perspectives held by our Mexican-origin and Puerto Rican respondents reflect similar attitudes and criticisms of American democratic politics. Their responses, however, are in radical contrast to the political attitudes held by our Cuban respondents. Nonetheless, Cuban political perspectives do share a common concern with the Puerto Rican and Mexican-origin peoples. The three Latino groups expressed concern over their political underrepresentation at all levels of government. They agreed that, if their political representation were to improve, Latino candidates must be elected to office.

Shared Political Attitudes in Mexican and Puerto Rican Communities

Nearly all of our Mexican-origin and Puerto Rican respondents were highly critical of the Republican and Democratic parties. They strongly believed that their ethnic groups were either discouraged or excluded from fully participating in electoral politics. According to our respondents, the political exclusion of the Mexican-origin people and the Puerto Ricans was manifested in the following ways: (1) the Democratic and Republican parties did not actively encourage Mexican-origin people and Puerto Ricans to vote because they were not perceived to be important voting constituencies; (2) both political parties failed to discuss how electoral campaigns affect the social welfare of the Mexican-origin and Puerto Rican peoples; and (3) elected officials were not responsive to the social needs of both ethnic groups.

From September 1 to November 15, the field researchers in the Mexican-origin and Puerto Rican communities found minimal evidence of any type of outreach on the part of the two parties. In the Mexican communities, neither party actively advertised campaign propaganda, distributed literature door to door, or initiated a local get-out-the-vote campaign. Only in the Pilsen and Magnolia sites did some Democratic candidates do some outreach. The intent of this outreach, however, was to remind Mexican Americans to vote Democratic because the party depended on their loyalty. For example, during two community celebrations in Pilsen, Democratic candidates encouraged the Mexican-origin community to vote for party members. The politicians did not discuss issues of significance to Pilsen, however, nor attempt to educate the audience about the differences between voting Democratic or Republican. In Magnolia, a similar phenomenon occurred. Only one candidate visited the site and asked people to vote Democratic. Political issues were not discussed.

Field researchers observed a similar lack of outreach in El Barrio. Campaign meetings were not held, only one political poster appeared during the election, a get-out-the-vote registration drive was not organized, and political propaganda was not distributed to the residents door to door. Although the Democrats opened a campaign office in El Barrio, the field researchers found it regularly closed, and telephone calls went unanswered. In an attempt to contact someone at the campaign office, one of our field researchers visited the office regularly for 2.5 months and observed that no one was there in the morning, afternoon, or evening. Our field researchers also observed that very little campaign literature was distributed from this office. Only a newsletter appeared in the barrio reminding people to vote for one of the Democratic candidates. When the site coordinator spoke to one of the incumbent Democratic candidates about the lack of Democratic involvement in getting out the Puerto Rican vote, the candidate responded, "if my constituents do not know at this point what I do, then they do not deserve me as their senator. . . . I, therefore, did not send . . . a little paper saying: re-elect Senator . . ."

Our field researchers also found that in their Mexican-origin and Puerto Rican research sites the Spanish-language media were rarely used by the Democrats or the Republicans to disseminate electoral information. Political parties seldom used the Spanish-language media to educate the Mexican-origin population or Puerto Ricans about campaign issues. Only on occasion did the Democrats use Spanish radio to remind Latinos to go out and vote. Once again, however, their intent was to remind Latinos to be loyal to the Democratic party, not to educate them about political issues. Our field researchers observed that, had it not been for the efforts of Latino political activists and media reporters, electoral information would not have reached Latinos monolingual in Spanish. The Spanish dominant constitute a sizable element of the Puerto Rican barrio. Most electoral information was disseminated by Latino reporters, radio hosts, and political activists. Moreover, without the efforts of these individuals, many Latinos would not have received any analysis of the relevancy of the electoral campaign to their communities.

Cuban Political Attitudes: Cubanismo

In the case of the Cuban community, the Democrats did not actively pursue the Cuban vote, in contrast to the Republicans, who sought out Cuban support. In the case of the Cubans, one does not see the same pattern of political neglect as witnessed in the Mexican and Puerto Rican sites. The overwhelming view of our Cuban respondents was that the Republican party adequately represented their political concerns. The Cubans' apparent satisfaction with the Republican party centered on the issue of "hard-line politics" with respect to anything dealing with communism and, in particular, Fidel Castro. To the Cuban community of Calle Ocho, anti-Castro and anticommunist persons were friends of the Cuban community and would be supported by them. General sentiments of the Cuban respondents indicated that they would not vote for Democratic candidates unless they supported "*Cubanismo*," a platform that placed Cuban interests first and that featured a hard-line anticommunist position. A large number of our Cuban respondents also remarked that the Democratic party did not pursue their vote because the party preferred to cater to the special interests of the black and Anglo American communities.

Our field researchers' observations indicate that the Cubans' political attitudes were strongly reinforced by the behavior practiced toward them by the Democratic and the Republican parties. That is, the Democratic party did not appear to be interested in changing the attitudes of the Cuban community or in gaining its electoral support. For example, it was uncommon for the Democrats to use the Spanish-language media, which is central to Miami political life, to obtain Cuban support. The Democrats did not open an office in Calle Ocho, nor did they distribute literature door to door, nor was there any Democratic political propaganda in the streets. Moreover, although during the primaries two Democratic candidates attempted to reach out to the Cubans, in the runoff there was no such effort.

The Republicans, on the other hand, made it very clear that they valued their Cuban constituency. The Republican party's strategy in dealing with Cubans, however, concentrated on getting them to vote Republican, with little attention to explaining issues or discussing problems affecting their community. For example, the Republicans bombarded the Spanish-language media with advertisements that emphasized that a vote for a Republican was a vote for *Cubanismo*. The Republican party, however, did not explain how voting Republican would help to ameliorate the social problems in Calle Ocho. In short, to get the Cuban vote it was common for the Republican party to appeal to *Cubanismo* and to sidestep or to pay lip service to social problems such as transportation for senior citizens and low-cost day-care centers.

Our field researchers also found that, although Cubans were disappointed with some Republican candidates, most were unwilling to criticize the party. This behavior differed from that of the Mexican-origin and Puerto Rican respondents. That is, although most of our Cuban, Puerto Rican, and Mexican-origin respondents can be characterized as working-class, only the Puerto Ricans and the Mexicans were inclined to voice their displeasure with political representation perceived as inadequate. We now turn to this issue.

Latino Perspectives of Elected Officials

Nearly all of our Puerto Rican and Mexican-origin respondents perceived a close relation between persistent community social problems and the failure of the Democratic and Republican parties to fulfill campaign promises. In general, Mexican-origin and Puerto Rican respondents felt that, because their communities were deemed unimportant by both political parties, candidates ignored their social needs. Indeed, Mexican American respondents attributed most of their com-

munities' social problems to political neglect. A high crime rate in
their neighborhoods, insufficient low-income housing, the growth of
gangs, uncontrollable drug trafficking, and inferior education were attributed to the failure of the Democratic and Republican parties adequately to address their constituencies' needs. Excluding the gang problem, the Puerto Ricans voiced similar complaints. The Puerto Rican
and Mexican-origin communities wanted their elected officials to
provide better schools, more police protection, more accessibility to
low-income housing, and an effective drug control program to protect
their children. Both ethnic groups, however, were disillusioned with
the government's inaction and did not envision any change. In essence,
the respondents felt that the government treated them as undesirable
second-class citizens who should be satisfied with what they had.

Though most of the Mexican-origin and Puerto Rican respondents
did not foresee any change in the immediate future, they believed
that long-term change would occur. Most Mexican-origin respondents
felt that, as the size of their population increased, more Mexican
American candidates would be elected to office, and these officials
would be more sensitive to their concerns. The Mexican-origin respondents also believed that only elected officials of Mexican descent had
an interest in advocating for their social needs. In Los Angeles, city
councilwoman Gloria Molina was often cited as the type of elected official who was committed to her community.[5] According to some respondents, Molina fought for many issues that benefited the Mexican-
origin community, even if the outcome of her actions hurt her career.
For example, she fought against the construction of a state prison and
an incinerator in the center of East Los Angeles, even though her colleagues favored the construction of these projects in the Mexican
neighborhoods.

Most of our Puerto Rican respondents concurred with the opinions of
the Mexican-origin population. They agreed that electing Latino candidates to office was beneficial and believed that social problems
affecting Latino communities would be acted on only by Latino elected
officials.

Although the Puerto Rican respondents held positive opinions about
Latino elected officials, they also held critical views. They recognized that most elected officials could become corrupt. In particular,
they commented that whenever Latino politicians held office for
several years and were re-elected without opposition, they eventually
became irresponsible and perhaps corrupt. The Puerto Rican respondents believed that Latino elected officials would compromise their
principles and support policies that did not benefit Latinos, if it
benefited their careers. The majority of our Puerto Rican respondents

stated that to avoid this problem it was necessary for Latino voters to have several Latino candidates to select from. In their eyes, competition among Latino candidates would help to reduce corruption.

The Cubans of Calle Ocho overwhelmingly concurred that having Latino elected officials was desirable. They were very proud that people of their ethnicity were active in national, state, county, and local politics. Our Cuban respondents generally felt that because there was sufficient competition among Cuban politicians they were able to select the best candidate. Several of our respondents also commented that they would not support a Cuban elected official who was not loyal to the community. Such a person was a Cuban who no longer practiced *Cubanismo* and had minimal contact with the community.

Furthermore, when our field researchers conducted the exit poll interviews, a common concern voiced by the Cubans was that there were very few Mexican American and Puerto Rican elected officials. They considered this to be a serious problem and to be counterproductive for all Latinos. In particular, they felt that if Mexican-origin people were represented in numbers relative to their population, this would benefit Cubans at the congressional level. Several Cuban respondents also offered the following sentiment: How can Mexicans and Puerto Ricans advance if they have no one to speak for them?

The Views of Community Activists

In the Mexican American neighborhoods, our field researchers gathered additional information about how Mexican Americans could become politically empowered. These interviews were conducted with priests, political activists, and social service professionals. The priests were active in Magnolia and Pilsen. The political activists and social service professionals lived in the three Mexican American neighborhoods we studied. The political activists were members of organizations that included United Neighborhood Organization, Pilsen Neighbors, the Metropolitan Organization, League of United Latin American Citizens, and Mothers of East Los Angeles. The Mexican American social service professionals managed government agencies ranging from day-care centers to alcohol rehabilitation centers.

In their analysis of electoral politics, the Mexican American political activists and social service professionals shared similar views. They concurred that the government ignored the social and economic needs of the Mexican Americans and inadequately funded local social service programs. They commented that the Mexican-origin population was not actively encouraged to participate in the Republican and

Democratic parties. On the other hand, our respondents also offered in-group criticisms of Mexican American voting practices. A common criticism was that Mexican Americans needed to be more politically active and needed to form bloc-voting interest groups. They alleged that until more political organizations were formed in the barrios Anglo American politicians would ignore the voices of the Mexican Americans. Our respondents commented that, to become powerful, Mexican Americans must register to vote and Mexican immigrants must naturalize. To enact this type of political activism, however, it would be necessary first to lift the political spirit of their communities.

No general plan was offered by our respondents to realize this kind of change, however. Instead, they offered different plans of action suited to their communities. In Magnolia, several respondents suggested that at-large district elections be changed to single-member district elections. For example, the director of an educational program suggested that, if such a system were instituted, Mexican Americans would be able to elect Mexican American district judges and other county-level positions. This system would lift the Mexican Americans' community spirit and people would eventually vote in larger numbers. She also proposed that the at-large election system currently practiced in the county discouraged Mexican Americans from voting because it was difficult to elect Mexican American candidates. In Pilsen and Los Angeles, our respondents stated that their communities must show the Democrats and the Republicans that neither party controlled the Mexican American vote. They proposed that Mexican Americans should support only candidates, be they Democrats or Republicans, who have a history of advocating for Latino issues. Our respondents in Boyle Heights suggested that their community could become politically empowered by forming a coalition of Latino organizations whose main goal would be to get their candidates elected to office. In this manner, the community would be able to elect candidates who advocated on behalf of Latino issues.

Two Anglo American Catholic priests in Magnolia and one in Pilsen also offered comments regarding the political empowerment of the Mexican American community. According to the priests, Anglo American politicians react differently to the needs of their Latino and Anglo American constituencies. Elected officials listen carefully to their Anglo American constituencies and immediately act on their demands. On the other hand, elected officials often ignore the voices of their Latino constituents. This occurs allegedly because politicians believe that the Mexican American community is unorganized. Although the priests did not envision any change in the near future, they did comment that political activism in their barrios was increasing and they predicted that within a few years community activists would be able to organize the Mexican American vote into powerful interest groups. According to the priests, the Immigration Reform and Control Act of 1986 and its amnesty triggered political mobilization in the barrios. When IRCA was enacted, many Mexican American organizations apparently were formed to protect the rights of undocumented families. Today these organizations are expanding their agendas and are becoming social-civic organizations such as tenant advocacy groups, youth Christian leagues, women's groups, and nonpartisan voter registration groups. Based on the priests' observations and interaction with Mexican Americans, they envision that in the near future these community organizations will become important political advocacy groups.

Conclusion

Our research teams found that Mexican-origin and Puerto Rican respondents shared similar political views. These two Latino groups overwhelmingly considered themselves to be politically disenfranchised. On the other hand, Cubans felt that the Republican party adequately represented them. Overall, the political spirit of the Mexican Americans and the Puerto Ricans appeared to be low. In the near future they did not expect the Democratic or Republican parties to represent them adequately. They envisioned political change only when they were represented by Latino elected officials. In contrast to these beliefs, the Cubans' political spirit appeared to be healthy and hopeful. Cuban respondents were content with the political representation they received from the Republican party. Our researchers' ethnographic observations suggest that the Cubans' anticommunist agenda has served as a rallying point of peoplehood and traditionally has triggered community political activism.

Notes

1. In the discussion that follows, I will use the term Mexican-origin to denote all people of Mexican descent who reside in the United States. I will use Mexican American to refer to people of Mexican descent who are eligible to vote in the United States.

2. In the Boyle Heights area, only one researcher began his observations on September 1, 1990. The other Boyle Heights researchers began their observations by September 14.

3. In Boyle Heights the principal investigators used focus groups to conduct

the formal interviews. This consisted of speaking to informants in groups. The twelve core questions were asked and the discussions lasted approximately one hour.

4. The research sites conducted the following number of exit polls: Magnolia, 52; Pilsen, 63; Boyle Heights, 38; El Barrio, 30; and Calle Ocho, 200.

5. When our study was conducted, Gloria Molina had not yet been elected county supervisor.

References

Edmonson, Munro S. 1957. *Los Manitos: A Study of Institutional Values.* New Orleans: Middle American Research Institute, Tulane University.

El Grito. 1967–1973. Berkeley, Calif.: Quinto Sol Publications. Vols. 1–4.

Foley, Douglas E. 1977. *From Peones to Politicos: Ethnic Relations in a South Texas Town, 1900 to 1977.* Austin: Center for Mexican American Studies, University of Texas Press.

———. 1988. *From Peones to Politicos: Class and Ethnicity in a South Texas Town, 1900–1987.* Austin: Center for Mexican American Studies, University of Texas Press.

Geilhufe, Nancy. 1979. *Chicanos and Police: A Study of Politics and Ethnicity in San Jose, California.* Washington, D.C.: Society for Applied Anthropology.

Hernández, Deluvina. 1970. *Mexican American Challenge to a Sacred Cow.* Berkeley and Los Angeles: University of California Press.

Kluckhohn, Florence, and Fred Strodtbeck. 1961. *Variations in Value Orientation.* Evanston, Ill: Row Peterson.

Knowlton, Clark S. 1962. "Patron-Peon Pattern among the Spanish Americans of New Mexico." *Social Forces* 41: 12–17.

Kutsche, Paul. 1979. "Introduction: Atomism, Factionalism, and Flexibility." In Paul Kutsche, ed., *The Colorado College Studies: The Survival of Spanish American Villages,* pp. 7–20. Colorado Springs: Research Committee of Colorado College.

Kutsche, Paul, and John Van Ness. 1981. *Cañones: Values, Crisis, and Survival in a Northern New Mexico Village.* Albuquerque: University of New Mexico Press.

Leonard, Olen. 1970. *The Role of the Land Grant in the Social Organization and Social Processes of a Spanish-American Village in New Mexico.* Albuquerque: Calvin Horn.

Levy, Jerrold. 1968. "Perspectives on the Atomistic-Type Society: Some Anazagorean Thoughts on Atomism, Dualism, and the Effects of the Mind on the Monad." *Human Organization* 27: 230–235.

Madsen, William. 1964. *Mexican Americans of South Texas.* New York: Holt, Reinhart and Winston.

Menchaca, Martha. 1988. "Chicano-Mexican Conflict and Cohesion in San Pablo California." Ph.D. dissertation, Stanford University.

———. 1989. "Chicano-Mexican Cultural Assimilation and Anglo-Saxon Cultural Dominance." *Hispanic Journal of Behavioral Sciences* 11 (3): 203–231.

Miranda, L., and J. T. Quiroz. 1989. *The Decade of the Hispanic: A Sobering Economic Retrospective*. Washington, D.C.: National Council of La Raza.

Paredes, Américo. 1978. "On Ethnographic Work among Minority Groups." In Ricardo Romo and Raymund Paredes, eds., *New Directions in Chicano Scholarship*, pp. 1–37. San Diego: Chicano Studies Monograph Series, University of California.

Rosaldo, Renato. 1985. "Chicano Studies, 1970 to 1984." *Annual Review of Anthropology* 14: 405–427.

Rubel, Arthur. 1960. "Concepts of Disease in Mexican American Culture." *American Anthropologist* 62 (5): 795–814.

———. 1966. *Across the Tracks: Mexican Americans in a Texas City*. Austin: University of Texas Press.

Rubel, Arthur, and H. J. Kupferer. 1968. "Perspectives of Atomistic Type Society." *Human Organization* 27 (3): 189–190.

Spicer, Edward. 1972. "Introduction." In Edward Spicer and Raymond H. Thompson, eds., *Plural Society in the Southwest*, pp. 1–5. New York: Interbook.

———. 1975. "Persistent Identity Systems." *Science* 174: 795–800.

Takash-Cruz, Paule. 1990. "A Crisis of Democracy Community: Responses to the Latinoization of a California Town Dependent on Immigrant Labor." Ph.D. dissertation, University of California-Berkeley.

Van Ness, John. 1976. "Spanish-American vs. Anglo American Land Tenure and the Study of Economic Change in New Mexico." *Social Science Journal* 13: 45–52.

3

Puerto Rican Politics in East Harlem's "El Barrio"

Anneris Goris and Pedro Pedraza

This chapter examines the 1990 election in an East Harlem neighborhood (El Barrio) in order to understand the relationship between the electoral process and Puerto Rican politics in New York City as experienced by this community.[1] As we will suggest, the level of Puerto Rican electoral participation in the 1990 elections in El Barrio reflects the weak voting strength of this population. The low level of Puerto Rican electoral participation can be partially explained by structural factors outside of El Barrio. The 1990 election had no presidential race. Further, the two state-level offices offering the most direct contact with the community—the state senate and the state assembly positions—were uncontested in the general election.

Yet, 1990 offered several opportunities for empowerment around which more organized political communities could organize and potentially capitalize. The most important state-level offices were up for election, including the governor, the lieutenant governor, the comptroller, and the attorney general. The research site's congressional seat was also up for re-election. In addition, the 1990 election was the last prior to redistricting at several levels of elective office. In 1991, the New York City Council was to be expanded. The creation of the new seats was designed, in part, to increase the power of minority communities. Further, the post-1990 census redistricting at all other levels of elective office offered further potential for community mobilization. A strong showing from El Barrio in the 1990 elections could have increased the bargaining power of the community's representatives in redistricting debates. These factors should be considered as we discuss the low levels of community interest in the 1990 campaign and the virtually nonexistent efforts by campaigns and candidates to mobilize the residents of El Barrio.

A History of Puerto Rican Electoral
Participation in El Barrio and New York City

For the Puerto Rican community and El Barrio, the low levels of electoral participation and mobilization manifested in the 1990 elections are an exception to the historical experience. As early as 1927, Puerto Ricans participated in party politics.[2] In 1929, two thousand Puerto Ricans voted in the general election. They formed their own party clubs in 1935 and, in 1937, helped to elect Oscar García Rivera, the first Puerto Rican state legislator in New York (Sánchez-Korrol 1983: 172-193). By the 1940s, Puerto Ricans had become very active in electoral politics.[3] Not only did they manage to register over thirty thousand voters (Rodríguez-Fraticelli and Tirado 1989: 184), but they also organized to support Vito Marcantonio, an Italian-American Democratic congressman who was recognized as a champion of the poor. He allied himself with Puerto Ricans in El Barrio to fight racism and discrimination and advocated the independence of Puerto Rico (Meyer 1989: chapter 7).

In the late 1940s and the early 1950s, several organizations were created to address social welfare problems faced by Puerto Ricans. The mid-1950s saw the Puerto Rican community mobilized to defend its civil rights and organized to present cultural events such as the Puerto Rican Day Parade.

With the creation of the Great Society and the War on Poverty programs of the 1960s, many Puerto Rican groups were able to take advantage of federal funds. Several foundations also provided funds for the creation of services to assist Puerto Rican youth. War on Poverty programs helped many community-based organizations in Puerto Rican neighborhoods to create and develop an economic and social infrastructure while channeling funds to enhance the leadership structure of the community. As a consequence of the politics and ideological underpinnings of these programs, however, certain groups became institutionalized, thereby leading to entrenched leadership and financial dependence on government funds.

In the late 1960s, the Young Lords, an organization of Puerto Rican youth, decided that the time had come to change the conditions of poverty in the Puerto Rican community in the United States and to demand the liberation of Puerto Rico. This group of college students and other youth would, in a very short time, become a political party that organized the community for "offensives" against various governmental institutions.

Some of the very same people who took part in this movement, however, now view electoral participation as an important tool in the political struggle of Puerto Ricans. In the words of a former Young Lord, "We are beginning to develop an understanding of organization building, leadership development, direct action, litigation, lobbying, and other tactics in combination with effective electoral participation" (Pérez 1989: 59).

Despite this history of political organization and activism, only 3 percent of 26,343 elected officials in the state of New York were Puerto Rican in 1990. Only 3.3 percent of the state senate, 2.7 percent of the state assembly, and 8.6 percent of the city council were Puerto Rican (Institute for Puerto Rican Policy 1989). In 1990, there were 11 elected Puerto Rican officials in the city of New York: 3 council members—Víctor Robles, José Rivera, and Rafael Colón; 2 state senators—Olga Méndez and Efrain González; 4 assembly members—Angelo Del Toro, Roberto Ramírez, Héctor Díaz, and David Rosado; Bronx borough president Fernando Ferrer; and Congressman José Serrano. There were also a host of Puerto Ricans who were elected to positions of leadership within the Democratic party, such as district leaders (Institute for Puerto Rican Policy 1989: ii).

Project Methodology

This chapter presents a historical snapshot of the present-day political participation of Puerto Ricans in El Barrio as observed during the 1990 election campaign. The research focused on the daily life of the community in order to develop a comprehensive understanding of the texture of the community, the links between the community and the rest of society, the importance of ethnicity to neighborhood residents, and the manner in which this neighborhood engages in the electoral process.

The research team comprised four student research assistants and two principal investigators. We selected census tracts 166 and 172.01, encompassing an area between Third Avenue and Park Avenue in Manhattan. Along with three adjacent census tracts that we did not include in our research site, these five tracts constitute a two-block-by-twelve-block rectangular section of East Harlem that is the heart of El Barrio. The five tracts combined have a population of over ten thousand and are some of the most densely populated Latino tracts in Manhattan. The site is in State Assembly District 68 and contains nine electoral precincts.

The fieldwork began the second week of September. The first week served as an orientation period for the research assistants while the entire team participated in developing a research plan. We began by making informal visits and by strolling through the twenty-four-block area, which served to familiarize the team with the area and to identify strategic observation sites, such as *bodegas* (small grocery stores), *casitas* (vest-pocket parks with improvised structures that function as unlicensed bars and serve as social clubs and neighborhood gathering places), laundromats, bakeries, and a playground, for future visits. At this stage, our conversations with people were informal and exploratory.

During our first week in the field, New York State held a primary election. We found this primary to be a nonevent in the community. Most residents were unaware that an election was occurring.

After the primary, we took a more direct approach by asking community residents questions about the election. We supplemented these informal interviews with a formal questionnaire used to interview people at different locations throughout the neighborhood. We also used a formal questionnaire to interview candidates, political party functionaries, and community activists and leaders. Throughout the course of the study, we conducted 35 formal and 12 informal interviews. A multidimensional approach toward the project—incorporating participant observations, interviews, an exit poll, and historical data—provided a rich composite picture of the community with which to decipher the complexity of its relationship to the political process.

Description of the Research Site

As we have indicated, our research site is within El Barrio in East Harlem in Manhattan. This area is the traditional center of New York's Puerto Rican community. El Barrio is considered "la cuna de la comunidad puertorriqueña" (the cradle of the Puerto Rican community) in the United States. It was the first area of residence for many Puerto Ricans coming to the United States and continues to be dominated by Puerto Rican leaders. El Barrio refers not just to the physical and geographical boundaries, but to a community with much social, cultural, and historical significance for the members of the diaspora coming from Puerto Rico. Residents include some who are third- or fourth-generation descendants of the initial turn-of-the-century migrants, as well as first-generation migrants.

El Barrio still functions as a point of entry for many new arrivals, although the majority of these newcomers are not Puerto Ricans, but residents of other Spanish-speaking Latin American and Caribbean countries. The neighborhood recently has become a locus for Mexican migration into New York City. Today, the Puerto Rican residents of "Spanish Harlem," as the neighborhood has been called, do not amount to more than 50 percent of the total population, although they are a plurality. Nonetheless, there are areas that still exhibit a pattern of residence reminiscent of most of East Harlem twenty years ago, when it was viewed as the capital of the Puerto Rican colony in the United States.

In order to describe the demographics of the research site, we examined census data and New York State electoral jurisdiction data. As we have mentioned, the research site encompasses two census tracts—166 and 172.01—and part of Assembly District 68. Although we cannot pinpoint demographic and electoral information specifically for the research site, we will describe the site by presenting information on these three bureaucratic divisions.

In 1980, Assembly District 68 contained 46,294 households made up of approximately 123,266 persons. The ethnic breakdown of the population reveals that 45.7 percent were black, 41.3 percent were of Latino origin, 11.1 percent were white, and 1.1 percent were American Indian or Asian American (see Table 3.1). Among the Latinos in Assembly District 68, Puerto Ricans made up 87.7 percent; "other" Latinos, 10.6 percent; Cubans, 1.1 percent; and Mexicans, 1.1 percent (Institute for Puerto Rican Policy 1991a).

The area has seen an increasing proportional concentration of Puerto Ricans and other Latinos over the past decade. The population of Assembly District 68 decreased 9.23 percent from 1980 to 1990—from 123,266 to 112,845. Despite this decline in population, the Puerto Rican and Latino population increased by 7 percent.

As mentioned, the neighborhood has seen an increase in the number of Mexican immigrants. Dominicans have also established roots in the area, although not always as residents, but as owners of restaurants, beauty parlors, and grocery stores.

TABLE 3.1 Population by Census Tract for the El Barrio Research Site, 1980

Tract	Total Population	% Latinos	% Whites	% Blacks
166	6,148	73.1	5.3	20.3
172.01	4,641	73.2	2.9	22.8

Source: Institute for Puerto Rican Policy 1991a.

In 1980, the combined population of census tracts 166 and 172.01 in our research site was 10,789. Latinos made up 73 percent of the population of these two census tracts; whites, 5 percent; and blacks, 22 percent. Of the Latino subgroups, Puerto Ricans were 86 percent, "other" Latinos were 10 percent, Mexicans were 4 percent, and Cubans were 1 percent.

According to 1980 census data, Latinos in tract 166 had the following demographic characteristics: 2,261 people were sixteen years old or younger and 2,526 people were twenty-five or older. The median household income for Latino families was $6,574 and the mean was $9,478. An examination of the educational levels revealed that, of the tract's Latinos, 21.2 percent had finished from one to three years of high school, 16.2 percent had completed high school, and 0.10 percent had four years of college or more.

Puerto Ricans do not have a strong hold on any sector of the economy of the research site. For instance, many of the *bodegas*, restaurants, and dry cleaners are owned and operated by Dominicans who do not live in the neighborhood. Koreans own variety stores and vegetable stands. Mexicans have opened restaurants, flower shops, and video stores. Some Puerto Ricans and Dominicans also have small informal service, repair, and construction businesses that provide services to the area.

Despite El Barrio's image as the home to the city's Puerto Ricans, it has been steadily losing its preeminence to other parts of the New York metropolitan area. Since the 1970s, Puerto Ricans have come to constitute a higher percentage of the Bronx's population (39 percent) than of Manhattan's (23 percent). These population figures reflect both the migration of non-Puerto Ricans to traditionally Puerto Rican areas of Manhattan and a movement of Puerto Ricans out of Manhattan during the 1970s and the 1980s (Governor's Advisory Committee for Hispanic Affairs 1984).

The 1990 Election

As we have indicated, Puerto Ricans have been involved in electoral politics since the late 1930s. In recent years, however, Puerto Ricans have become less active in formal politics. An examination of the voter turnout in El Barrio in Assembly District 68 reinforces this assessment. Unregistered eligible voters in this election district totaled 19,468 in 1989. This means that almost 20 percent of the residents who were eligible to vote were not registered (Institute for Puerto Rican Policy 1991a). Registration, of course, does not equal turnout. In fact, the data show that, in 1988, 54 percent of registered voters in

District 68 actually voted. This percentage decreased to 48 percent in 1989 (Voter Assistance Commission 1990), and 25 percent in 1990. Thus, the combination of citywide geographical dispersion of Puerto Ricans, the number of unregistered eligible voters, and low turnout rates among the registered inhibits the electoral power of Puerto Ricans at the local level (Fitzpatrick 1987*a*: 42).

Interviews

We gauged the attitudes of the community toward electoral politics with participant observations, interviews with elected officials, directors of agencies, and community residents, and exit polls. We began our fieldwork in September, when the weather was still warm and the streets were full of people. On our first day, few people seemed to be aware of the primary on September 12. We spoke to a couple on Lexington Avenue. The woman was able to provide specific details about the primary, but the man stated that the last time he voted was in the 1949 [*sic*] presidential election. As we continued down Lexington Avenue, we noticed a group of six older men playing dominoes. One stated that he did not know anything about the upcoming primary, but claimed that once inside the voting booth, he would find out. Another group of men sitting on the steps of the building said that they were not aware of the election, but were able to name the site of the polling place.

On the day of the primary, we visited El Barrio to document the level of political activity. We observed few people coming out to vote. Of those on the street whom we stopped to ask about the election, many did not know that an election was taking place. At La Casita, we observed five adults; no one mentioned the elections and politics was not discussed. During these visits to the community, we noticed a few fliers and newsletters promoting the campaigns of several candidates.

Almost two weeks after the primary, we spoke with two older Puerto Rican men in front of a *bodega* on 104th Street near Park Avenue. After they inquired about our study, we took the opportunity to probe them about politics in El Barrio. One man had lived in the community for over thirty years and remembered when Vito Marcantonio organized the Puerto Rican community in the 1930s. He went on to explain that, during those days, Lexington Avenue ("La Avenida") was the center of political activity in the community. He stated that this was no longer the case because politicians and organizations had moved away. "Now, for us to see Olga Méndez [the Latina state senator from El Barrio], we have to go to Third Avenue and 116th Street, and 'nadie va allá' (nobody goes there)." According to this man, drugs were the main problem in the community.

On the other side of Lexington Avenue, at the Aguilar Senior Citizen Center, we met an old man sitting on the steps of the building. He said that he visited the center every day and spoke at length about it. The current director, he said, was a black woman, but her predecessor was a white man. "I do not know why the director is not Hispanic; maybe there were not Hispanics qualified for the position," he offered.

On October 1, while conducting observations at Los Gavilanes restaurant, we overhead a conversation between two men who were discussing rent increases in El Barrio. One said that he did not worry about them, because he earned $350 for working five hours a day, six days a week, "pasando numeros" (running numbers).

Several days later, we ran across a voter registration drive at a public school, organized by the Central Elections Board and conducted by black and Latina women. One of the women, Mildred, said that older people and men voted more often than others in the community. She added that Olga Méndez "does not do anything in the community."

An insightful interview with a prominent neighborhood leader, Antonio Rivera, provided another dimension of life in El Barrio. Rivera was the director of the Ombudsman Unit of the City Council of New York. His dual roles as a longtime community member and as a mediator/liaison ("defensor del pueblo") between his neighborhood and the city council placed him in a unique position from which to comment on the community's political experiences. His remarks about the lack of competition in local races were similar to those we had heard from other residents:

> When there are primaries and there is a campaign, people come out to debate. Then the politician is obligated to come out to debate positions and to talk about the accomplishments during that time. . . . There are people who dominate their positions, and they don't permit others to enter. . . . I find this a little destructive because when that occurs, there is no competitiveness and one can not change the leadership. . . . It is for this reason that people don't want to participate.

To summarize, from August to October, the only political activity we noted was the presence of fliers and newsletters. The primary did not draw much attention and was not "a big deal in the community," according to several informants.

Organizations

Another interview with a "famous" neighborhood resident, musician Johnny Colón, revealed equally fascinating insights. Colón is a well-known Puerto Rican musician in New York City and is politically active as well. He is a product of El Barrio, having graduated from junior high and high school there. He currently runs a music school in the neighborhood. Colón believed that the paucity of financial resources for community organizations was to blame for the lack of unity in the neighborhood. Without a stable economic base, organizations find themselves having to get loans at high interest rates to pay salaries.

Another community organizer and activist, Fernando Salicrup, offered a second explanation for the absence of community organizations (whether political or not) in El Barrio. He was politically involved because of a series of personal relationships with the elected officials. Yet he reported that many other residents felt more marginalized because the "political machine" that operated the city viewed the Puerto Rican community as "low profile," or politically inactive.

He suggested that this inactivity was a function of two phenomena. First, activists from the 1960s realized that the changes they were fighting for would take too long to accomplish, so they lost interest. Second, the Puerto Rican community as a whole failed to move beyond the poverty programs of the 1960s to such issues as housing. As a result, Puerto Rican leaders did not assure their own leadership role in the city programs that emerged in the 1970s and the 1980s, despite the fact that many Puerto Ricans relied on the services being offered. In sum, he suggested that Puerto Ricans in El Barrio had failed to take advantage of opportunities that would have been available had they organized around specific issues. He argued that elected officials were too busy and too dependent on core supporters to take the lead in this necessary community organizational effort.

Issues

The issues discussed in the neighborhood tended to revolve around the drug problem, mainly crack. Residents were concerned about losing their young people to this drug. When asked if they thought that political officials were addressing this issue, they said that if they were, they were not doing a very good job.

One of our informants mentioned a drug problem of a different nature. He pointed out the drug center nearby, not far from the elementary school. Yet the drug center he was referring to was not your typical drug market; instead, it was a medical office or "Medicaid mill," where people got drugs. "You should see the number of people who go to the doctor's office to get drugs. The children in the community see this every day." He concluded by saying, "The politicians are not doing anything about this. . . . It is hard to contact the politicians in this area."

Both community activists and one of the elected officials we interviewed mentioned educational budget cuts as a serious issue facing the state. They reported that this was not a mass issue in the 1990 elections because cuts that had already been enacted would not take effect until after the elections.

Our interviews identified just one local issue tied to a state electoral initiative. The ballot included a bond issue that would have allowed *casitas* to be declared cultural recreational sites. Further, the bond issue would have allocated resources to develop parts of El Barrio as historical sites, development that we thought would attract more business to the neighborhood.

No specific Latino issue emerged during our discussions with people. The only political issue we heard much about was the plebiscite in Puerto Rico, which was obviously not pertinent to this election.

Just as no clearly Latino issue emerged in the campaign, no issue of particular interest to women developed. The state senator, Olga Méndez, reported that she was the first Puerto Rican woman elected to a public post in the United States as well as the first Puerto Rican woman or Latina elected to a leadership post in the New York Senate. In our interview, she indicated that she "imagines that [if] instead of being Senator Olga Méndez, [she were] Senator Méndez, politically things would have been very different."

Candidates

Candidates for statewide offices, such as governor and lieutenant governor, made no direct outreach efforts to El Barrio. Citywide efforts such as advertising and rallies, however, spilled over to residents of the community.

According to the residents we interviewed, the local candidates in the 1990 election seemed uninterested in El Barrio. They did very little active outreach, with the notable exception of the day of the primary, when fliers were posted and distributed. Candidates did not draw special attention to their election or re-election and did not pay particular notice to El Barrio. The offices of political parties that were located in our site seemed to be perpetually closed.

One of the local candidates, Senator Olga Méndez, in fact, prided herself on not having to campaign. She reported that:

I do not use my time to run after newspaper reporters so that they can give me time. In the last four elections, I have had [sic], it is seven years that I have not [had] a fund-raiser party to get funds for my elections, that means I have no money, which means that when re-election time comes I tell myself: if my constituents do not know at this point what I do then they do not deserve me as their senator and I do not deserve them as my constituency.

In sum, we observed considerable distance between the community and the candidates.

Advertising

We saw no political advertising on television during the primaries. Several judges made announcements on radio immediately before and during the primary election. Atrévete, a citywide organization coordinated by the government of Puerto Rico, placed advertising in the local Latino newspapers encouraging people to vote.

Conclusions: The Campaign in El Barrio

In sum, our overwhelming impression was that the community was not involved in the electoral process. Although people we talked to expressed a range of political opinions, the majority did not know whom they would vote for in November. We noted an astonishing lack of campaigning in El Barrio, despite the fact that candidates at all levels of government were up for re-election. The governor, the lieutenant governor, the comptroller, the attorney general, the state senator, the state assembly member, and the member of Congress were up for re-election, yet most of these politicians were distant strangers to the community. At this point, we began to suspect that the absence of campaigning might be due to the lack of any real opposition.

Election Day in El Barrio

On election day we began conducting observations at 8:00 A.M., recording and documenting the political activity of the day. On arriving at the polling site, we noticed a Latino man distributing fliers in support of Olga Méndez and saying to voters, "Go inside and do your thing." Many smiled at him and said things like, "Well, you know, that is how it should be." When the voters emerged, the man would approach them and ask, "Did you do your thing? Did you vote for her? Do it for one of us, a Latina." People would respond with, "Sure, brother, always." About 9:00 A.M., we approached a Latina who had just voted. She was interested in talking about politics in El Barrio, yet was unwilling to speak with us by the polling place; we scheduled an appointment to interview her in depth later.

Later in the morning, we noticed that Olga Méndez's office was open—the only time we had seen it open during our research. With no traffic in or out, we wondered why the office was open at all. One community resident explained that the office is open on election day for the purpose of "spying on the community." This person said that from Méndez's office "*alcahuetes* (panderers) kept an eye on everybody . . . they see who comes in and out, and if you do not vote, they let you know later that you did not vote." According to one informant, "they count the votes later, and if they do not even out, then they could tell that some of her followers lied."

We spoke to another Latino exiting the polling place, who seemed hostile to our questions. He said, "I come out to vote. What else can I do? What do you want from me?" We were given the impression from more than one person that people felt obligated, almost pressured, to vote for a certain candidate. Another woman admitted, "I come out to vote early, because I did not want anybody to see me; nobody is going to intimidate me . . . the vote is my way of saying no to the things that I know are going on here." When asked why people do not get involved in formal politics, she stated:

> It is very difficult to participate in the political process in New York City. . . . Minorities and Latinos seem to be caught up in the system all the time, and it is hard for us to take part in the political process when we are located outside the political machinery. Latino politicians who are elected to positions do it with the help of the Democratic machine or are blocked by the system. . . . Our votes do not count because the elected officials are already entrenched in the system, and our new candidates do not have the resources to challenge them or the established system.

Exit Poll Results

Our observations of voting on election day indicated that few people turned out to vote. During the entire morning, early afternoon, and evening, fewer than 150 people voted at the polling place where we were stationed. On election day, the team conducted exit polls and interviewed 30 people. Our data revealed interesting results regarding the public's thoughts about their reasons for voting, their reactions toward candidates, and their identification with issues. When we asked people why they had turned out to vote that day, 23 percent said they did so out of party loyalty. Forty percent told us they voted out of a sense of responsibility, 18 percent said they came out to vote for their candidates, and 20 percent reported that a combination of factors compelled them to vote that day.

We also asked people to name specific issues that were important to them in this election. The bond act to develop parts of El Barrio as historical sites and to declare the *casitas* as historical areas was mentioned by some respondents. Of the people we polled, only half voted on this measure. Of the half that voted, 39 percent voted no, 20 percent voted yes, 31 percent did not state their preferences, and 10 percent did not answer.

The voters were probed about their reasons for voting for certain candidates. The majority, 83 percent, said that they voted for the Democratic party's candidates. In response to the question of why they voted for a particular candidate, 33 percent said they did so out of loyalty to the candidate, 20 percent said they did so because they agreed with the issues raised by the candidate, 23 percent said they thought the candidate represented them, and 26 percent stated that they did not have any other choice.

The last question we asked related to issues of particular importance to the voter that were not raised by the candidates or the parties. Only 17 percent felt that problems such as war, housing, drugs, and education were not discussed by the candidates, while 50 percent believed that all the important issues were raised by the candidates. Another 33 percent did not answer. These responses reveal that at least half of the voters we interviewed seemed to believe that the candidates were at least discussing pressing issues in the community.

Election Results

Approximately 25 percent of registered voters in New York's Puerto Rican and Latino communities voted in the 1990 elections. The low level of participation exhibited in El Barrio characterized the 1990 elections throughout New York State; the percentage was the lowest turnout since the early nineteenth century. The competition for governor was one-sided. Mario Cuomo beat his Republican opponent, Pierre Rinfret, by more than two-to-one. Just 3 million of New York's 7.6 million registered voters voted in the gubernatorial race (U.S. Bureau of the Census 1991: Table 4). The other statewide races were similarly lopsided and generated little electoral interest.

In congressional and state legislative races, the general election saw campaigns without major party competition. The incumbent member of Congress, Charles Rangel, ran unopposed in both the primary and the general elections on the Democratic, Republican, and Liberal party tickets and received 97 percent of the vote. Similarly, the incumbent state senator and member of the assembly faced no electoral opposition.

Conclusion

As this chapter is being written in the summer of 1991, there is already evidence of community-level outreach and activity that was totally absent in the 1990 election. Because of a unique set of circumstances, the 1991 city council election promises to offer a situation in which there will be a truly open election process, that is, new city council districts with no incumbents. East Harlem will be electing a new representative to a much more powerful city council. There are eight declared candidates and some have already spoken to one of the community groups we know of on the topic of housing. There is a group forming to develop an agenda that they plan to have all candidates address and that they hope will form the discourse for the election campaign. This campaign and those that follow in the 1990s can learn two important lessons from the 1990 election.

First, the Puerto Ricans whom we met in El Barrio cannot be categorized as isolated from or fatalistic about the system of government, and they did not show apathetic attitudes toward the system. These people were very aware of the process in which, like it or not, they were involved, and they wanted changed.[4]

One gets the impression from many of the people we spoke to that the residents of this neighborhood felt they were fulfilling their obligation as voters by not coming out to vote for people who were not doing their jobs. The feeling was that the degree of political involvement could not be measured by how many people came out to vote. The act of consciously not participating was itself an act of rejecting an unauthentic system of representation. For at least some Puerto Ricans in this neighborhood, the only way to deal with the problems that afflict them is to remove some Latino elected officials from their present posts.

Thus, the information gathered in our research contradicts the widely held notion that the poor in the ghettos are less likely to take part in the formal political process because of their class status. Instead, we would argue that many are consciously deciding *not* to use their votes in order to make what they consider a political statement. The issue for some of the community residents, however, is not whether they feel politically efficacious if they vote. Rather, the lack of participation is a mechanism that can be used effectively to remove some politicians from their posts, especially those who run unopposed.

The second lesson that can be learned from the 1990 election relates to the importance of off-year elections. There was neither a presidential nor a mayoral office at stake. There was the perception among many in the community that the offices being contested were not significant, even though the governorship and state senate and assembly seats were at stake. The popular perception of an irrelevant state government (or less relevant than national offices) must be challenged, given the forfeiture of many social and governmental responsibilities to the states by the federal government during the 1980s.

At the community level, it can be argued that state government on a day-to-day basis may be the most influential level of government in the majority of people's lives; however, most members of the community do not recognize this.

In another sense, this election could prove to be significant for this community in the near future because of the coming together of two different, but important, processes. These processes may in fact define the political clout of this community for the next ten years. The first event is redistricting, which will occur in 1991, and the second is the new charter revision of the city government, which will create sixteen new city council seats in a greatly enhanced and powerful city council. These smaller city council districts (representing between 139,000 and 143,580 people) ostensibly were created to increase minority representation in city government. A poor showing at the polls in 1990 could conceivably translate into limited influence on the mapping process that determines the population base on which these more powerful city representatives will be chosen.

The past elections as measured by voter turnout and interest did not, however, depict a unique historical juncture whereby the community increased its power or influence. We found that, to most people in El Barrio, well-being and electoral politics were not even related, much less synonymous. As we have documented, there may be a very good reason for such views to dominate the Puerto Rican community of East Harlem, given the present reality and recent history of this "democratic" institution we call electoral politics.

To conclude, a brief examination of the political trajectory of Puerto Ricans in New York City, particularly in El Barrio, indicates that important changes have occurred over time. The situation is more complex than the ability to elect and re-elect Puerto Ricans to important political positions within the Democratic party. In fact, we have learned that, in El Barrio, some of the established Puerto Rican politicians may not be re-elected to their political posts because the community believes they have not done their jobs. There is a precedent for this turn of events: recently a white female council candidate beat an incumbent Puerto Rican for a council seat. There seem to be two ways of the community's manifesting its dissatisfaction with the status quo: by not turning out to vote and by supporting opposition candidates.

We have briefly described different aspects of the political participation of Puerto Ricans in East Harlem. Based on the data gathered in this investigation, we would suggest that the new path in Puerto Rican politics would be to develop a broad agenda that focuses not only on how to increase political representation, but also on how to use the electoral process to empower the community. As should be clear from our argument in this chapter, we would strongly recommend greater involvement of the community in the political process before elections and before candidates are selected. This task of accountability can be accomplished in several ways:

1. All Puerto Rican elected officials must use every opportunity available, such as primaries and general elections, to inform the public about the political process.
2. Through other public forums, the community must know about the issues and problems that affect the neighborhood.
3. Latino politicians must come to the community and not wait for the people to make the first move; politicians like Vito Marcantonio won the hearts of the Puerto Rican people because they were able to establish good rapport ("un ambiente familiar") with the community.
4. Latino politicians should remember that their job is also that of mediator between the people and the establishment.

Incorporation of these principles into the linkage between elected officials and barrio residents will allow community residents to exercise their political beliefs in a positive manner (by choosing among candidates) instead of a negative manner (by not voting to express their displeasure with the opportunities available through electoral politics).

Notes

1. The project's principal investigators wish to thank the project's research assistants: Samuel Crespo, Vicky Gonzáles, Bruno Aguancha, and Carlos García.

2. Puerto Ricans were granted U.S. citizenship in 1917.

3. It has been stated that during this period Puerto Ricans were drawn into the political arena as a way to deal with discrimination and racism (Rodríguez-Fraticelli and Tirado 1989: 36).

4. In a sense, the ideology of what has been called fatalism, *el que será, será* (what will be, will be) or *que sea lo que Dios quiera* (let God's will be done), is being challenged by these people in a direct way. See Fitzpatrick (1987b: 135).

References

Fitzpatrick, J. 1987a. *Puerto Rican Americans: The Meaning of Migration to the Mainland.* Englewood, N.J.: Prentice-Hall.

———. 1987b. *One Church, Many Cultures: The Challenges of Diversity.* New York: Sheed and Ward.

Governor's Advisory Committee for Hispanic Affairs. 1984. *New York State Hispanics: A Challenging Minority.* New York.

Institute for Puerto Rican Policy. 1989. *Towards a Puerto Rican-Latino Agenda for New York City, 1989.* New York: Institute for Puerto Rican Policy.

———. 1991a. "Political and Demographic Data for East Harlem Political Ethnography Project."

———. 1991b. *New York as a Majority Minority City: 1990 Census Tract Databook.* New York: Institute for Puerto Rican Policy.

Meyer, Gerald. 1989. *Vito Marcantonio: Radical Politician 1902–1954.* Albany: State University of New York Press.

Pérez, R. 1989. "Challenges Facing Puerto Ricans in the 1989 New York Mayoral Election." *Centro Bulletin* (Spring).

Rodríguez-Fraticelli, Carlos, and Amilcar Tirado. 1989. "Notes Towards a History of Puerto Rican Community Organizations in New York City." *Centro Bulletin* (Summer).

Sánchez-Korrol, V. 1983. *From Colonia to Community: The History of Puerto Ricans in New York City, 1917–1948.* Westport, Conn.: Greenwood Press.

U.S. Bureau of the Census. 1991. *Voting and Registration in the Election of November 1990.* Current Population Reports. Population Characteristics. Series P-20, No. 453. Washington, D.C.: U.S. Government Printing Office.

Voter Assistance Commission. 1990. *Annual Report of New York City, January 1989–December 1989.* New York.

4

Political Mobilization in Houston's Magnolia

Néstor P. Rodríguez, Noelia Elizondo, David Mena,
Ricardo Rojas, Adolfo Vásquez, and Frank Yeverino

The study of Latino political mobilization in Houston in the November 6, 1990, election centered around a residential and commercial section in the barrio of Magnolia, the largest Latino neighborhood in the city. Located in the city's southeast quadrant, the Magnolia research site, with an area of 0.65 square miles, is bounded by a large residential section and the Houston Ship Channel to the north; more residential sections and a city park to the east; a golf course, cemetery, and another city park to the south; and a commercial strip and a mixed Latino-white residential area to the west.

Socially and culturally, the Magnolia research site resembles the many Mexican barrios of the U.S. Southwest. It contains the usual set of barrio institutions, such as Catholic and Protestant churches, community parks and centers, bars and pool halls (some for Mexican Americans and others for Mexican immigrants), dance halls, public schools, Mexican restaurants, tortilla factories, neighborhood grocery stores, *panaderías* (bakeries), and small retail centers. Ethnic enterprises abound, and the coexistence of *yerberías* (herbalists) and medical offices illustrates the traditional-modern spectrum of the barrio's residents. English and Spanish are spoken throughout the barrio, and the two languages help to distinguish the long-term residents from new immigrants (de la Garza, Rodríguez, and Pachon 1990). In the 1980s, newcomers to the barrio included undocumented Salvadorans, Guatemalans, Hondurans, and other Central Americans (Rodríguez 1987; Rodríguez and Hagan 1989).

In and around the Magnolia research site, we found that, while Latinos raised many issues affecting their neighborhood, they generally remained aloof from electoral politics. The virtually unopposed candidacy of a local resident, the dominance of a single party, and the large proportion of immigrants living in the area were some factors related to the lack of political interest and involvement. The Magnolia fieldwork, however, sought to go beyond the identification of causal factors such as these in order to explore the nature of political mobilization (or the lack of it) in the research site. The questions that the study investigated to understand political organizing in the Magnolia research site, and that are answered in

TABLE 4.1   Electoral Races Followed in the Magnolia Research Site and Votes Cast in Precinct 64

Candidate	Votes Cast	% of Total Precinct Votes Cast in Race
Governor		
Clayton Williams (R)	84	17.6
Ann W. Richards (D)	380	79.8
Jeff Daiell (L)	12	2.5
Total for race	476	
Attorney General		
J. E. Brown (R)	38	8.3
Dan Morales (D)	417	90.7
Ray E. Dittmar (L)	5	1.1
Total for race	460	
State Representative, District 143		
Mario V. Gallegos, Jr. (D)	429	96.2
Joe Johansen (L)	17	3.8
Total for race	446	
Judge, County Criminal Court No. 12		
Rick Brass (R)	45	10.5
Joe T. Terracina (D)	382	89.5
Total for race	427	
Straight Party Vote		
Republican	27	5.5
Democrat	236	48.1
Libertarian	4	0.8
Not a straight party vote	224	45.6
Total precinct vote	491	

Registered voters in precinct: 2,174
Ballots cast in precinct: 491
R = Republican; D = Democrat; L = Libertarian

this chapter, were the following: Who are the political actors in the neighborhood? Who raised issues affecting the neighborhood and what were the issues raised? How did candidates reach the people in the neighborhood? How important was the election in the neighborhood? Table 4.1 lists the electoral races we followed closely in Magnolia.

Historical Background

The history of the Magnolia barrio starts in the 1910s, when Mexican working-class families settled in the previously all-white Magnolia Park neighborhood. It was a time when Houston's booming economic growth depended significantly on labor immigration (Feagin 1988). According to Arnoldo De León (1989), the construction of the Houston Ship Channel and port facilities acted as a powerful magnet attracting large numbers of Mexican workers. Mexican American workers migrated to the new *colonia* from the Mexican communities in Texas. Immigrant workers also came from northern Mexico, and some arrived by way of labor-recruiting agencies in San Antonio. Political and economic problems in Mexico in the 1910s and the 1920s were among the conditions that motivated this migration.

Men in the developing *colonia* of Magnolia found low-wage work in cotton compresses, cement plants, and construction. Many of the women found work in textile plants, factories, and stores (Sheldon et al. 1989).

By 1920, the Mexican-origin population in the Magnolia Park neighborhood had grown to such a number that the local school trustees decided to build a separate school for the Spanish-speaking children. A separate Catholic church, Immaculate Heart of Mary, was built for the Mexican residents in 1926, the year Magnolia was incorporated into the city of Houston (De León 1989).

Continued in-migration from other Texas localities and immigration from Mexico produced the social and cultural resources necessary for Magnolia to develop into a full-scale Mexican-origin community (Sheldon et al. 1989). The barrio became, as it remains today, a dual community of Mexican Americans and Mexican immigrants. More than an immigrant generation kept the two groups apart, and, yet, more than physical proximity brought the two groups together.

At the same time that some Magnolia residents strove to build community organizations that contrasted with the larger society, other Mexican American residents of the barrio worked to build organizations that brought Latinos closer to the U.S. mainstream. A small group of Mexican American business owners established a chapter of the League of United Latin American Citizens in Magnolia in 1934 (Sheldon et al. 1989).

As a large *colonia*, Magnolia was home to many community organizations and thus played an important role in the early civil rights struggles of Houston's Latinos. During World War II, Magnolia still boasted a community leadership segment of business owners and other civic actors. This segment provided leaders for combatting anti-Latino practices in the city's schools and other public agencies (De León 1989).

In the 1950s and the 1960s, Magnolia experienced substantial change. The pre-1950s Magnolia *colonia* described by De León contrasts sharply with the Magnolia barrio we see today. These changes reflect the social-cultural contrast between a *colonia* community and an inner-city barrio. The *colonia* had a vibrant Mexican-oriented social life in which much of the leadership was determined by relationships to social and cultural organizations *within* the *colonia*. The barrio, in contrast, has a bicultural social life that seems to offer fewer opportunities for leadership growth. In the barrio, election to the major offices (city council member, state representative, etc.) is determined by relationships to governmental entities *outside* the barrio, entities in which the barrio representatives are minority members. The *colonia*, once a dynamic center of Mexican society, has become a community with underclasslike conditions, including the diminution of the community's leadership segment (Rodríguez forthcoming).

Description of the Research Site

The area we selected as our research site in Magnolia forms the eastern half of the city's census tract 310. In 1990, census tract 310 had 6,214 residents in 1,644 households (U.S. Bureau of the Census [hereafter Census] 1991). Sixty-four percent of the census tract's population was eighteen years of age or older. Forty-one percent of the residents in the census tract were foreign-born. The 1990 census also showed that the median household income in the census tract was $18,483. The census also found that only 25.5 percent of the census tract's residents age twenty-five and older had completed high school (Census 1992).

In 1990, 94.3 percent of census tract 310 was Latino (Census 1991). Mexican-origin persons accounted for 92.5 percent of the Latinos in the census tract. The census tract's Latino population, which had increased by 88.5 percent during the 1970s (Census 1983), decreased by 6.6 percent between 1980 and 1990. Most of this small population loss undoubtedly occurred during the city's sharp economic recession from 1982 to 1987. Given the undocumented immigration into the barrio of Magnolia, it is likely that the true Latino population in the census tract has remained unchanged or grown slightly since 1980.

While our research site forms the eastern half of census tract 310, it also forms the southern half of Precinct 64. Precinct 64 has an estimated population of 14,900 residents, with 57 percent age eighteen or older. In the November 6 election, 2,174 people in Precinct 64 were registered to vote.

Research Methods

To explore political mobilization in the Magnolia research site, we developed a multifaceted fieldwork approach. This approach involved observing settings and activities, conducting formal and informal interviews, and monitoring media sources. A bilingual crew of six Latino students (four males and two females) was involved in the fieldwork.

Our ethnographic observations focused on election-related activities in and near the Magnolia research site. The setting we initially selected for observation was a residential area; however, given the almost complete absence of election activities in this area, by October we branched out to nearby areas. These included an adjoining retail center and major avenues that ran adjacent to the selected residential area. In October, we also branched out to observe small establishments (bars, restaurants, pool halls, etc.) in adjacent residential neighborhoods. Since almost no major election events involving Latinos took place inside Magnolia, we conducted our observations of voter registrations, political rallies, meetings, and fund-raisers in settings outside, but usually close to, the barrio. Several members of the research team also traveled from three to five miles outside Magnolia to observe political gatherings.

To carry out the fieldwork, the research team initially divided into teams of two researchers, each taking responsibility for observation on specific days, covering the whole week. After the researchers became familiar with the project site, a more natural approach evolved wherein some of the researchers specialized in certain activities and candidates.

We conducted formal interviews with candidates, with members of a voter registration project, and with persons working in community organizations in Magnolia. A total of thirty-two formal interviews were conducted during the study, including eight with non-Latinos. The formal interviews ranged from an hour to an hour and a half in length. Informal interviews were generally conducted in the form of conversations and chats with Magnolia residents, families, business owners, candidates, and other persons in election-related organizations with whom researchers became familiar. In several cases, we used informal interviews to gather information from persons who had originally participated in formal interviews. The study's researchers conducted ninety-two informal interviews, which ranged from ten to thirty minutes. Twenty-one of the informal interviews were conducted with non-Latinos.

Researchers also gathered election information from television, radio, and newspaper sources. One researcher read English and Spanish newspapers and monitored radio and television stations.

Political Actors

Our fieldwork found that only a small number of persons and organizations were actually involved in promoting political interest and behavior in Magnolia. These political actors can be grouped into four categories: individuals, neighborhood organizations, businesses, and outside organizations. In this section we identify these actors and describe some of their activities that affected Magnolia.

Individual Actors

Only one person emerged as an individual actor who was consistently involved in election-related activities in Magnolia. This person was Mario Gallegos, a thirty-five-year-old Magnolia resident running for state representative of District 143, which includes Magnolia. Gallegos, a Houston fire fighter from a politically involved family, usually attended political activities near Magnolia to talk with people, shake hands, and pass out campaign materials. Often, his campaign workers and family members would accompany him to political gatherings. Gallegos also attended community events within Magnolia to meet people and pass out campaign literature.

A few other individuals also participated in political activities that affected Magnolia, but in a remote way. City council member Ben Reyes, for example, was very active in promoting festivals and other community activities in the adjacent barrio of the Second Ward that were meant to draw Latinos to hear politicians or register to vote. Yet, these activities drew only a handful of people from Magnolia. In another case, Rick Brass, running for a county judgeship, placed some of the biggest campaign billboards in Magnolia to promote his candidacy. While his billboards helped give a political ambience to a few blocks in Magnolia, Brass never actually visited the neighborhood and expressed little knowledge of it during an interview.

Neighborhood Organizations

Within Magnolia we found two Catholic churches and a few businesses to be sites of political activism.

At the Immaculate Conception, Father McKenna stated that the Metropolitan Organization (TMO), a community-based organization with an office located outside Magnolia, used the church to conduct voter registration drives. Father McKenna said that he placed announcements in the church bulletin to encourage parishioners "to vote in fulfillment of Christian duties and duties as an American."

At the Immaculate Heart of Mary, Father Ray-John Marek also promoted political interest among the parishioners by coordinating TMO meetings at the church. A flier announcing an upcoming TMO convention was taped to a window in his office. Father Marek was well informed about Magnolia's needs and got involved with political matters, for example, by encouraging members of the church to register to vote.

Several other organizations in Magnolia promoted political involvement through voter registration drives. These organizations included VFW Post 472, a LULAC chapter, and the Magnolia YMCA.

Businesses

The fieldwork in Magnolia also found that some business owners in Magnolia attempted to generate political interest by placing campaign and other election materials in their establishments. Indeed, much of the political advertising displayed in Magnolia was found in business establishments. At an early stage in the election we found a bumper sticker supporting Dan Morales for state attorney general and a sign promoting voter registration in Memo's Record Shop.

El Mirasol restaurant also displayed political materials. At the restaurant a bumper sticker on the mirror behind the bar promoted Hannah Chow for a court position. We also noticed a large sign that read "ELECT RICK BRASS—JUDGE. COUNTY CRIMINAL COURT NO. 12" at the far end of the restaurant's parking lot.

The Island Club, a Latino nightclub at the western edge of Magnolia, allowed the Southwest Voter Registration and Education Project to set up a voter registration booth during its Tejano Festival '90. The club also held a fund-raiser for Gallegos. A few other smaller businesses in Magnolia displayed some political signs, including Jiménez's Barber Shop and Tony's Drive In.

Outside Organizations

SVREP, based in San Antonio, opened its Houston-Harris County office at the Latino Learning Center just northwest of Magnolia. SVREP was the biggest organization registering Latino voters for the election. Magnolia residents were among the two thousand persons registered to vote by SVREP before election day. The SVREP Houston office plans to register one hundred thousand voters in Houston by 1995.

TMO, which operates through a network of churches and is headquartered in the northwest sector of the city, works with Magnolia residents on several issues (crime, city services, etc.) affecting the neighborhood. A week and half before the election, TMO sponsored an "accountability" day on the "near northside," a barrio just north of downtown. A number of Magnolia residents attended the event to meet and question several local candidates.

Catholic churches and small businesses seemed to have promoted the election more than any other group in Magnolia. With the exception of Gallegos, candidates did not actively campaign in Magnolia.

The Issues

The fieldwork in Magnolia did not find a striking or pressing issue that generated political interest and activity in the neighborhood. What we did find were sets of issues that reflected the different perceptions of groups and of neighborhood residents.

Business Owners and Organization Members

Business owners in Magnolia were concerned about several neighborhood issues. The owner of a Mexican restaurant was concerned with the drug problem in the neighborhood. Drug problems spark other problems in the neighborhood, specifically, the problem of inadequate police protection. According to some business owners, the neighborhood was not receiving its share of tax-supported services, such as police protection. At Fernández Supermarket, the issue of police protection was raised. The owner felt he had adequate protection. He stated, "Having an extension of the police station in the immediate area gives a sense of security because I have never been robbed." According to the owner of Memo's Record Shop, important issues in the neighborhood were education and the large number of bars. Commenting on the need for neighborhood improvement, the record shop owner described some recent improvements: "There has been an effort by politicians to upgrade the conditions in the neighborhood. Certain streets were repaired, sewage systems were upgraded, a center for senior citizens, a multiservice center, and a Houston Police substation were established, and the Edison Middle School and neighborhood public library were rebuilt."

Father Marek, who worked with TMO, called Magnolia "a forgotten neighborhood." He explained, "The city and state government do not want to deal with us, the poor, unlike the more beautiful neighborhoods where more educated, intelligent people live. The quality of education in the neighborhood is inferior."

During a meeting at Immaculate Heart of Mary to prepare for a TMO state convention, Father Marek and other TMO members enumerated several issues they felt affected Magnolia. The issues included drugs, education, prostitution, and the bars in the neighborhood. Father Marek stated, "Most people do not care for the governor's election. Those who vote tend to be one-issue voters. That is why candidates know what issues to focus on in the Magnolia neighborhood." Father Marek also viewed the issues of military spending and equal rights as having significant implications for Magnolia residents. Another Magnolia priest and TMO representative felt the major issue for the neighborhood was one that had been around for a long time—poverty.

Other TMO and church members viewed crime as another important issue affecting the neighborhood. Estela González, member of TMO and Immaculate Conception Church, listed burglaries and prostitution as major problems in the neighborhood. She stated, "Crime is rampant and the church has been vandalized numerous times as have been church members' homes in the area."

Rachel Lucas, the director of Magnolia's Chicano Family Center, indicated that the biggest problems in the neighborhood were related to education and drugs. Concerning education, she explained, "We don't have a good educational system. We have a very uncaring, except for a few exceptions, a very uncaring educational system. And we don't seem to feel that our kids are being educated, not with the kind of quality education that is required to enter the mainstream." She went on to explain why issues affecting the Hispanic community received attention: "Issues raised right now are being raised [not] because it is . . . [solely] a concern of ours. It has become a concern across the board, particularly in education."

According to Frank Velásquez with Unión y Progreso-El Centro, a social service agency located in Magnolia, the major issues in the neighborhood were education, transportation, and social services. He commented on the issues as follows:

These are not new issues, especially to Magnolia. The high school dropout rate has always been high and is reinforced through society and ingrained in the Mexican American community that we will not graduate from high school. Here in the 1990s, only 4 percent of Mexican Americans entering college will graduate. So the general attitude of society towards Magnolia is "do the best with what you get and be happy with that even if there are not sufficient resources."

The director of the Magnolia Senior Citizens Center thought that important issues in Magnolia were the homeless problem, the need for more free services, and projects to help senior citizens repair their homes. Medicare and Social Security were also important national issues affecting the elderly in Magnolia, according to her.

At the police substation in Magnolia, a police officer listed drugs, burglaries, homicide, taxes, sanitary conditions, and gangs as the set of issues that most affected Magnolia residents.

Issues Raised by Residents

Residents of the neighborhood also raised various issues, including education, taxes, lack of political debate, voter registration, homelessness, the environment, budget problems, jail overcrowding, abortion, minority issues, and mental health programs. In addition, an elderly resident indicated that discrimination against Mexicans was an important issue for all Mexicans. Other residents agreed that discrimination against Mexicans was a problem.

Residents also stressed the inefficiency of the police department. According to one neighborhood resident, "The police could be better; their lack of interest combined with their sore attitude is not helping the situation any."

Issues Raised by Candidates

Candidate Gallegos stated that the most important issues in his campaign were education, crime, employment, and the environment. Revitalizing Magnolia's physical environment and assuring that senior citizens received adequate services were his major concerns.

Libertarian Joe Johansen, Gallegos's opponent, stated that the most important issue in the election was what could be done to improve the quality of life for the people in the Magnolia area. According to Johansen:

There needs to be a lot of improvement for the people in this area and this can be accomplished without raising taxes. Poor people in this area are hit hard through increases in excise taxes and do not receive the immediate benefits. Money can be saved in many ways, including the elimination of high salaries for politicians and commission members in Austin. Big issues such as burning the flag do not mean much to a person that cannot read or lives in a box. Private businesses within the immediate community need to get involved. Private sector interaction is very productive because the purse string is there in the community as opposed to way off at the Capitol.

Armando Rodríguez, who ran unopposed for re-election for a precinct judge position in Magnolia, listed crime and education as the most important issues affecting the neighborhood. He elaborated on the educational issue:

> In the last two years I have seen an increase in interest in education. It is a very popular issue today, but I know that Hispanics have always cared about education and have always been concerned with the lack of it. Education has not been approached very effectively and it is an issue that is always at the forefront. Images are present in our society which portray the Mexican American as a group of uncaring, lazy, drunks and of course this is untrue. We are no different from any other race—we only want the best for our children and ourselves.

Outside of Magnolia, Mary Leal, who ran for a position as county school board trustee, listed education, jail overcrowding, and the criminal justice system as important election issues. Concerning the education issue, she stated: "For Magnolia, equalization of the monies in the schools is important. Hispanics in general are feeling discriminated against especially due to the language barriers. There are not enough school administrators and teachers who are Spanish-speaking role models. . . . Parents cannot communicate with their children's school personnel. . . . HISD [Houston Independent School District] neglects discrimination but it exists." Leal explained further: "What is needed is a Hispanic superintendent because the majority of the students are Hispanic. Out of the nine county school trustees, only two are Hispanic. All they are doing is awarding contracts and education is getting lost in the shuffle."

A second candidate for the county school board, Paul Tittsworth, also listed school funding as a major issue. He stated, "[I]f I am taking this much money and putting it into nothing, look at how much education I am wasting. There is a federal court order for school districts to get an even share; it's a redistribution of funds. The school districts are not being funded equally."

A third candidate for the county school board, Ronnie Harrison, listed taxes, abortion, crime, and leadership as major issues in the election. According to him, these were the issues that Magnolia residents should be concerned about.

Rick Brass, who ran for a judgeship in county criminal court, saw the drug problem and an effective court system as the major issues in the election. Furthermore, he viewed Magnolia issues to be the same as in the rest of the county. "I can only surmise," he said, "that issues important to the citizens of Magnolia are the same issues of importance to the rest of Harris County citizens, and that is to have a court system that is doing something constructive toward increasing public safety. The issue has been around for quite some time."

Issues Raised at a Community Rally

Local elected officials and candidates for state offices also raised several issues at a Houston Hispanic Unity Rally held in the Second Ward barrio just northwest of Magnolia ten days before the election. City council member Ben Reyes opened the rally by explaining the importance of voting and getting involved in elections. He spoke about Latinos converting to the Republican party despite the fact that it was the same party that vetoed the 1990 Civil Rights Act.

John Sharp, a Democrat running for state comptroller, addressed the audience on the difference between the Republican and Democratic parties' views on several issues. He stressed the issue of school finance: "[T]he Democratic party stand on education is one that entails an equal amount of money used per each child in the State of Texas. Equality in civil rights cannot occur until the equality in educational rights exists, because according to me, every single child is equal in the State of Texas."

The next speaker was former mayor of San Antonio Henry Cisneros. He emphasized the ability to place a Latino (Dan Morales) in public office at the state level as well as a black leader (Morris L. Overstreet). He also spoke about the importance of participating in the election within the Democratic party, "a party for all people of Texas." After Dan Morales, candidate for attorney general, spoke, Constable Víctor Treviño addressed the audience. His opening lines were in Spanish. He stressed the importance of unity among Latino families and individuals as a means to further progress for Latinos in politics. He stated, "Future goals may be to elect a Hispanic as governor of the state or even mayor of Houston." He also stressed that parents should emphasize the importance of voting to children and socialize them into the electoral process.

The last speaker was Ann Richards, the Democratic gubernatorial candidate. After being introduced by Treviño, she received a standing ovation. She thanked everyone for their support and their presence. According to her, a "tough" issue that needs to be resolved in the next ten years is education. Richards gave the audience statistics on teenage dropout rates and suggested that these stemmed from problems in education. She also gave alarming statistics on children living in poverty. She called this "a sin, a shame, and a crime." She raised the issue of rising health insurance costs, especially for older people. She promised to be "a governor who cares for the people buying insurance and not for the people who sell it."

Overall, we did not find a major difference between the sets of issues raised by organizations, residents, and candidates. In the exit poll interviews in Magnolia, 69 percent of the voters indicated that there was no issue of particular importance to them that was being neglected by candidates or parties. Yet, this did not mean that the voters and political leaders had achieved a high degree of alignment. In our view, it indicated that issues played a small role in the election in Magnolia. Party identity—Democratic party identity—and not issues is what motivated political interest in the barrio. For the political leaders, on the other hand, generating interest for the election was the real issue.

Latino Issues

Almost invariably, the issues cited in Magnolia by residents, organization members, and political leaders were given as Latino issues. Table 4.2 indicates the range of issues identified as Latino issues by these groups. While problems with bars and immigrant quotas are clearly related to the Latino population, it is less clear why issues such as job training and the state budget are identified as Latino issues. Why do Latinos worry about issues that affect other populations besides their own? Magnolia residents react to issues from a Latino ethnic perspective, which in Magnolia is heavily associated with low-income status. From this ethnic and social/class perception, social issues are not seen in an abstract or general form but as concretized in the daily Latino community experience. Many of Magnolia's low- and moderate-income residents understand that the issues that trouble them are not felt in the affluent neighborhoods in the city.

Education ranked first among the Latino issues identified by people we spoke to. Education was presented as a question of the quality of education being offered to Latino children attending schools in the Magnolia area. Lorenzo Cano, whose children attended schools in Magnolia, expressed frustration with the issue: "Not even current legislative efforts that are being attempted seem to be working . . . [to]

TABLE 4.2 Frequency of Latino Issues Raised by Magnolia Residents, Organizations, and Candidates

| | Number of Responses | | | |
Issue	Residents	Organizations	Candidates	Total
Education	4	6	6	16
Political activism	3	5	3	11
Drugs	4	4	2	10
Police protection, crime	4	3	3	10
Discrimination	2	0	1	3
Taxes	0	1	2	3
State budget	1	1	1	3
Revitalizing Magnolia	1	1	0	2
Senior citizens	0	1	1	2
Jail overcrowding	1	0	1	2
Home ownership	1	1	0	2
Communication	0	1	1	2
Prostitution	0	1	0	1
Puerto Rico allowed to vote	1	0	0	1
Homelessness	0	1	0	1
Free social services	0	1	0	1
Job training	0	1	0	1
Immigrant quotas	0	0	1	1
Cantinas	0	1	0	1
Abortion	0	0	1	1
Leadership	0	0	1	1
Total issues addressed	11	13	15	

change the quality of our education." Belia López, who worked with TMO, saw education as the most important issue for Magnolia: "Parents need to get involved in the educational system while the schools have to be more sensitive to Latinos." Rachel Lucas, director of the Chicano Family Center in Magnolia, saw the need for more equality in education: "equality in education that is required to enter the mainstream." Candidate Gallegos, who saw education as "particularly important to Latinos," emphasized the need for more bilingual education programs.

The need for greater Latino political involvement ranked second among the Latino issues identified in the study. Father Marek attributed Magnolia voter apathy to the neighborhood's population composition: "Individuals residing in Magnolia are not all American; most are immigrants." Another reason given for the low political involvement in the neighborhood was that "some Mexicans do not see the point of voting because it does not help their people." Frank Velásquez stated that it was important to inform Latinos about the election process and to help reduce the fear of politics among newly arrived immigrants. Not surprisingly, Latino candidates took the position that Latinos needed to exercise their voting potential.

The issues concerning drugs, police protection, and crime ranked third and were seen as interrelated. At times, people in Magnolia offered different views on how these issues were related. While some business owners felt that the level of police presence in the neighborhood was adequate and effective, the owner of the Mirasol restaurant felt that the neighborhood's drug problems were the result of poor police protection. Many other residents also felt that rising crime in the neighborhood was related to what they perceived to be poor neighborhood police protection. At the Chicano Family Center, which helps youth with drug problems, Lucas felt that poverty was the root of drug problems, which in turn led to crime: "Poor youth deal drugs because they make a quick profit."

Among the candidates, Republican Rick Brass particularly focused his campaign on the drug problem. His campaign signs in Magnolia carried antidrug messages. Brass felt that inefficiency in the court system was partly to blame for the rise in drug problems.

As this discussion has shown, issues abounded in the research site and in the larger barrio of Magnolia; however, neither political leaders nor Magnolia residents connected the issues to the election campaigns. In the following section we describe how political leaders and organizations involved in the election reached (or failed to reach) the Magnolia residents with their political and electoral messages.

Getting the Message to the People

During the election campaign period, political actors used several means to encourage people to become politically interested and to vote. These included political events, printed materials, the media, and telephone banks and mail-outs.

Political Events

Political events included festivals, meetings, voter registration drives, and fund-raisers. Magnolia residents participated in these events when they occurred close to the barrio. SVREP members almost always used political events as an opportunity to register voters. A chronological account of the major events held near Magnolia follows.

On September 12, the Mexican American Student Organization (MASO) at the University of Houston, located a few miles from Magnolia, sponsored a Hispanic Political Summit in which Dan Morales, candidate for attorney general, was to make the keynote address. The summit was organized so that elected and appointed Hispanic officials could convene a round-table discussion on quality education, voter participation, and political empowerment. Eight officials attended, ranging from a school board member to a state representative. Two of the eight officials were women—one a municipal court judge and the other a Houston Community College trustee. Isaias Torres, an immigration law attorney, came in place of Dan Morales and also represented SVREP. He explained how SVREP's efforts to register the Latino community to vote had wider implications for empowerment, such as reapportionment of district lines for congressional seats. The audience consisted of a few college students, professors, professionals, and community activists.

On September 14, SVREP held a grand opening of its Houston-Harris County office, located in the Latino Learning Center, a community center in the Second Ward barrio, bordering Magnolia. At the opening, many Latino political figures and supporters were present. Lisa Hernández and Isaias Torres, SVREP activists in Houston, explained how they planned to register two thousand voters by election day and one hundred thousand voters by 1995. A sense of hope and enthusiasm prevailed among the mostly Democratic Latino crowd.

On September 29, SVREP held a breakfast meeting to train volunteers to register voters. Hernández and Torres provided plenty of breakfast taquitos, juice, and coffee and sent out "soldiers" to register Latinos in supermarkets around the city. SVREP had obtained permission from Fiesta Grocery Stores to register voters on store premises. Fiesta stores are known for their *mercado* (market) atmosphere and cater to a large Latino population. A Fiesta store is located near Magnolia.

On the first Saturday of October, SVREP intensified its efforts by holding a televised voter registration telethon in conjunction with KTMD, Channel 48-Telemundo, a Spanish-language station. Again, SVREP used the Fiesta stores as registration sites. A talk show featuring Judge David Mendoza, Jr., Torres, and Hernández discussed the importance of the Latino vote. During the discussion, the television station would break to live shots of people registering to vote at the Fiesta stores.

SVREP used other organizations to meet their registration goals. MASO members from the University of Houston, for example, helped register about one hundred voters in the Fiesta store near Magnolia.

But the MASO efforts were surpassed by the Latino Veterans of Vietnam, who registered more than one hundred voters.

SVREP also took its voter registration drive to the 11th Annual Chicano Music Festival, held on October 6 at a public outdoor theater several miles from Magnolia. Spanish radio personalities encouraged the festival attendees to register to vote as six Latin groups performed throughout the night. About fifty people approached the SVREP booth to register.

On October 7, the Organization of Spanish Speaking Officers (OSSO) of the Houston Police Department sponsored Tejano Festival '90 at the Island Club. A large crowd of middle- and working-class Chicanos listened to the music of Robert Pulido, David Lee Garza, and Ramiro "Ram" Herrera. The crowd averaged about thirty years of age and had an equal number of males and females. OSSO members registered forty-five Latinos during the festival.

On October 18, SVREP held an awards presentation at the Latino Learning Center to recognize individuals who had helped register two thousand voters before the election. The main speaker was Andy Hernández, the national director of SVREP. The charismatic Hernández gave a rousing speech about the success of the organization in Latino communities in ten states. He envisioned the same kind of success for Houston. With community support, according to Hernández, SVREP could register some one hundred thousand new voters in Houston within five years. The awards were well attended by Latino political figures and supporters and the crowd remained enthusiastic throughout the night.

On October 25, state representative candidate Mario Gallegos held a fund-raiser at the Island Club. Having won the Democratic primary election in a runoff in the spring, Gallegos was running virtually unopposed against a Libertarian candidate. Several local elected officials and other political leaders spoke on his behalf and encouraged people to vote and not become complacent. A group of Anglo fire fighters from San Antonio and a black representative of the Houston school maintenance workers also came out for Gallegos; the latter presented Gallegos with a donation collected from the maintenance workers. Forty-five persons attended the fund-raiser and dined on the club's Mexican food.

Printed Materials

Printed materials used by candidates to get their message to the voters in Magnolia consisted of bumper stickers, fliers, brochures, posters, and signs on yards and street posts. The majority of these materials, however, appeared only a few weeks or days prior to the election.

Bumper stickers appeared as sort of a poor-person's poster in several establishments in Magnolia. A record store in Magnolia displayed two bumper stickers supporting Dan Morales for attorney general. Bumper stickers promoting various candidates were also seen in several bars in Magnolia. Some were written in English and Spanish and were readily visible to people entering the bars. Bumper stickers also appeared on traffic signs and light posts. Bumper stickers were usually distributed at rallies and at SVREP booths (*Su Voto Es Su Voz*—Your Vote Is Your Voice) throughout the campaign period.

Fliers and brochures providing election information also were distributed in Magnolia. A bilingual flier from the office of city council member Ben Reyes provided information on upcoming events that affected the community. Fliers were also observed at the Immaculate Heart of Mary Church in Magnolia announcing an "accountability day" sponsored by TMO. Most of the fliers and brochures found in Magnolia were usually written in English and distributed in public places. Only one Magnolia resident reported seeing a candidate distributing fliers in the neighborhood, "sometime in August or September, but none since then."

Candidates also placed posters and signs in yards and on street posts. Most of these materials were placed in commercial areas where pedestrian and car traffic was the heaviest. All but one of the posters and signs was written in English. The one poster in Spanish was in Memo's Record Shop and it promoted voter registration. Only a few yard signs were visible and most were for statewide candidates.

Media

Candidates also attempted to reach the neighborhood through television, radio, and newspapers. Several candidates mentioned that television reached a larger audience. Candidates placed political ads on English and Spanish television stations. Republican gubernatorial candidate Clayton Williams had a commercial on Spanish television Channel 45. Some candidates and Magnolia residents believed the English media were more important because most of the people who could vote could speak English, and that those who could not speak English were not citizens, so they could not vote. Others, however, believed that the Spanish media were more important because candidates needed to appeal to Hispanic voters in Spanish, especially to the elderly monolingual Latinos—"so the people will see that the candidates are concerned with Hispanic people," according to one Magnolia resident. Several Magnolia residents reported that the only thing they knew about the election and the candidates was what they had seen and heard on television.

Candidates also used the radio. Magnolia is one of the largest audiences for the city's several Spanish radio stations. Candidates placed political commercials and participated on talk shows on Spanish radio stations. Radio Station KQQK (Radio Trece) was a popular station for several candidates. In the latter phase of the campaign, Republican gubernatorial candidate Clayton Williams's shouts of "Viva México!" could be heard on radios in Magnolia homes.

Candidates used newspapers very little to get their message to Magnolia, or to other communities, for that matter. As the election got closer, the city's two major newspapers, the *Houston Chronicle* and the *Houston Post*, ran articles about the candidates and covered the campaign extensively. The city's several Spanish newspapers (*El Sol, La Voz*, etc.) covered the election less extensively.

Telephone Banks and Mail-Outs

Two other strategies used by the candidates to reach people were phone banks and mail-outs. Several people involved in campaigns and voter registration efforts reported having reached voters in Magnolia through telephone banks organized by their organizations. Rachel Lucas, of the Chicano Family Center, for example, reported that her organization had children phone Magnolia residents to educate them about the candidates and election issues. Candidate David O. Fraga said he mailed information and political brochures to residents of Magnolia. Constable Víctor Treviño stressed the importance of mail-outs because they were a way to stay in touch with the people. Most candidates claimed that they used mail-outs, but our fieldwork in Magnolia found little evidence of this. A member of the research team who resided in Magnolia received only two fliers related to the election during the campaign period.

In general, candidates did not appear to have done a substantial job of getting their message out to the residents in Magnolia. While political materials were posted in some businesses and on street signs, whole sections of the barrio were devoid of any campaign material. Except for Gallegos, who lived in Magnolia, no candidates were seen interacting with Magnolia residents inside the research site or in the larger Magnolia barrio. While candidates, including statewide candidates, appeared at political rallies in the nearby barrio of the Second Ward, they did not hold similar rallies in Magnolia. It was clear that some of the candidates preferred the mass media of television and radio to reach the voters. This was a sharp contrast to Gallegos's style of personally meeting people with a firm handshake and a smile, a style that seemed to go over well with the barrio residents. In the end, however, it did not seem to matter that candidates were not reaching Magnolia with their messages. As Table 4.1 shows, the barrio seemed to listen to only one message: vote Democrat. While this message helped to create political power, the power of a political stronghold, it did little to generate political interest and activity beyond voting.

The Election's Saliency in the Neighborhood

From September to election day, the election had little saliency in Magnolia. In this section we convey this lack of significance by describing our observations and conversations with people in and near the research site during the campaign period.

September

In talking with a Mexican American family in the research site, we found mixed interest in the election. Some of the family members had resided in Magnolia for over thirty years. We conversed with two of the family members, a twenty-one-year-old man and a fifty-four-year-old woman. A third family member, a twenty-seven-year-old man, refused to participate in the conversation, though he claimed to be a registered voter. The twenty-one-year-old man was not familiar with the candidates but indicated that he intended to familiarize himself with the candidates before election day. The older female was not familiar with the candidates either. According to the two of them, no one discussed the election in their house. During the conversation, it became clear that they were not interested in lengthy discussions about the election.

Father McKenna, the priest at Immaculate Conception, said that TMO was active in encouraging people to vote. He believed the main reason for the election's low level of importance in Magnolia was the makeup of the neighborhood. He claimed: "Voting is not in their history; in some cases, their residential status is still pending." He compared immigrants who had recently arrived in the neighborhood to people who had lived in the neighborhood for many years: "Recent immigrants do not express a desire to push neighborhood issues in contrast with those who have been living in the area longer. These immigrants have entered the mainstream of society, and they have started to begin the process of naturalizing." His assumption was that recent immigrants did not get involved in electoral politics for fear of being apprehended by the *migra* (immigration).

According to Father Marek, Mexican Americans said, "Why do we have to vote? It is not going to accomplish anything." He believed that apathy developed because Mexican Americans voted but saw no improvement in their communities. He went on to say how TMO planned to emphasize the importance of the election in his parish. "TMO will have some type of get-out-the-vote drive, persuading leaders to get in tune with local issues, and announcing during Sunday mass the importance of registering and voting on election day."

Belia López lived near Magnolia. She worked with TMO and had been a member of Immaculate Conception for many years. She doubted that Magnolia was playing a very important role in the election. She thought there were large numbers of people (voters) to empower Magnolia, "but the people need to get involved."

At El Mirasol restaurant, a group of former employees indicated that they could not change present-day issues confronting the community because of their immigrant status. They did not discuss political issues among themselves.

During a visit to Merino's Ice House (a Texas-style drive-in tavern) near the research site, customers did not mention the election. Their attention was on a boxing match on a Spanish television channel. The customers were middle-aged Mexican-origin men who spoke primarily in Spanish. The ice house had a single political sticker, supporting a Democrat running for statewide office.

In an interview with State Representative Román Martínez, whose district is adjacent to Magnolia, he commented on the saliency of the election in Magnolia: "The 1990 election is very interesting, especially to people in the neighborhood. The governor's race is media-intensive and does not rely on grass-roots organizing. The Democratic candidate for attorney general, who is Hispanic, has not even attempted to spread his campaign into Magnolia and that is a shame. There are many people in Magnolia who are willing and ready to volunteer their time for political campaigns."

Overall in September, the election generated very little enthusiasm among the residents in the research site and in the larger Magnolia barrio. Most people did not talk about the election or seem interested in it. Others, like Representative Martínez, felt that the election's saliency would increase in October.

October

In sections of Magnolia, the significance of the election increased only slightly toward the end of October, when more political advertising appeared and candidates were seen and heard on television and radio.

The owner of Memo's Record Shop, who was a member of the Harris County Mexican American Democrats, provided information about voter registration and placed political posters in his store. He was obviously concerned about electoral politics and said he knew and talked with elected officials. Photographs in the store showed him with Latino, black, and white elected officials. When we asked about the low political visibility in Magnolia he responded, "The lack of material posted by candidates is not only occurring in Magnolia but throughout Houston." He did not think there was a lack of electoral activity occurring in Magnolia considering the paucity of political material throughout neighborhoods in Houston.

At Arbol Inn, a neighborhood pool hall, there was no discussion about electoral politics. The customers were Mexican Americans who identified themselves as Chicanos and Chicanas. In a discussion with us, a customer stated that he was registered to vote and voted in every election. He was not familiar with the candidates for the 1990 election, however.

Back at Merino's Ice House, which we visited in September, there was still no talk about the election. Conversations focused on social matters. When we asked the bartender about the political sticker in the window, he replied in Spanish that it had been there for quite some time. According to him, the owner of the ice house had always supported candidates in past elections but was not supporting any candidates this election.

In an interview with Rose García, director of the Magnolia Senior Center, the discussion focused on the mobilization of Magnolia residents in electoral politics. She stated in an optimistic tone:

> People in the neighborhood are becoming more mobilized because they feel that the government is doing less to help them, thus they feel if they can get someone up there [in government] they can get more response from the government. Consequently, the number of voters is higher, thus becoming a more important voting bloc for elections. The neighborhood has become more politically active during the past two years and this increase has provided for more positive changes in the community.

While observing SVREP voter registration at the Fiesta supermarket, near Magnolia, we overheard the conversations of people walking in and out of the store. Most of the conversations were in Spanish, and none pertained to the election. When we approached people to inquire if they were registered to vote, very few would talk about politics. A middle-aged man from Ecuador stated in Spanish, "I have lived in Houston for the past ten years but have not applied for citizenship. If I could vote, I would vote for a Mexican if one was running." Many older Mexican Americans indicated they were already registered. Others said they had no time to register. One person claimed that he was unaware of the upcoming election. Many of the people approached were Mexican immigrants ineligible to vote. Many of them, however, said they would vote when they became U.S. citizens.

At the Tejano Festival, featuring a mostly Mexican American crowd, no one talked about electoral politics, even though SVREP was registering voters at the festival. One Mexican American man explained why he was not interested in the election or politics: "I have no interest in registering because presidents never help Mexicans. The only good president was shot and killed in Dallas. Do you know who that was? John F. Kennedy! . . . I need to have some kind of proof on paper saying that politicians will assist the Mexicans."

At Beto's Place, a bar in the main shopping center in Magnolia, three middle-aged Mexican American men conversed in Spanish and English. The men joked about each other's citizenship status. One of the men called another a "mojado" (undocumented). The man responded, "If you have never seen a 100 percent Chicano you are looking at one now." The men, who said they had lived in Magnolia for several years, did not talk about politics.

As these encounters describe, the election did not gain any momentum in Magnolia in October. Except for the people working in campaigns or in agencies affected by election outcomes, the majority of residents in the neighborhood expressed little interest in the election or in political campaigns.

November

In the last week of the election campaign, we made a special effort to talk with Magnolia neighborhood residents to gauge the saliency of the election in the barrio just prior to election day. When we introduced ourselves to three elderly Mexican American women and explained our interest in Magnolia, one woman quickly called her husband. He appeared and said he allowed signs to be placed in his yard but only for certain candidates. When the women were asked if they voted, they said yes and shied away from the conversation. The man compared politics in Houston to politics in the Lower Rio Grande

Valley. Speaking in Spanish he said that Valley residents were much more involved in electoral politics than were residents of Houston.

In one of our walks through the neighborhood, we spoke with an elderly Mexican American woman. She stated, "I registered to vote and always vote in the elections." She usually decided who to vote for by watching television and by talking with family members who were regular voters. Her preferences were Mexican American Democrats. To her knowledge, none of the candidates in the election had visited the neighborhood. When asked about issues, she complained about trash pickup.

In a nearby street, a group of men conversed in front of a house. As we approached and introduced ourselves and began talking about the election, two of the men left. The man who remained indicated that he was registered to vote but did not vote. During the conversation he described a relationship between wealth and political power: "It is useless; if you have the money you make the laws." To his knowledge, no candidates visited the neighborhood during this election, only a state representative during the spring primaries. He concluded, "I am not familiar with the candidates in this election and I have lost interest anyway. . . . Unfortunately, greed has taken over; that is one of the reasons I have lost interest in politics."

Another day we approached a young Mexican woman. She said in Spanish that she could not vote because she "did not have papers" but hoped that someday she could. She knew about the election from watching television and she viewed the political disorganization of the residents as a problem in the neighborhood. She said she voted in Mexico.

On a street corner, four Mexican immigrant men were drinking beer in a parked car. Three of the men were permanent residents and one was undocumented. Speaking in Spanish, they said they knew about the upcoming election but had little interest in it. The candidates had not been in the neighborhood and their only exposure to them was from the media. One man compared the candidates to officials in Mexico: "It is all the same thing. People don't care because all they do is make promises and never keep them." Another man stated, "Why should I become a naturalized citizen? Para qué (For what)?" The men complained about discrimination Latinos face: "The Anglo will always be offered a higher salary than the Chicano even if both have finished school."

We approached a house with political signs in the front yard. An elderly Mexican immigrant woman lived in the house. She indicated in Spanish that the signs were posted by a man who asked her permission. She was not aware if the candidates visited the area. She knew about the election from watching Spanish television.

At a house with a garage sale, researchers spoke to an elderly Mexican American woman. She indicated that the candidates had not been in the neighborhood for this election, but two months earlier some people passed out political fliers to every house. She and her husband did not discuss politics but always voted straight Democrat. Speaking in mixed English and Spanish she indicated that her family had not experienced any problems in the neighborhood, even though she sometimes left her doors unlocked. She stated, "I do not understand the [criminal] stereotype that Mexicanos fall under."

When we approached two middle-aged men from El Salvador, the men explained they were permanent residents but not eligible to vote. Regardless, they were not interested in electoral politics because of their personal experiences in El Salvador. Their only interest, they said, was to work and better their lives.

As these findings indicate, even one week before election day the election did not gain a high level of saliency in Magnolia. On November 6, whole residential sections in the neighborhood remained devoid of any signs of political interest or behavior. It was hard to tell that a major election was in progress.

The opening of campaign offices in Magnolia no doubt would have heightened the neighborhood's interest in the election. In a September interview with Gallegos, he indicated that this was a strong possibility. As he explained, "Most of the candidates look to Magnolia to house their offices. A lot of the headquarters and campaigns originate in Magnolia. Magnolia is the center of Latino barrios and from there the candidates can expand." But candidates did not look to Magnolia to house their offices, nor did Latino campaigns originate in the neighborhood for the 1990 election. For example, the Houston campaign office of Dan Morales was opened in a nearby suburb that was turning Latino but still had a sizable Anglo working-class population.

The comments made by Father McKenna concerning Magnolia's large immigrant population may help explain why campaign offices were not located in the neighborhood. That is, candidates may have perceived the barrio to be too immigrant and thus low on political capital. Another relevant factor may have been that the center of gravity of the city's Latino political leadership was not located in Magnolia but in the Second Ward, where the major rallies were held.

There was no indication during the campaign period that Latino candidates were deliberately trying to keep a low profile in Magnolia. As we have described, several election-related events were held just outside the barrio at the Island Club and at the Fiesta supermarket.

With a few exceptions, candidates simply did not bother to work the barrio personally; instead, they relied on radio and television to reach the people. One political insider indicated that the Democratic campaigns simply did not have the financial resources to spend on Magnolia. According to him, in the case of the Democratic gubernatorial campaign in Houston, the decision was probably made to invest in the black vote over the Latino vote, since blacks had a higher turnout rate.

There was also no indication in Magnolia that organizations discouraged political involvement or channeled individual participation away from the electoral process. SVREP, the largest organization involved in the electoral process, recruited workers from Magnolia for its voter registration drives. Yet, with the exception of the Gallegos campaign, no well-developed organization emerged to establish a political power base in Magnolia.

Election Outcomes

From the standpoint of election results, the campaign ended successfully in Magnolia. Mario Gallegos, the Magnolia Democratic candidate for state representative of District 143, defeated Libertarian Joe Johansen with 96 percent of the votes cast in Precinct 64 and with 93 percent of the total votes cast in the district. In the statewide races, the Magnolia voters were also successful in helping to elect Democratic candidates, such as Ann Richards for governor and Dan Morales for attorney general. The voter turnout in Magnolia was very much a victory for the Democratic party (see Table 4.1). Almost half (48.1 percent) of the voters in Precinct 64 cast a straight Democratic vote, while only 5.5 percent cast a straight Republican vote.

But if the election was a victory in electing Hispanic and liberal candidates who would be more sympathetic to low-income communities such as Magnolia, it also represented a defeat on two issues related to the election.

One hoped-for possibility was that a popular Anglo city council member, Eleanor Tinsley, would be elected Harris County commissioner, thereby creating the opportunity for a Hispanic to be appointed interim replacement. But Tinsley lost the race. About a month after the election, a position did open with the death of black council member Judson Robinson. Latino leaders made a vigorous effort to have Robinson's at-large seat filled by Leonel Castillo, but after lengthy debates, a majority of the council (including Mayor Kathy Whitmire) voted to appoint Marguerite Robinson, the wife of the deceased council member.

The second defeat concerned low voter turnout in the neighborhood. Of 2,174 persons who were registered to vote in Precinct 64 on election day, 491 voted, or only 22.6 percent of registered voters. Three out of 4 registered voters in the barrio did not bother to vote. Of course, the question can be raised as to whether a greater turnout would have made a difference. Based on our sense of the community, we have no doubt the election results would have been the same even with a 100 percent turnout, since the barrio's favored candidates won their races.

The overall sense of defeat has to be measured in other ways. If SVREP sought to make a difference in turnout for the election, it failed in Magnolia. Neither the number of registered voters nor the turnout rate differed significantly from past elections (see Table 4.3). SVREP met its registration goal but in a way that, in our view, did not significantly affect any one area of the city.

There is a lesson here. Elections are organized through geographical, not ethnic, units. SVREP would have had a greater impact if, with its limited resources, it had concentrated on more specific neighborhoods, where a bloc vote could make a difference, if not electorally, at least psychologically. Moreover, voter registration is an empty accomplishment if the registered voters do not vote on election day.

A second defeat brought about by the low voter turnout was the failure to diminish the image of the city's Latino communities as poor political capital. This image was a critical factor in the decision by Anglo at-large council members not to support a Latino to fill the

TABLE 4.3 Selected Election Results in the Magnolia Research Site, Precinct 64

Election	Registered Voters in Precinct	Votes Cast	% of Registered Voters
1988 general (presidential) election	2,220	950	42.8
1989 city council runoff election (December 9)	2,231	344	15.4
1990 primary for state representative, District 143	2,245	337	15.0
1990 general election (November 6)	2,174	491	22.6

Estimated total voting age population in precinct: 8,493
Estimated U.S. citizen adult population in precinct: 4,246

council seat formerly occupied by Robinson. A *Houston Chronicle* (12/20/90: 15A) analyst explained the reason why Anglo council members in at-large positions supported a black:

> The reasons are simple. Blacks vote in large numbers and in blocs during elections. Hispanics don't. . . . Blacks account for at least 30 percent of the votes cast in a typical citywide election. Their turnout roughly reflects their percentage of the city's population. Hispanics, on the other hand, make up slightly more than 25 percent of the population. At election time, they cast somewhere between 5 percent and 10 percent of the votes.

Thus, blacks in Houston have political clout. Latinos, with their poor voter turnout, do not.

Conclusion

Overall, the neighborhood of Magnolia had little significance for the election as a whole. Several factors are related to this finding. These factors include the population composition of Magnolia and apathy among residents and candidates.

Magnolia's Population Composition

Magnolia's Latino population contains a large number of immigrants, almost half of the neighborhood's total population. Most of the immigrants are from Mexico, but some are from Central America. Magnolia's large immigrant population, which includes many who are not eligible to vote, creates the image for some political leaders that the neighborhood is a poor electoral resource. According to Father McKenna, "voter registration drives . . . could have been more successful [in Magnolia] if the large immigrant sector would not be so leery of registering." While his analysis is not universal, it does provide some insight as to how some politically active people view immigrant political power. For example, a TMO representative stated that Magnolia did not play a "very important role in elections, due to the high numbers of immigrants who are not citizens."

Resident Apathy

The fact that three out of every four registered voters in Precinct 64 did not vote illustrates the political apathy in the neighborhood. Many residents were not familiar with the candidates and did not discuss the elections. During registration drives, many Latino residents were reluctant to register. The absence of campaign posters and signs in many sections of Magnolia also indicated the lack of political interest in the neighborhood.

Frank Velásquez, of Unión y Progreso in Magnolia, attributed some of the residents' political apathy to the political image created by "special interest needs" of the candidates. For example, according to Velásquez, the interpersonal strife in the governor's race lessened the people's interest in politics and thus engendered apathy. As TMO member Belia López explained, "[I]t was hard to choose among the mudslinging between the candidates." Luis Ballestenos, who works in the Magnolia police substation, associated voter apathy with a sense of powerlessness among the residents: "They figure that their vote is not going to count."

Candidate Apathy

Nine of the ten candidates we interviewed were apathetic about campaigning in Magnolia; none of the statewide candidates visited the neighborhood. Some local candidates had little or no knowledge of Magnolia, Houston's largest barrio. For example, one of the candidates for county judge stated that he had never heard of Magnolia, nor had a candidate for county school board trustee. The latter was an incumbent running for re-election. Other candidates expressed only scant knowledge of the neighborhood. Needless to say, if candidates are not aware that the barrio exists, how can they view it as significant to their campaign?

When asked how important Magnolia was to the elections, some of the candidates indicated that the barrio had great importance, but they were not able to describe any significant involvement with the barrio. For example, Rick Brass, candidate for county criminal court judge, felt that Magnolia was important to his campaign but he could not campaign in Magnolia because of lack of funds (which meant that he invested money in other neighborhoods). A Latino candidate for a judgeship also recognized the importance of Magnolia because of its Latino roots, but he did not have the money or volunteers to campaign in the neighborhood. Another candidate for a judgeship also asserted the importance of Magnolia for his campaign, but noted that he was not financially able to campaign actively in the barrio.

Joe Johansen, the Libertarian candidate for the state representative position, also said the neighborhood was important to his campaign but admitted that he "conducted phone calls and door-to-door walks in Galena Park," a neighborhood adjacent to Magnolia.

Our exit poll interviews of fifty-two voters in Magnolia found that 49 percent of the interviewees voted because they viewed it as responsible behavior. The remainder indicated that they voted because they wanted to support a candidate (25 percent), a party (15 percent), or a specific issue (1 percent). Eight percent of the interviewees did not give a reason for voting. These interview results indicate that a large majority (74 percent) of the Magnolia residents who voted (who were a one-fourth of the barrio's registered voters) tended to be persons who had internalized the civic value of electoral participation or who were loyal to specific candidates. Issues had almost no weight in motivating Magnolia residents to vote. Moreover, the interviewees had no conspicuous demographic or social distinction. In terms of age, they were evenly spread from the twenties to the sixties and over; in terms of income, they were evenly spread between low- and middle income. Over two-thirds of the interviewees, however, responded to the exit poll in English.

Not having ethnographic data on other election campaigns in Magnolia (e.g, in city council or presidential elections), it is impossible to conclude empirically whether the apathy in the barrio is constant or situational, in other words, whether it was a factor in the statewide and congressional races of the 1990 election. The 42.8 percent turnout of registered voters in the 1988 presidential election (see Table 4.3) indicates a significantly greater interest in that election. It is axiomatic that presidential elections attract a higher level of voter participation because they generate much more publicity than local campaigns usually produce.

Given the origin of the Magnolia barrio as a Mexican settlement disenfranchised from core political institutions, it is difficult to avoid the conclusion that the barrio's political apathy is partially related to this legacy. In a barrio characterized by large numbers of poor working-class families and new immigrants, the transition to political incorporation is an arduous process. Barrio leaders have to both mobilize resources in the most disadvantaged community conditions and struggle for expansion into the larger political arena, where well-established groups are often unwilling to share power. For ordinary women and men in the barrio, however, the dynamics of this political process may seem almost irrelevant in the context of their daily struggles for economic survival.

Epilogue

On December 20, a day after Marguerite Robinson was appointed to the at-large city council seat left vacant by her husband's death, council member Ben Reyes (the sole Latino in the fifteen-member city council), newly elected state representative Mario Gallegos, and a number of other Latino community leaders held a press conference at city hall to announce a hunger strike in support of Latino voter registration. According to Reyes, Latino leaders and supporters would conduct one-week hunger strikes until the October 1991, registration deadline for the next city council elections. The hunger strikes would draw attention to the voter registration problem and the money saved by not eating would be donated to SVREP. Reyes stated, "It'll begin the empowerment for us. There's a lot of frustration in our community right now" (*Houston Chronicle* [December 21, 1990: 1A]).

Surrounded by many Latino leaders, and with a large painting of Our Lady of Guadalupe in the background, Ben Reyes, former city controller Leonel Castillo, and Catholic bishop Enrique San Pedro initiated the first week of fasting. Latino leaders hoped the hunger strike would help increase the current seventy thousand Latino registered voters in the city by forty thousand more.

References

de la Garza, Rodolfo O.; Néstor Rodríguez; and Harry Pachon. 1990. "The Domestic and Foreign Policy Consequences of Mexican and Central American Immigration: Mexican American Perspectives." In George Vernez, ed., *Immigration and Foreign Relations*, pp. 135–147. Washington, D.C.: RAND Corporation.

De León, Arnoldo. 1989. *Ethnicity in the Sunbelt: A History of Mexican Americans in Houston*. Houston: Mexican American Studies Program, University of Houston.

Feagin, Joe R. 1988. *Free Enterprise City: Houston in Political and Economic Perspective*. New Brunswick, N.J.: Rutgers University Press.

Rodríguez, Néstor P. 1987. "Undocumented Central Americans in Houston: Diverse Populations." *International Migration Review* 21 (Spring): 4–25.

Rodríguez, Néstor P. Forthcoming. "Economic Restructuring and Latino Growth in Houston." In Joan Moore and Raquel Pinderhughes, eds., *Beyond the Underclass Debate: Latino Communities in the United States*. New York: Russell Sage.

Rodríguez, Néstor P., and Jacqueline Hagan. 1989. "Undocumented Central American Migration to Houston in the 1980s." *Journal of La Raza Studies* 2(1) (Summer/Fall): 1–3.

Sheldon, Beth Ann; Néstor P. Rodríguez; Joe R. Feagin; Robert D. Bullard; and Robert D. Thomas. 1989. *Houston: A Study of Growth and Decline in a Sunbelt Boomtown*. Philadelphia: Temple University Press.

U.S. Bureau of the Census. 1983. *Census of Population and Housing: 1980*. Census Tracts. PHC80-2-184.

————. 1991. *1990 Census of Population and Housing.* Summary Tape File 1A. Census tract tabulations released by the Center for Public Policy, University of Houston.

————. 1992. *1990 Census of Population and Housing.* Summary Tape File 1 and 3. Washington, D.C.: U.S. Government Printing Office.

5

Latino Politics in Chicago: Pilsen in the 1990 General Election

John Valadez

Despite being the fifth-largest Latino population in the nation, Chicago's Latino population has often gone unrecognized or ignored by social scientists. Changing national demographics, however, have brought renewed interest in the potential impact of the Latino community on the political arena. Chicago provides a unique laboratory for the study of the political behavior of the Latino, for not only do ethnicity and race continue to play a major role in Chicago politics but the city's neighborhoods also remain sharply defined along ethnic lines. It is also a city where the Mexican American community (60 percent of the Latino population) is aware and proud of its ethnic identity and has begun to create for itself a political place in the governmental structure. Given that there are more than half a million Latinos in Chicago, a 30 percent growth from the 1980 census, this work will concentrate on the Mexican American community in one barrio called Pilsen.

This chapter analyzes the effects of the 1990 general election campaign on the Pilsen community of Chicago. We looked at those aspects of the campaign that positively or negatively affected the participation of the Mexican American community of Pilsen. We also sought to determine if this community saw itself as an important political actor in Chicago. To these ends, a political ethnographic study was developed that focused on Mexican American participation in the electoral arena.

One key variable that stands out is the role that the political machine, whether real or imagined, plays in defining the political activities of the Mexican American community of Chicago. An underlying current is clearly an internal conflict in the Pilsen community based on two key perceptions of politics in Chicago: (1) that the machine is waning in influence and voting can be used to increase political power, and (2) that politics has not changed and the old historical political constraints of a strong machine organization remain in force. This internal dynamic is important in understanding the political behavior exhibited by the Pilsen community during the campaign.

What the research also suggests is that community-based organizations (CBOs) play an important role in the Pilsen community. CBOs see themselves as representatives of the community and as challengers to machine control. CBOs are also vital in defining issues and strategies important to the Pilsen community. Finally, one begins to understand that, for the Mexican American of Pilsen, participation is defined more in terms of acting on issues than in terms of voting.

Methodology

Ours is a political ethnographic study of the Pilsen community. The project ran from September 1990 through November 1990. The investigative team consisted of four persons—the principal investigator and three research assistants. The research assistants (one woman and two men) could read, write, and speak Spanish and English. Two of the research assistants were Latinos from Pilsen who had graduated from the local high school. One still lived in the community and the other had relatives there. The third researcher was an Anglo male familiar with the Latino community of Chicago.

Each researcher was committed to the project and saw it as a means to add to his or her own knowledge of politics and the Pilsen community. One researcher was deeply involved in the activities of the community and served as participant observer. A second researcher concentrated on the media and women's issues, and the third concentrated on making contact with local residents to provide a sense of the electoral process at work in Pilsen.

A comprehensive array of activities was pursued to get an overall sense of Pilsen. For purposes of the research study, the Pilsen site was divided into a fifteen-block area of approximately three square miles. Each research assistant was assigned a section of approximately five square blocks and each spent approximately twenty to twenty-five hours a week visiting the site and talking to individuals in order to develop a thorough working knowledge of the area. Each of the researchers developed a regular pattern of travel in Pilsen to establish contact with local residents. These visits served to collect information through interviews and observation.

We conducted ninety formal and informal interviews with community leaders, political candidates, campaign officials, and members of the community at large. On election day, we also conducted sixty-three exit poll interviews. In addition, each of the researchers attended various civic functions, including two major city-sponsored Mexican Independence Day events, which all major candidates attended or sent representatives to. Also on our agenda were a number of publicized local events called to make public endorsements of the various candidates and two parades held in Pilsen organized by Democratic candidates.

Research Site

Chicago has a diverse Latino population living in four identifiable barrios (Kerr 1976). Although Mexicans and Mexican Americans make up 60 percent of the Latino population, there is also a noteworthy Puerto Rican community, a significant Cuban presence, as well as a growing number of Central and South Americans. Of the four barrios, three are generally considered to be Mexican and one Puerto Rican. The latter, though dominated politically by the Puerto Ricans, is demographically composed almost equally of Mexican Americans and Puerto Ricans (Latino Institute 1986).

This study focused on the Mexican American community in Pilsen, a neighborhood located midway between two far south side Mexican American barrios and the north side Puerto Rican barrio. In reality, Pilsen is one-third of a major Mexican American barrio located on the near southwest side of the city. What geographically may be considered a contiguous area that stretches the width of the city is viewed by residents as three separate barrios—Pilsen, Little Village, and 26th Street. Physically, Pilsen is not a large community, covering approximately three square miles. It is bounded by a freeway on the East (the Dan Ryan), and by a railroad viaduct on the North (Sixteenth Street), with the Chicago River as its southern boundary, and a major avenue (Western Avenue) as its westernmost limit.

Pilsen covers census tracts 3101 to 3155. Its population is estimated to be 47,623. As seen in Table 5.1, it is an overwhelmingly Mexican American community. Table 5.2 indicates low numbers of registered voters but at the same time shows the potential for political power if even half of the unregistered eighteen thousand were converted into actual voters.

Other demographic data reflect a population of low economic and educational status. For example, the median income for Pilsen, according to the 1980 census, was $13,633. Further, 29.3 percent of the Latino population of Pilsen lives below the poverty level. The 1980 census shows educational attainment in Pilsen at a very low level. Of

TABLE 5.1   Population of Pilsen, by Race and Ethnicity

	Number	%
Total white, not Hispanic	7,620	16
Total African American	476	1
Total Latino	39,527	83
Mexican-origin	33,598	85
Puerto Rican	3,162	8
Cuban and other Latinos	395	1
Latinos not identified by national origin	2,372	6
Total population	47,623	100

Source: City of Chicago (1985).

TABLE 5.2   Voting-Age Population in Pilsen

	Number Voting Age	% Registered	Number Registered
Latino	23,576	23	5,323
Other	7,046	64	4,509

Source: City of Chicago (1985).

the more than fourteen thousand Latinos twenty-five years and older, 69.7 percent have less than an eighth-grade education; furthermore, only 13.3 percent have had one to three years of high school. These demographic characteristics are traditionally associated with low levels of political participation (Wolfinger and Rosenstone 1980).

Politically, Pilsen is part of the 25th Ward and is one of Chicago's oldest communities, dating back to before the great Chicago fire of 1871. Partly because of its age and location, Pilsen has over the years acquired the reputation as a port of entry for the many waves of immigrants who have continually flowed into the city (Fremon 1988). Initially established as a German-Irish community in the mid-nineteenth century, by the early 1900s the neighborhood began to take on a Bohemian (thus the name Pilsen), Eastern European character, which it maintained until the late 1950s. With the onset of the 1960s, Pilsen began to change from a predominantly Eastern European community to a predominantly Mexican American community (Kerr 1976).

Pilsen began to evolve as a Mexican American community during the social and political turmoil of the mid-1960s and the 1970s. Urban renewal policies that displaced Latinos from adjacent communities were a major influence in this transformation. Between nine thousand and sixteen thousand people, many of Mexican origin, were forced to relocate during this period (City of Chicago 1971). Urban renewal projects such as new upscale housing and a major new university (the University of Illinois at Chicago Circle) were built on sites with large pockets of Mexican families, who then found themselves displaced. Pilsen's proximity to these sites, as well as its older housing and thus cheaper rents, proved to be the answer for this newly dispossessed community (Padilla 1985). Pilsen also gained many new Mexican immigrants, who were attracted not only by its affordability but also by the neighborhood's ethnic flavor. These two factors, affordability and ethnicity, contributed to making Pilsen in a very short time one of the largest Mexican barrios in Chicago (Kerr 1976).

Pilsen has until recently been a transient community, with most of its residents moving west to the Little Village and 26th Street communities after their income and job situation become stable. A prominent community organizer and leader explained, however, that many residents have now begun to establish themselves as permanent residents of Pilsen. This new tendency to establish roots has been a critical factor in the growth of political activity in the community. Community agencies find it easier to mobilize residents who have a stake in resolving community problems and are motivated to become involved in the resolution of key issues facing their barrio.

Although not large geographically, Pilsen has been among the most politically active Latino communities in the city. This ethnic political awareness and development is partly due to the influence of the Chicano movement. The movement coincided with Pilsen's becoming a Mexican American barrio and helped provide the community with the motivation to develop its own political identity (Kerr 1976). Since that time, Pilsen has been identified as a community involved in ethnicity-based political issues and solutions. Further, even though Pilsen has only a short history as a Mexican American barrio, it is viewed by many as the symbolic political leader of the Mexican American community of Chicago (Kerr 1976). It has been able to achieve and maintain this important political role for itself mainly through its effective infrastructure of community-based organizations.

Pilsen has also positioned itself as potentially one of the key centers of Latino ethnic power in the city. A meaningful example of the kind of activity that marked Pilsen as a major Latino political actor was the role it played in demanding that the Chicago Board of Education build a high school, Benito Juárez High, in Pilsen (Valadez 1986). Another example of the use of its ethnic identity and emerging political consciousness to define itself within the polity of Chicago was its participation in and support of the conflict that brought about the redistricting plan resulting in four Latino seats on the city council in 1985.

In conjunction with the Little Village and 26th Street barrios, Pilsen has been a key player in an effort to create new political power for Latinos in Chicago. This effort was abetted by Harold Washington's campaign as an independent Democrat and his emergence, after the 1983 election, as the mayor of Chicago. His victory set in motion a new political awareness not only in African American communities but in Hispanic communities as well (Kleppner 1985). The regular Democratic organization not only saw its machine defeated by an independent African American, but, more importantly, saw its 1980 ward map of Chicago challenged and overturned in 1984 by the federal courts. The court ordered that six wards be redrawn and that two of the wards be given African American super majorities and four of the wards, two in the Puerto Rican and two in the Mexican American communities, be given Latino super majorities (Kleppner 1985). In the election of 1985, the 25th and 22nd wards elected the first two Mexican American aldermen in the city's history, both of whom claimed to be independent of the regular Democratic party. It should also be noted that two Puerto Rican aldermen were elected at this time in the near north side.

The Role of Community-based and Neighborhood Organizations

Community-based organizations have been historically important to Latino communities because of the leadership and services they provide (Tirado 1974), a characteristic that remains true of the many CBOs in Pilsen. The CBOs have proven time and again to be effective voices in identifying issues of importance to the community. I shall suggest that ethnicity plays a decisive role in creating and maintaining the various CBOs in Pilsen. The community groups were in turn able to provide solutions to issues that reflected community concerns. Thus, the reality of Pilsen is that the CBOs remain the principal means for creating issues and making demands of local political institutions. As a result, we focused on the relationship between the CBOs and the 1990 elections.

Many of the CBOs began in the late 1960s and the early 1970s, galvanized in part by the Chicano movement and its emphasis on ethnic identity. Although ethnicity was a major influence in helping to create and give identity to community organizations, another element helped motivate these organizations to political action. That element was the anti-Daley and antimachine sentiment that dominated political organizing in the early 1960s and the 1970s in Chicago (Valadez 1986). These views helped structure the conflicts that were vital to the political organizations of Pilsen. That is, the conflicts helped define the boundaries of the competing groups in Pilsen.

Although most of the more than thirty CBOs in Pilsen provide direct social services such as day care, educational programs, counseling, and shelters, at least three organizations are active in the political arena— Pilsen Neighbors, the Pilsen Resurrection Project, and the United Neighborhood Organization (UNO). Each of these is umbrellalike in structure and seeks support and membership not only from individuals in the community but, more important, from the CBOs and churches in Pilsen. The United Neighborhood Organization is the only one of the three that has a citywide constituency, much of it parish-based.

Our research documented that women are beginning to attain leadership roles and play major roles in a number of the CBOs in Pilsen. As one key male leader pointed out, "Women are the backbone of many organizational efforts." It is certain that women are poised to begin voicing their issues (e.g., child care, abuse, alcoholism) and placing them on the political agendas of Pilsen. Yet one female activist was puzzled as to why "women who are extremely qualified to be leaders will concede power as soon as a male steps in. What happens to women that they develop these notions? It is as if they don't think that they belong in the public spheres."

In addition to using local CBOs to organize Pilsen's politics, political organizers in Pilsen regularly focus their recruitment efforts on church congregations. Churches are particularly important because they have a substantial, ethnically identifiable constituency, and so can be mobilized by the political organizations to legitimize community issues and solutions. One of the more politically active CBOs working in Pilsen during the campaign was the Pilsen Resurrection Project, which started as a coalition of the various groups in the parishes of Pilsen.

For Mexican Americans, the church remains an important political catalyst. Our interviews with priests revealed that they supported community leaders in their endeavor to increase political participation. Priests usually aided community activists in their efforts to create a political identity for Pilsen.

Research Findings

From the outset, our research indicated that CBOs directed and motivated the community to identify, define, and provide answers to critical issues in Pilsen, a highly important role in light of the community's low rate of electoral participation. CBOs organized and developed what could be termed nonvoting political participation in community action. Community action includes such activities as involvement in demonstrations, sit-ins, petition drives, and other legal or extralegal activities. To a large degree, community members believed that they were successful in the political arena when they acted as antagonists to the politically entrenched establishment. The battle for Benito Juárez High School and the fights over redistricting are the most well known examples. Individuals in the community responded positively toward and supported organizations that confronted the establishment.

The nature of many of these successes led many people to believe that success could come about only through confrontation rather than electoral participation. This point of view was echoed in people's responses to the question of whether they saw any connection between voting and what happened in the community. To paraphrase the responses, "Voting is not the only way to get things done. Demonstrations and confronting politicians often are the best ways to get things done in our community." The successes resulting from this activism can ensure that governmental responses reflect community concerns rather than traditional machine concerns.

Yet, even though CBOs have achieved some political successes, they are also part of the problem faced by Pilsen. The problem stems from the inability of CBOs to work with each other on the problems facing the community. For example, many of the leaders and organizational spokespersons often identified as important the very same issues (e.g., housing, education, drugs, and gangs), yet, these individuals disagreed over how to define problems and over solutions. Community leaders were concerned that solutions and control over solutions be maintained by the "community," often a euphemism for their own organization.

This continuing conflict between competing political activists over who speaks for the community affected the agencies involved in the campaign. One of our researchers, a principal actor in a major political organization in Pilsen, provided anecdotes about the conflicts among organizations in Pilsen. He noted an unwillingness on all sides to accept solutions that did not stem from their own groups. An example of this occurred during the campaign. It centered on the debate over how the housing issue should be handled in Pilsen. All parties agreed that housing was a major problem and that the city must take the lead in rectifying this problem. There was no agreement, however, as to which local group would be the lead agency in the community. Two alternatives were developed—one by the Pilsen Resurrection Project and a second by Pilsen Neighbors. Each felt that its plan was the most beneficial for Pilsen and best reflected community concerns. A confrontation between the two groups emerged over who really "represented" the community and who was the "opportunist" taking advantage of a new and potentially important program. The conflict reached the point where one group circulated a letter accusing the other of being controlled by Anglos who did not really understand the problems of the Mexican American community of Pilsen. Both continued to insist that they were the only true representative of the Pilsen community.

In part, CBOs also function as protection against the long-established view, held by community members, that voting accomplishes nothing if done outside the Democratic party organization. This attitude reflects, I would argue, the socialization of machine politics, a process that helped create a sense of superiority for the machine. This sense of superiority makes it difficult for nonactivists in Pilsen to believe they can change their own political conditions.

The Political Setting and the Machine

A discussion of the role of the CBOs in Pilsen should introduce the notion that, even though Pilsen and other Latino communities have begun to take an active role in Chicago politics, the political milieu in which they must operate must be understood in the context of the political machine of the regular Democratic party and its legacy (Gosnell 1968; Royko 1971; Hirsh 1983). Chicago is unique in that the machine grew in scope and power during a period when "good government" reforms permeated the rest of the nation (Royko 1971; Raykove 1975). Unlike other communities that experienced Machine Era politics in the mid- to late-nineteenth century, Chicago's Machine Era began in the mid-twentieth century and remained virtually unchallenged until 1980. Developed in the 1930s by Anton Cermak (Gottfried 1962), Chicago's machine was controlled by the Irish for fifty years (Royko 1971), reached its zenith under Mayor Richard Daley (Peterson 1975), and continued as a dominant element of politics in Chicago even after Daley's death in 1978 (Simpson 1991). The similarity of the Washington administration to the old Democratic machine became evident especially toward the end of Washington's tenure. Given the historical patterns of political control and patronage set up by the machine, it is hardly surprising that Washington wielded a strong and disciplined control over the political life of Chicago (Simpson 1991).

As the machine grew in power, it was able to control and minimize the struggle by ethnic and racial groups for political control of the city (Hirsh 1983; Kleppner 1985). The machine helped produce an environment that allowed white ethnics and some African Americans to exercise political power jointly (Hirsh 1983). For African Americans, however, this sharing of power was limited to the few who could contribute to keeping the machine in power. Thus, deep divisions persist among the major racial and ethnic groups that are played out in the political life of the city (Kleppner 1985).

That the machine relies on ethnicity as a way to attain and maintain political power might be seen as an asset to Pilsen. Yet, because other ethnics controlled political positions, the machine created an environment that was open only to established political entities, thus making it difficult for new, emerging groups to compete as equals. This political reality contributes to the belief by Latinos that politics remains closed and unresponsive.

This conflict resembles a zero-sum game. That is, groups understand distribution of political power only in the context of one group's attaining power at the expense of another. For the Latino community, this perception of how power is lost or won is even more important, given the community's emergence as a new player in the political arena. This was emphasized by a spokesperson from the Chicago Urban League who, while talking to a group of Latinos discussing the 1991 reapportionment process, stated that the impression in both the African American and the Latino communities was that "Latinos gain at the expense of blacks and vice versa." This perception is compounded for the Latinos of Chicago not only because they are viewed as newcomers to politics and as competitors for power, but also because they are competing in an arena that may already be stretched too thin, particularly given the present political tension between the African American community and the ethnic white community.

The Machine and the Demobilization of Pilsen

The machine created a mindset that has made it hard for the community to appreciate the long-term benefits of electoral participation. At the grass-roots level in the Mexican American community, people perceive that the machine does not need to broaden its base in order to maintain its political control. A resident of Pilsen reflected this notion when he stated, "I think it is because power has been consolidated in fewer and fewer hands and the non-powerful have become disenfranchised. People here [in Pilsen] also feel that they don't have the right to question the powerful—there is no collective sense of the fact that they have a right to access institutions." In the same vein, another respondent who was well known in the community stated, "all politicians are the same. My clients could all care less about who gets elected because nothing changes." Many in the community consequently believe that electoral politics in Pilsen is still dominated by the machine, even in light of its apparent demise since the death of Mayor Daley in 1978.

Mexican American communities like Pilsen view the election process as having failed to bring them any political benefits. People in Pilsen experienced years of machine control when important issues were either ignored or addressed in a superficial manner (Valadez 1986). The ordinary individual in Pilsen senses that access to political power for the powerless is out of reach within the context of the machine. It is difficult for them to perceive any change in a system that has been closed to them for so long. As one respondent stated, "Pilsen never benefits from an election." So even as Pilsen evolved into a potentially legitimate political and visible entity outside the realm of the machine, it also witnessed and realized the extent of and the preeminence of machine politics in the city of Chicago.

Our research for the project on the 1990 elections reinforces this concern about the lack of access to power. People in the community continually said things like, "The politicians only come around on election day," and "Why vote? Nothing ever changes." Many residents feel that relying on machine politicians and the electoral process changes nothing. The community's perception is that the machine still dominates and distributes all of the political resources in Chicago; therefore there is little value in participating in the electoral process. Some of this lack of participation may be attributed to what may be called Latino fatalism, an attribute often associated with the Mexican community (Paz 1961). A better explanation for Latino lack of participation is revealed in interviews with Mexican Americans in Pilsen, who see little connection between voting and the redistribution of resources to the community. Community members felt out of the loop and, in fact, saw little attention paid to them as voters. Reflecting on this situation, one respondent stated, "since Pilsen has been disenfranchised for a long time, the community has two options—revolt or accept the status quo. Pilsen has accepted the status quo." Especially for those at the grass-roots level, the status quo reflects a sense that the machine does not address community concerns.

Paul Kleppner, in his study of Harold Washington's 1983 election campaign, places this phenomenon in a broader context. He labels the machine's disregard for nonelectoral participation as "the demobilization" of select segments of the voting arena, a behavior that would appear to be the opposite of the standard machine practice of controlling as many votes as possible in a community. This demobilization demonstrates the machine's need to control and limit voters to only those who benefit the machine. In describing this process, Kleppner states: "The machine has developed a new formula for victory: high mobilization and cohesive support from both of the city's white ethnic areas and demobilization of the uncontrollable majority of its black electorate. That change in electoral strategy was enormously significant, both for what it revealed and for the ways in which it shaped the policy reaction of Daley and his successors" (1985: 140).

The dichotomy of Pilsen's voting patterns is a recurring phenomenon. The nonpolitical actors and nonactivists view politics as a function of the machine and therefore see the election process as bankrupt and of no use in changing conditions in Pilsen. On the other hand, the activists in the community are cognizant that voting is vital if one is to become active in the political arena of Chicago. These two attitudes are important elements for understanding the events in Pilsen in 1990 election.

The 1990 Election

In the general election of November 6, 1990, thirty-nine candidates were seeking twenty nonjudicial offices. In addition, many judicial races were being contested, including two state supreme court judgeships, three appellate court judgeships, and fifty county circuit court judgeships (*Chicago Tribune* [November 5, 1990]). Table 5.3 lists races and candidates that were mentioned at least once by respondents during our interviews. Omitted are candidates running on the Solidarity party

TABLE 5.3   Candidates on the Pilsen Ballot in the 1990 General Election

Office		Party	
	Democrat	*Republican*	*Harold Washington*
National			
Senate	P. Simon	L. Martin	None
Congress	W. Lipinski	D. Shestokas	None
State			
Governor	N. Hartigan	J. Edgar	None
Atty. general	R. Burris	J. Ryan	None
Secretary of state	J. Consento	G. Ryan	None
Treasurer	P. Quinn	G. Baise	None
Controller	D. Netsch	S. Suter	None
Representative, 20th District	B. Martínez	None	None
Cook County			
President	R. Phelon	A. Deangels	B. Norman
States attorney	C. Partee	J. Ommaly	J. Robinson
Sheriff	M. Sheahan	J. O'Grady	T. Brewer

ticket, as they were given little chance of winning a significant portion of the vote.

Only one Latino, Ben Martínez, the Democratic candidate for the 20th State Assembly District, ran for office in the November election, and he ran unopposed. No other major race featured a Latino candidate. The two races that attracted the most attention in the community, based on our interviews, were the Senate race between incumbent Democratic senator Paul Simon and Republican representative Lynn Martin, and the governor's race between Democrat Neil Hartigan and Republican James Edgar. All of these candidates attempted to appeal to the Latino community for support. Thus, our attention was focused on these two key races.

In assessing political activity during the campaign, it must be noted that this election was not decisive for Chicago's politics. Most of the important local contests were decided during the Democratic primary. In talking to various political actors and activists, the 1990 elections were perceived as having a minimal effect on the local political arena. One Mexican American elected official explained, "People don't really get very involved except for local elections. People can relate to the [local] candidates and the [local] issues and to the significance of who ought to be the officeholder. In larger elections, this is more difficult." A Pilsen community activist put it this way, "This election, however, is not that important to us. It doesn't mean as much as the mayoral race, which is closer to home. Community people are just not sure how the governorship affects them, whereas the mayoral and aldermanic elections seem a lot closer [to the community]." Given Pilsen's experience with Chicago governance, it is hardly surprising that the community does not get excited or even become aware of politics when a local contest is not at stake. Thus, we found individuals who had only limited awareness of or, for that matter, did not care about who controlled national and state offices.

The issues discussed by community members reinforced the notion of a local focus. The four most often mentioned issues in our interviews were gangs, drugs, housing, and employment. While each of these issues can be influenced by national-level policy, each also has a local dimension. Gangs and drugs reflect a perceived weakness in law enforcement. Housing and employment reflect respondents' integration into the community. As I shall suggest, these community issues were neglected by the candidates and campaigns during the 1990 elections.

As the election campaign unfolded, it became obvious that candidates were not going to focus their attention on any one particular Latino community in Chicago; rather, they would appeal to the Latino community as a whole. In place of a concrete agenda detailing a point-by-point program aimed at alleviating the problems of the Latino community, their basic strategy could be characterized as requesting support by eating a taco or walking in an ethnic parade. This strategy, called "fiesta politics" (McWilliams 1948) or "taco politics" by many, is typically used by politicians trying to attract a Latino constituency.

Early in September, several events took place that exemplified fiesta politics. A number of politicians came to Pilsen to participate in the city-sponsored El Grito celebration commemorating Mexican Independence; they also came out for the Mexican Independence parade in Pilsen and Little Village. Also in September, politicians addressed crowds at the city-sponsored Fiesta Latina. As one community activist said, "they [politicians] only come to Pilsen for public relations reasons—to make themselves look good. By coming to Pilsen, they justify that they are friends of Hispanics and then they claim that Latinos support them."

The Campaign in Pilsen

Early in September the only "major" issue addressed by most of the candidates, particularly the gubernatorial and senatorial candidates, was the lack of Latinos in policymaking positions. The candidates all promised that they would change this if elected; however, even though candidates mentioned issues important to Latinos (i.e., gangs, housing, drugs), they did not directly attempt to identify themselves with issues that solely reflected problems in the Pilsen community. Instead, they presented these as citywide or statewide issues.

The major gubernatorial and senatorial candidates had Latino liaisons on their staffs and to some degree made direct media addresses to the Latino community. Republican gubernatorial candidate Jim Edgar attempted to create Latino ads that were not just Spanish translations of his regular campaign material. One researcher found that Edgar also made some effort to acknowledge the ethnic differences between the Mexican American and the Puerto Rican communities. One of his Spanish-language television ads was shot in a park in the Puerto Rican neighborhood with Puerto Rican flags as a backdrop. A second ad showed Edgar posed in front of a local elementary school in the Pilsen community; however, Edgar's and Hartigan's Latino campaigns were mostly limited to "media opportunities," which minimized the need for paid advertisements.

As the campaign evolved in September and October, we noted little activity. It was not until the end of October and the first week of November that we witnessed significant electoral activity. During the last week of the campaign, two Democrats organized parades aimed at the Latino population at large but held in Pilsen. Even these events were minimal and targeted party regulars rather than the community at large. That is, the get-out-the-vote drive was aimed primarily at getting regular party members to the polls, with little attention paid to new voters. Thus the level of interest going into election day provided little impetus for those not already electorally engaged. One of our researchers commented that he saw no attempt to call or take people to the polls. He contrasted his election day experience in Pilsen with what he saw as vigorous activity in neighboring communities.

One interesting note about the campaign was Jim Edgar's Spanish-language appeals, which did not mention that he was a Republican. This tactic was no doubt a recognition of the strong Democratic party loyalty of Mexican Americans. To some degree, it was a successful ploy. As an Edgar worker said, "39.9 percent of the Latino vote was for Edgar, which points to the fact that Latinos are voting for candidates and not for a particular party." The Democratic candidates, on the other hand, depended on the party loyalty of Mexican Americans. As a Democratic party media consultant related in an interview, "Edgar has been active [in his Latino media campaign]; Hartigan has not been because the community is already overwhelmingly Democratic."

The Role of Community Organizations in the 1990 Campaign

Our research showed that activists from community-based organizations understood the importance of politics and Pilsen's potential as a key player in Chicago, though not necessarily the importance of the value of the 1990 elections. Political organizers also recognized the value of voting. Throughout the campaign, community leaders, in interviews both with the press and with our team, emphasized the potential and future importance of the Latino vote. Most of their comments reinforced the idea that the 1991 elections for mayor, alderman, and committeeman would see a more active community. Many felt the real test of their resources and political influences would not come until the 1993 elections, with the anticipated influx of new voters resulting from the Immigration Reform Act of 1986.

Thus, community organizations are more aware of the value of voting than are community residents. Therefore, as advocates, their attention remains on mobilizing the community as a means of helping it become a legitimate actor in the political arena. Yet, even as these leaders emphasized the importance of electoral participation, the community at large showed little enthusiasm for the 1990 election. In reality, community organizations saw the election campaign as a forum in which to voice issues rather than to get out the vote.

There were two major voter registration drives in September. Of the two, only one was organized by a local community group, the Pilsen Resurrection Project, and it failed to have any real impact, registering only fifty people in a monthlong campaign. This campaign was organized with the help of various churches in Pilsen. The other voter registration drive was a citywide attempt that also failed to attract many new registrants. This latter campaign, VOTES, was widely supported by Latino politicians, businesspersons, and community activists alike. The initial publicity announced that this was an attempt to try to make the Latinos of Chicago viable actors in the political arena. One of the more important members of the VOTES coalition was the Latino advocacy organization UNO.

UNO has a citywide constituency and organizes around several issues with broad Latino appeal. UNO identified itself early with the voter registration drive. In discussing the registration drive with an official from UNO, it was apparent that the thrust of the drive was more long-term than geared toward the 1990 election. The official explained that this drive would serve as an educational process in which individuals in the community could begin to learn about the vote and its importance to the community.

Besides targeting those who were already eligible to vote, UNO targeted amnesty participants who would soon become eligible voters. Emphasis was to be on educating people in the amnesty program who in the next few years would help to make the Mexican community of Pilsen much more important. The thrust of this political education accented the importance of voting and the need to work independently of the local party organization, while stressing the potential of the community to affect issues and policies outside the constraints of traditional machine politics. The leaders of this campaign maintained that voter registration would remain a top priority for Pilsen and the Latino community for the near future.

The 1990 election was not as important to the Pilsen community leaders as was the preparation for future elections. We heard such comments as "the real election will come next year." Others cited the upcoming amnesty-eligible voters, who would "be independent of traditional influences" and might be used to create an independent political voice for the Latinos of Pilsen. Many people thought that the local elections of 1991 and the potential for creating a new Latino congressional district would be the real political goals for the Latino community. One respondent characterized this as the start of a long educational process to ensure an independent Latino electorate.

The Results of the 1990 Elections

We examined two aspects of the results of the 1990 elections—turnout and voter preference. In discussing projected turnouts with various political and community leaders, we were told that "turnout will be low—in the 30 to 40 percent range." The actual turnout in the 25th Ward was 43 percent of the registered voters (approximately five thousand of the twelve thousand registered voters). On a precinct basis, the ten precincts with more than 90 percent Latino voters had a turnout rate of nearly 43 percent. In four precincts with 40 to 60 percent Anglo voters, the turnout was nearly 59 percent. Citywide, voter turnout was approximately 53 percent. Within the context of Chicago elections, a 40 percent turnout is considered to be low, although in other areas of the country, it might be viewed differently.

I have already indicated two possible reasons for this low turnout. The most important factor was the lack of any real local contest on the ballot; secondarily, the election featured only one major Latino candidate, who ran unopposed.

The research also suggests several other reasons. First, the issues of interest to the Pilsen community were not addressed by the candidates, nor were they debated in the campaign. Second, the Democratic organization made only a minimal effort to get out the vote in Pilsen. Third, our research team found a sense of frustration on the part of many community members, who felt they were not respected by the political establishment. In response to the question "Why don't you vote?" many answered with the same type of response, "Nothing changes," or "Our vote does not count, so why vote?"

Why, then, did people vote? Among those voters we talked to in our limited election day polling and postelection interviews, we heard repeatedly that people voted out of a "sense of duty" or "obligation" rather than to change conditions. Our election day polling revealed strong party loyalty as another motivating factor. This sentiment, combined with the high turnout in Pilsen relative to the barrios in other cities studied in this project, indicates the influence of the political machine over those who did vote.

Shifting the Focus from State and National to Local Elections

Our research reflects that, for the most part, Pilsen residents think that electoral politics has little to do with how things get done. In reviewing the election from the community's perspective, a number of factors stand out. With its focus on state and national offices, the election was perceived to offer only minimal benefits to Pilsen. This apathy in turn generated little enthusiasm from the organizations or the campaign. This is reflected in our interviews with activists and nonactivists alike, who made it clear that the local arena of politics in Chicago is where communities like Pilsen can have an impact. Our interviews found that the neighborhood sensed it was at the local level of politics where a difference could be made.

Our interviews further suggest that, even though some residents had little knowledge of the political process, they still relied on CBOs rather than on politicians for solutions to their problems. The community, as represented by CBOs, seemed to be aware that the policies that most affected it were a result of local political activity. Most, in fact, failed to make the link between state and national politicians and local political issues. The community depended on its organizations to define not just issues but solutions to its problems. Thus, it could be argued that community members are political actors within the context of organizations.

Individuals in the community recognized that political participation involved activities other than voting and saw these nonvoting forms of participation as more productive. Therefore, because local organizations can mobilize individuals on particular issues relevant to day-to-day problems, Latinos come across to the political establishment as a mobilized community whose issues must be addressed in order to maintain order. Within this framework, local organizations play a key role in effecting long-term inclusion in the political arena of Chicago. Organizations actually reflect individual concerns and provide the individual community member with a sense of political participation.

Thus, the community sensed a need for government to respond to its problems. Yet, they felt alienated because, as Mexican Americans, they have historically been left out of the political process, a process that determines which resources (i.e., contracts, jobs, services) should be distributed, and to whom. The 1990 general election provided little impetus around which to organize the community.

After this extensive discussion of Pilsen voter turnout, I offer brief comments on voter preference. In the two races of interest to the community, only one turned out to be competitive. Statewide, Republican Jim Edgar beat Democrat Neil Hartigan to become governor. Edgar's victory margin of 51 percent to 48 percent makes it unlikely that Illinois's or Pilsen's Latino voters could have had an influence on the outcome. The other major race, the Senate race between Paul Simon and Lynn Martin, turned out not to be competitive, with Simon taking 65 percent of the vote statewide. Pilsen's member of Congress, William Lipinski, won re-election with a 66 percent to 31 percent margin of victory districtwide. State Representative Ben Martínez had no opposition.

Conclusion

Our research unveiled a relatively low level of electoral activity by Mexican Americans in Pilsen. This is especially true when viewed within the context of Chicago's electoral process. The lack of interest in the campaign can, in part, be attributed to the fact that no local office was being contested and that only one Latino candidate ran for office. The Pilsen community's perception of governance was that only Latinos or local politicians could be made to respond to local concerns.

In addition, political institutions made only minimal efforts to target or motivate the Pilsen community to vote. These efforts can be described as the demobilization strategy of the political machine. The campaign consisted primarily of politicians making periodic forays into the community, paying little attention to a particular Latino community and its issues. Toward the end of the campaign, candidates used the Latino media, both electronic and print, yet neither political party made any real attempt to identify itself with a Latino issue. Most of the campaign materials, except for those of gubernatorial candidate Edgar, were little more than translations of existing literature and not directed at a Latino audience. Even the Latino media did little out of the ordinary to attract or maintain interest in the campaign. In general, the candidates also neglected to address local political agendas, in part because of the tendency by politicians to view local communities like Pilsen only as a subset of the larger Latino community of Chicago. This campaign revealed the political establishment's failure to understand the potential that local issues have to excite Latino constituents and to get them to vote.

We noted different levels of awareness that affected the political behavior of Pilsen residents. As a result, activists and leaders in the community see the arena of politics very differently from the community at large. That is, the average community member's behavior is based on a traditional understanding of how politics operates in a machine environment; the activists, on the other hand, approach politics with the idea that change will occur once the community begins to act as an independent political actor.

The research helped us conclude that Pilsen's community organizations typically take the lead not only in organizing the community but also in disseminating information to the community. Organizational leaders play the role of advocates for their constituents, developing relationships with officials and candidates. Organizations provide the community with the means for attending political events and at times organize the events themselves.

One fact seemingly ignored by nearly all candidates was the role of women and issues that reflect women's concerns. As I have suggested, women play major roles in the organizational structure of Pilsen. Traditional "women's issues" were mentioned by community members during interviews, yet candidates did not address these themes. One national issue in particular—abortion—had little impact during the election. All major candidates had similar positions and therefore abortion was not viewed as a point of distinction among them.

While the 1990 election was of little interest to the average Pilsen resident, neighborhood leaders and activists viewed the electoral process as vital, if not for 1990, then for the future. People inside the political establishment, as well as those who worked as political and community leaders, and to some degree even those outside these circles, argued that the real competition for electoral benefits would come in the future. They hoped that the Pilsen community would become more involved once its residents understood the electoral process and the importance of a political stance independent of the political machine.

To prepare the community for participation in the electoral arena, the CBOs in Pilsen developed an educational approach to registration and the naturalization process. This approach revolved around registering those currently eligible to vote, and equally important, those who would become eligible under the 1987 Amnesty Program. The potential of registering many new Latinos is perceived by many in the Latino community as vital to their political future. By expanding the number of registered voters, Latinos can look forward to greater political strength at all levels of governance.

The issue of political independence dominates the agenda in Pilsen. In part, independence is seen as a resource that can take advantage of the current racial polarization in Chicago. An election outcome that pointed to the break in traditional voting patterns was the ability of Jim Edgar to attract a significant percentage of the Latino vote. The large Edgar vote gave signs that the Latino community might no longer be relied on to support candidates simply because they run as Democrats.

The campaign showed that the Pilsen community views political participation in ways that transcend voting. It was obvious that the discussion of issues and their solutions remained the strongest criterion by which the community judged its own level of participation. The campaign also established that the Latino community still remains outside the political mainstream of Chicago. It became apparent that the potential for political power for a community like Pilsen is, in the final analysis, just that—potential. Most political analysts would agree that Pilsen, along with the rest of the Latino community, must begin to translate potential into some type of voting strength or in the end lose all credibility as a major political player in Chicago. The Latino community must begin to understand that the election process, like other arenas of participation, can be made to respond to community demands.

References

City of Chicago. 1971. *Chicago Statistical Abstract*. Chicago: Department of Planning.

————. 1985. *Chicago Statistical Abstract*. Chicago: Department of Planning. March.

Fremon, David K. 1988. *Chicago Politics Ward by Ward*. Bloomington: Indiana University Press.

Gosnell, Harold. 1968. *Machine Politics: Chicago Model*. Chicago: University of Chicago Press.

Gottfried, Alex. 1962. *Boss Cermak of Chicago*. Chicago: University of Chicago Press.

Hirsh, Arnold. 1983. *Making the Second Ghetto: Race and Housing in Chicago, 1940–1960*. New York: Cambridge University Press.

Kerr, Louise. 1976. "The Chicano Experience in Chicago, 1920–1970." Ph.D. dissertation, University of Illinois at Chicago Circle.

Kleppner, Paul. 1985. *Chicago Divided: The Making of a Black Mayor*. DeKalb: Northern Illinois University Press.

Latino Institute. 1986. *Al Filo/At the Cutting Edge*. Chicago.

McWilliams, Carey. 1948. *North from Mexico: The Spanish Speaking Population of the United States*. New York: Greenwood Press.

Padilla, Félix. 1985. *Latino Ethnic Consciousness*. Notre Dame, Ind.: University of Notre Dame Press.

Paz, Octavio. 1961. *The Labyrinth of Solitude*. New York: Grove Press.

Peterson, Paul. 1975. *School Politics Chicago Style*. Chicago: University of Chicago Press.

Raykove, Milton. 1975. *Don't Make No Waves, Don't Back No Losers*. Bloomington: University of Indiana Press.

Royko, Mike. 1971. *Boss: Richard J. Daley of Chicago*. New York: Dutton.

Simpson, Richard. 1991. "The Chicago City Council 1971–1991." Paper presented at the annual meeting of the Midwest Political Science Association, Chicago.

Tirado, Manuel Richard. 1974. "Mexican American Community Political Organization: The Key to Chicano Political Power." In F. Chris García, ed., *La Causa Política: A Chicano Political Reader*, pp. 68–93. Notre Dame, Ind.: University of Notre Dame Press.

Valadez, John. 1986. "Chicano Political Development: The Role of Political Participation and Agenda-Building in Expanding the Biases of the Polity. A Case Study." Ph.D. dissertation, University of Washington.

Wolfinger, Raymond, and Steven J. Rosenstone. 1980. *Who Votes?* New Haven, Conn.: Yale University Press.

6

Grass-Roots Politics in an East Los Angeles Barrio: A Political Ethnography of the 1990 General Election

Harry Pachon and Lourdes Argüelles, with Rafael González

If one area typifies the Mexican American urban experience in the American mind, that area would indisputably be East Los Angeles, or East L.A. Twenty years ago, one researcher described East L.A. as "the largest single concentration of Mexican Americans; it is a center of Poverty Program work, produces the most militant Mexican Americans, and is an area which social scientists have been studying for the past twenty years, thus providing an invaluable storehouse of data" (Dworkin 1973).

As Ambrecht and Pachon (1974), Acuña (1984), and others have noted, East Los Angeles has also been associated with such historical events in the Mexican American experience as the Sleepy Lagoon case, the Pachuco riots, the East Los Angeles school walkouts ("blow-outs"), and large-scale rioting in the 1970s. It is currently perceived as having the most politically and socially mobilized Latino community in the state of California. Organizations ranging from the Community Service Organization, the Brown Berets, United Neighborhoods Organized (UNO), and the East Los Angeles Community Union (TELACU) have all used East Los Angeles as their base. Hollywood feature films depicting the Mexican American urban experience—from *Colors* and *Boulevard Nights* (dealing with Chicano gangs) to *Stand and Deliver* (the story of Jaime Escalante, a nationally known educator) have used East Los Angeles as their setting. East Los Angeles is also the area represented by nationally known political figures such as Congressman Edward R. Roybal and County Supervisor Gloria Molina.

East Los Angeles, encompassing several hundred thousand residents, is not one homogeneous area. While not a large geographical area (approximately nine square miles), it encompasses a wide range of urban settings, including parts of the Los Angeles manufacturing distribution and warehouse areas, a county general hospital, widespread light manufacturing firms, single-family housing, apartment complexes, and several public housing projects. No clear demarcation separates these multiple land uses, and one would be hard-pressed to use any single term to describe this urban mix except to note its heterogeneity.

When defining East Los Angeles for the context of this study, however, respondents—focus group participants, interviewees, and key informants—made the authors acutely aware of the historical boundaries of the area, which are not politically or legally recognized outside the community. The perceptions of the respondents of East Los Angeles define a territory underlying much of the political activism in our study area and crossing political and jurisdictional boundaries. Respondents, for example, described the eastern border of East Los Angeles as being as far east as the city of Pico Rivera and as far west as Olvera Street in the downtown area of Los Angeles.

Within East Los Angeles, residents also describe neighborhoods: Belvedere, Boyle Heights, City Terrace, Maravilla. Again, exact boundaries are not clearly delineated but offer smaller geographical units that are perceived as more homogeneous racially and socioeconomically. These units are also seen as home territory—a familiar environment of people, buildings, and spaces tied to family and household interests (Plotkin 1990).

The Boyle Heights Neighborhood

This study focused on two locations in the Boyle Heights neighborhood of East Los Angeles. It was conducted over a two-month period immediately preceding the general election of November 1990.

Boyle Heights has been an ethnic enclave for different immigrant groups since the turn of the century. As Romo (1983) has observed, Boyle Heights, considered a Jewish ethnic enclave in the 1920s and the 1930s, was in reality an immigrant community where Italians, White Russians, Poles, and Mexicans lived side by side. Since the 1960s, however, Boyle Heights has been predominantly Mexican American and Latino (UCLA 1965). In 1990, Boyle Heights was estimated to be over 90 percent Latino (U.S. Bureau of the Census [hereafter Census] 1991*a*).

Driving through Boyle Heights in the 1990s, one sees the urban heterogeneity that characterizes Greater East Los Angeles. Entering Boyle Heights from downtown Los Angeles by crossing the concrete-sided Los Angeles River, one sees single-family homes with fenced, well-tended lawns coexisting with auto repair and body shops—often in the same block. Heavy commercial factories with smokestacks are but blocks away from yards where chickens and roosters are still kept. Multilevel freeway interchanges run throughout the north and southwest corners of the area. Boyle Heights, like much of East Los Angeles, is a study in contrasts.

According to the Los Angeles City Planning Department, Boyle Heights has the following boundaries:

Northern boundary: San Bernardino Freeway (I-10)
Southern boundary: City of Vernon
Eastern boundary: City Terrace
Western boundary: L.A. River

A study of Boyle Heights, cosponsored by the City of Los Angeles Planning Department and the Urban Design Advisory Commission (Los Angeles City Planning Department 1990), substantiated the following points about the neighborhood:

Housing units are very old; 81 percent of the units were constructed before 1960 and many units were constructed in the early 1920s.

There is extensive overcrowding in the area. Units designed for a single family now house several times that number. However, there are few homeless people in the area.

There is very limited home ownership in the area—less than 20 percent. It does not appear that the children of older homeowners are interested in occupying their parents' homes or living in the area.

Thirty percent of the households have an income of less than ten thousand dollars.

Safety concerns prevent many youth, as well as adults, from involvement in activities unless the activities are within one or two blocks of their homes.

Toxic contamination on several of the industrial sites makes these parcels unreasonably expensive because of the costs of toxic clean-up. Cleaner industries are dissuaded from locating in the area because of the fear of toxic contamination.

The adjacency of the residential neighborhoods to the tremendous truck traffic causes safety concerns for the pedestrian traffic attempting to cross major intersections.

There is an abundance of publicly assisted housing currently under public and private ownership. There are negative social impacts to the community by concentrating "housing projects." For example, there are an estimated two thousand units between Wyvernwood, Estrada Courts, Aliso Gardens, and William S. Mead homes (close to ten percent of all housing).

Previous government projects such as the freeway system, the Los Angeles River aqueduct, the L.A. prison, and the Vernon incinerator have stirred public controversy.

The Political Demographics of Boyle Heights

Analyzing voter registration rates in Boyle Heights highlights a large discrepancy between the actual population (98,879) and the population registered to vote (17,079). In large part, three demographic factors particularly relevant to the Latino community account for this discrepancy.

The first demographic factor is the high number of immigrants among California Latino adults. Statewide, close to 50 percent of Latino adults are not U.S. citizens. In the city of Los Angeles, the rate of noncitizenship among Hispanic adults is 46 percent (NALEO 1990). In other words, close to one out of two adult Latinos in the Boyle Heights area are not eligible to register to vote because of noncitizenship.

The second factor is the relative youth of the Latino population (Census 1991b). According to the Census Bureau, approximately 30 percent of all Hispanics were under nineteen years of age in 1990. This is disproportionately high when compared to the majority population—only 20 percent of all Americans are nineteen years or younger.

The third factor limiting voter registration in Boyle Heights is related to the first demographic factor. Over the past decades Boyle Heights has served as a port of entry for undocumented immigrants.

Evidence of the high number of undocumented immigrants can be garnered by analyzing the U.S. Immigration and Naturalization Service's data on applicants who applied for legalization under the provisions of the Immigration Reform and Control Act of 1986 (NALEO 1989). This report identifies legalization applicants by residence zip code. An analysis of the three zip codes (90023, 90033, 90063) that make up Boyle Heights reveals that over twenty-two thousand legalization applicants lived in these three zip codes alone. To comprehend the significance of this number, the legalization applicants in these three zip codes outrank all but two California cities with large legalization populations. Taking all three factors into account—youth, legal residency versus U.S. citizenship, and the high number of legalization applicants and undocumented immigrants—the figure of only seventeen thousand registered voters becomes somewhat more understandable.

Before describing our methodology and the findings derived from studying the 1990 general election campaign in Boyle Heights, it is useful to describe the political institutions and processes that characterize the general East Los Angeles and Boyle Heights area.

Formal Political Structures in the Boyle Heights Area

Like other urban areas in the United States, Boyle Heights has many overlapping layers of political representation. We list these offices, their incumbents, and years in office in Table 6.1.[1]

Under California's system of government, the offices of school board member, city council member, and county supervisor are "nonpartisan" positions. In the November 1990 election, with the exception of the county supervisor's position, Boyle Heights's representatives in each of these offices were long-term Latino incumbents.

TABLE 6.1 Boyle Heights Elected Offices, Elected Officials, and Years in Office

Office	Officeholder	Years in Office
U.S. Congress (25th District):	Edward R. Roybal	27
State senate (24th District):	Art Torres	16
State assembly (56th District):	Lucille Roybal-Allard	3
L.A. City Council (14th District):	Richard Alatorre	5
L.A. School Board (5th District):	Leticia Quezada	3

Average number of years in office: 10.8

The long-term incumbency of each of the candidates had implications for the study. Boyle Heights is approximately 75 percent Democratic in party registration. Given the overwhelming number of registered Democrats, those who win the Democratic party primary—in the case of congressional, state senate, and state assembly offices—are also most likely to win the general election. All of the incumbents representing Boyle Heights are Democrats. Thus, in addition to the advantage of their incumbency, candidates who ran for partisan offices benefited from strong party loyalty in the general election. Some, such as Assemblywoman Roybal-Allard, ran unopposed.

Moreover, not all offices—such as positions on the school board—were up for election in 1990. Thus, for the 1990 election, only several statewide offices, most notably the governor's race, were contested.

It is also important to note the number of referenda and initiatives that voters of Boyle Heights faced on the ballot. The number of initiatives actually outnumbered the number of races (thirty-five versus fifteen). Many of the initiatives were extremely complex and only the most dedicated voter could be expected to have formed opinions about each of them. In fact, an emerging body of literature suggests that the initiative process has "gone out of control" in California politics and that voters are simply ignoring the countervailing political messages associated with most initiatives (League of Women Voters 1987). Two examples from the 1990 ballot should suggest the complexity of these ballot initiatives (County of Los Angeles 1990):

Proposition 135 PESTICIDE REGULATION INITIATIVE STATUTE—Expands monitoring program for produce, processed foods. Eliminates some industry fees. Modifies penalties, regulations training. Fiscal impact: One-time state General Fund cost of approximately $6 million for pesticide and food monitoring and research programs. Estimated annual state revenue loss of approximately $1.5 million due to repeal of industry fees. Additional state administrative and regulatory costs ranging from $200,000 to, possibly, several million dollars annually.

Proposition 141 TOXIC CHEMICAL DISCHARGE. PUBLIC AGENCIES. LEGISLATIVE STATUTE. Extends to specified public agencies Proposition 65 toxic discharge and release prohibitions, warnings. Fiscal impact: Unknown costs potentially exceeding $1 million beginning 1991 for notification requirements. Unknown costs, beginning in 1992, potentially in the tens of millions of dollars depending on extent existing waste discharge controls are not sufficient to comply with discharge prohibitions of Proposition 65 [sic].

Methodology

Site Selection

The large population of Boyle Heights, the geographical size of the area (four square miles), and the differing levels of communal and territorial identity within the area prevented us from treating Boyle Heights as one study site. Instead, in consultation with several key informants from the area, we selected two sites that represented different locales highlighting the diversity of the area.

The first site was the Estrada Court projects. Estrada Courts is a public housing project in the southern area of Boyle Heights, bounded by Soto Street and Lorena Street from west to east, and Olympic Boulevard and Eighth Street north to south. The projects consist of one- and two-story dwellings. The homes are in a park atmosphere with many trees and lawns. Estrada Courts is well known for murals that depict the Mexican American community and its struggles. South of Estrada Courts are commercial warehouses and factories. Commercial traffic is heavy on the west side of the projects. Voting precincts 1902 and 1904 (with 1,321 registered voters) encompass this site.

The second site consists of a Boyle Heights residential neighborhood made up of single-family homes bounded by Lorena Street and Esperanza Street from east to west, and by Opal Street and Whittier Boulevard from north to south. People have lived in the area for years and, in some cases, generations. Resurrection Church is active in community affairs. The local boxing gym is popular in the community. This is a quiet community with many senior citizens. Voting precinct 1899 (with 508 registered voters) is in this site.

These two sites have a total of 1,829 registered voters (see Table 6.2). Approximately 80 percent of the registered voters are Democrats and 10 percent are Republicans.

TABLE 6.2 Electoral Characteristics of the Boyle Heights Research Site

Precinct	Number of Registered Voters	Number of Households	% Democratic	% Republican
1902	582	403	77.32	11.68
1904	739	431	81.33	11.64
1899	508	338	83.27	8.86

Source: County of Los Angeles (1991).

Field Visits

A team of four student ethnographers under the direct supervision of the project's research assistant visited the sites regularly. They conducted eighty informal interviews in the streets, in factories, homes, stores, laundromats, parks, and beauty parlors. A selected number of these interviews were videotaped. The students based their interviews on an interviewer guide that included questions and probes on the following themes: (1) impression and salience of electoral and grass-roots politics, and (2) voting behavior in local, state, and national politics. Half of the interviewees were men and half were women.

Student ethnographers also took note of campaign materials such as posters, leaflets, and yard signs. They visited each of the three sites four times per week and interviewed the campaign staff of the two gubernatorial candidates, Pete Wilson (R) and Dianne Feinstein (D). Field notes as well as videotapes provided documentation of this assessment.

The Use of Focus Groups

To complement these field visits and interviews, student ethnographers and the project's research assistant conducted focus groups in order to elicit further reactions to the general election in Boyle Heights. We believed that focus groups would allow us to elicit information closer to the emic side of the continuum insofar as we would encourage and allow participants to describe the election in their own words with their own categorizations and perceived associations. In these focus groups, although the moderators did ask questions, they did not furnish the participants with categories in which to fit their answers.

In addition, we felt that focus groups would greatly complement our ethnographic interviews. The combined efforts of interviews and focus group discussions produced a wider range of information, insight, and ideas than the cumulation of individual responses secured privately. We also believed that the "bandwagon" effect that often operates in a group discussion, whereby a comment by one individual triggers responses from other participants, would greatly enrich our information base. Finally, we felt that, because no individual is required to answer any question in a group interview, the responses would be more spontaneous and at times less conventional. In a focus group, we and other investigators have learned, people tend to speak only when they have definite feelings about a subject and not because a question requires a response (Stewart and Shamdasani 1990).

Our focus groups were brought together after we identified certain patterns of responses from selected key informants. The patterns of responses were identifiable primarily by gender (men versus women) and by length of residency (longtime residents versus newcomers).

The groups were developed from membership lists of community organizations and amnesty and citizenship education classes. The project's research assistant also used his own family and friendship networks to identify these groups. We took care to include residents from both study sites. We identified forty-eight potential group participants. We invited each to participate in one of four ninety-minute focus group interviews. They were offered fifteen dollars for their participation.

Forty-two people participated in four separate focus groups. All focus groups began with four or more participants, with some of the participants arriving late and others leaving early. Members of two major gangs were contacted for individual interviews after we decided that a focus group approach was not feasible for these groups.

We videotaped all sessions with the focus groups. We conducted two of the sessions in Spanish (participants in these groups were male and female undocumented newcomers). Two focus groups were conducted in English (participants in these groups were male and female community activists and long-term residents).

Contested Races and Issues in the 1990 General Election

While the 1990 elections did not have highly contested races for local political offices in East Los Angeles or Boyle Heights, several major races were clearly salient to the community. The first was the governor's race, where the former mayor of San Francisco, Democrat Dianne Feinstein, and Republican U.S. senator Pete Wilson were in a close race, particularly at the beginning of the campaign. Moreover, several initiatives received much attention in the media and were heavily publicized. These included the following:

Proposition 128: The "Big Green" initiative, which set forth new environmental controls in the state for pesticides, air, and water.

Proposition 131: Term limitation initiative, which limited terms for elected officials and established ethics standards and partial campaign financing.

Proposition 140: A harsher term limitation initiative, which limited terms to eight years in office and reduced state legislative staff by 40 percent.

The 1990 elections in Boyle Heights have to be seen in the context of a presidential off-year election with few races truly offering the prospect of a close election (again, with the exception of the gubernatorial race) and a confusing host of initiatives confronting the voters.

Given all of the factors discussed above, how did the general elections of 1990 actually play themselves out in the Boyle Heights community?

Findings

Student ethnographers in September found few traditional indicators of campaign activity, such as leaflets, posters, and placards. Of these, and of these few, the majority were in English. Some people commented that this absence of political advertising was a clear indication that the parties and elected officials were not counting on the Latino vote. Others felt that it was all for the better in that the streets would remain cleaner. These ecologically oriented comments fit well in a community increasingly concerned with issues of contamination and pollution and their related health threats.

Interviews with members of the Feinstein and Wilson campaign staffs confirmed the low level of electoral activity in the area in September. According to the East Los Angeles director of the Feinstein gubernatorial campaign, the campaign did not spend any money on voter registration during the summer. The Democratic campaign, which traditionally sees East Los Angeles as a rich area for votes, was not able to open its offices until late September, one week before the deadline for voter registration. In October, there were only two major rallies in the east side that drew Boyle Heights residents. One of these rallies was held at one of the housing projects and focused on the problems of gangs and crime. It received television coverage.

The formal party campaign for the Democratic vote, Victory 90, however, did conduct get-out-the-vote drives. These included targeting the Boyle Heights areas through telephone banking.

After the middle of October, the election began to receive notice. Posters on telephone poles and yard placards began appearing. On Spanish television, paid political advertisements also began. More attention was focused on the ballot initiatives, especially the one increasing the alcoholic beverage tax (Proposition 134). It was vigorously opposed by liquor store owners in the area, who placed placards in their windows. Bilingual placards for Feinstein appeared in a few isolated instances. Mail advertisements began to arrive in the households of regular voters. Student ethnographers reported, however, that in November, election campaigning did not reach an expected crescendo. Rather, campaigning seemed to be a continuation of October activities.

Interviews with key informants further confirmed that this electoral campaign was not following a traditional model of public campaigning. Respondents repeatedly noted that there was heavy use of telephone banking and direct mail to contact first-priority voters (regular voters) of one's own party and, when resources permitted, other voters. Thus, there was a high level of political outreach for regular voters. Yet there were few traditional indicators of political activity, such as posters and yard signs.

Community Perspectives on the Campaign

Most interviewees reported that they felt that electoral politics was highly salient to their lives. Yet, almost all respondents voiced distrust and a sense of alienation that they felt was inherent in the American political system. They associated corruption, greed, and backstabbing with politics. Most of the eligible voters reported that they were more likely to vote in local elections, for two reasons. One had to do with feeling overwhelmed by life and not having time to become informed and go out and vote. The other was a sense that voting made no difference, given the unresponsive nature of the American political system. Many of the older interviewees had in fact stopped voting. This attitude was captured in the following statement: "Twenty-six years ago I was voting . . . I was politically active . . . I was working hard to change the system to make it a better place for us all. Today, however, I find that I am still behind the African Americans who are yet behind the Anglos in almost all respects of social and political life. I am tired. I have learned that I cannot change things for myself and my community" (elderly Latino male).

Women interviewed on the streets and in the front yards of the residential neighborhood site tended to mention local politics quite often, as did people who identified themselves as longtime residents of the area. They mentioned that they blocked construction of a prison in East Los Angeles and prevented the building of a waste incinerator. Human ecological issues were high on the list of priorities of these women, as were gangs and other perceived threats to the environment and the community. The women, more than the men, noted the importance of voting in what they considered a less than perfect system.

Recent arrivals, mostly undocumented, tended to speak of the harassment and brutalization of street vendors by the police as important issues that were not being discussed by elected officials. Street vending was seen by many of these respondents as a major route of social mobility for immigrants that was being closed off by the police. Interviews with street vendors confirmed these impressions. These vendors, however, rather than blaming the police, pointed the finger at the established Latino shopkeepers in the neighborhood.

Gang members and gang admirers were adamant in portraying electoral politics as a "whitewash." Their notion of the East Los Angeles community was more fluid and possibly reflective of "deal zones," that is, areas where narcotics trafficking takes place.

The Role of Community Organizations in Community Politics

Two organizations were routinely mentioned by respondents as constituting bulwarks against further community deterioration: the Mothers of East Los Angeles and UNO. Most of the respondents who identified these organizations were longtime residents, though a few newcomers also seemed aware of and supported these organizations.

The Mothers of East Los Angeles, according to our informants, was the preeminent grass-roots political group in the area. It was founded circa 1984, when a group of women who were longtime residents of the area and parishioners at Resurrection Catholic Church organized to battle plans to build a state prison adjacent to Boyle Heights. By 1990, the group had grown to approximately four hundred men and women who claim to have modeled themselves after the legendary Argentinean group—the Mothers of May Square—who for years denounced state repression in their country. Their strategies fulfill the three textbook principles of direct-action organizing: (1) winning real, immediate, and concrete improvements in peoples' lives; (2) giving people a sense of their own power; and (3) altering the relations of power. Supported by private donations from the local community, the group has no paid staff and meets in the homes of members.

The Mothers have addressed threats to health, safety, physical environment, and property values. More recently, they have added child care, racism, and educational issues, while keeping an eye on further negative land uses in East Los Angeles in general and Boyle Heights in particular. The Mothers have a wide net of supporters, including university-based activists and elected officials, such as Assemblywoman Lucille Roybal-Allard and Supervisor Gloria Molina.

The group's consciousness was one of beleaguered membership in an endangered enclave whose potential demise was due to a lack of political power. In this context, neighborhood deterioration meant the end of the integrity of the family and household life. The Mothers' instrumental connection between the defense of traditional family values and defense of the neighborhood, as well as their keen understanding of the connection between environmental degradation and political powerlessness, are key in understanding their not-in-my-backyard approach to political activism.

United Neighborhoods Organized (UNO) is a group modeled along the same lines as Communities Organized for Public Service (COPS) in San Antonio, Texas. UNO uses community organizing techniques centered around the parishes in the area. It has been active in car insurance issues as well as self-help efforts organized around crime and police protection. Although UNO is perhaps better known at the national level, activists saw it as playing a minor role in Boyle Heights politics; the Mothers were seen as the truly active organization.

In addition to these community groups, respondents felt that the churches were important sources of community activism, particularly Santa Isabel and Resurrection Church. The Dolores Mission, they noted, served as a site for community organizing.

Focus Group Insights

Each focus group discussion began with participants giving their impressions of the level of electoral activity in their neighborhood. They were given the opportunity to volunteer their knowledge and impressions of what was happening in the community and in the 1990 election campaign. The student ethnographers' observations of little traditional campaigning in the area were confirmed by members of all four focus groups. Some typical comments on this matter follow:

I think they aren't interested in our community. . . . There are no billboards of Feinstein or of Wilson. (WA)[2]

There are no fliers. I always expect fliers. (WA)

They [Wilson and Feinstein] have not visited our neighborhood. (WA)

We do not even know who the candidates are. . . . They have not taken the trouble to put up posters in Spanish telling us who the candidates are and what they are running for. It is their obligation. (MI)

We don't even know their political platform. We do not have the elements to make an informed decision. (MI)

There have been one or two rallies . . . but I don't know much about them. (WA)

I think they think we do not care and we are not going to vote. (WI)

Campaign Styles. Several of the newcomer participants felt that when politicians addressed survival issues they did not do so in an appropriate fashion. For most people, the methods for disseminating political information to Latinos left much to be desired. Participants recommended approaches that were more personal and less electronically mediated, such as visits to neighborhoods, door-to-door canvassing, informational posters, and rallies. A typical comment was, "I do not have a television and I am on the street most of the day so I cannot listen to the radio. So I need posters on the walls. Also I like to see them in person and see how they really look" (MI).

Abstract Versus Concrete Issues. Many participants, particularly ineligible voters, felt that elected officials were only interested in abstract issues or in sensationalism. They reported a distrust for the political process at the state and the national levels. The difficulty of making informed decisions in a context of competing propositions was addressed. Respondents preferred grass-roots organizing and the definition of issues at the local level. Representative comments concerning these topics included the following:

Politicians are for sensationalism, for issues like pro-choice or pro-life, not for survival issues. (WA)

They need to address things like what is happening to street vendors. They are being beaten and humiliated because they try to get ahead. (MI, WI)

They need to address the abuses of the regular police and of the immigration police and why they don't do anything against drug dealers. (MI, WI)

They only talk about what they have already done, not about what they are going to do. (WA)

Policy Issues Identified. Participants voiced many opinions that reflected the broad range of Latino concerns. Issues that were barely touched on by the statewide campaigns were elaborated on in detail by focus group participants. One respondent stated that "a big issue in the Latino community has been the decision to construct an incinerator in the Vernon area whose waste products would go directly into East Los Angeles" (MA).

As we have suggested, the predominance of incumbents among the Latino candidates limited the attention paid to any Latino candidate. The race with a Latino candidate that received the most community attention was outside the study area. Xavier Becerra ran to fill the California Assembly seat left vacant by the decision of State Assemblyman Charles Calderón to run for the state senate.

Both male and female activists, as well as immigrant newcomers, did not see elected officials effectively addressing the gang issue and the lack of safety in their neighborhoods. As a result, they perceived (not without a considerable amount of regret) that the general election had little immediate relevance to their lives and to their community. Paradoxically, however, most insisted on the need to make Latino voices heard at the ballot box. Their commitment was to a political process inclusive of Latinos. Yet, they realized the limitations of the political process.

This commitment to politics stood in sharp contrast to the marginal elements' outright dismissal of political participation. Activist feelings were encapsulated in one comment: "They will not discourage us by not paying attention to us. We need power and we will try every avenue to get it" (WA).

Grass-Roots Activism. A number of participants from the activist groups were frustrated that the Mothers of East Los Angeles did the bulk of political organizing in the community. Others expressed frustration that it was the same people—usually the long-term residents and the Mothers—who bore all the responsibility for political organization; they reported that they believed that other segments of the community needed to be politicized. Some saw the churches as future centers of political activism, while others saw women as the backbone of political organizing. Among the statements to that effect were the following:

Boyle Heights doesn't have other organizations like the Mothers. When it does, it will have political power. (WA)

Unions don't do anything outside the halls. You don't see them in the community. (WA)

All of the churches, not just Resurrection, are organized. (WA)

There is no electoral participation outside the groups of longtime residents. We have to find ways to draw other people in the political process. (WA)

Participants in the newcomers' group and some activist participants differed and reported that many neighborhood residents were politically involved. The following exemplify those comments:

Every community is fighting. There are meetings in schools and in churches on drugs, dropouts, teenage pregnancies, incinerators. . . (MA)

People are getting organized around issues. (MI)

Women's Concerns and Activism. Female participants in our study seemed resigned that the issues they thought were most crucial to the community would not be addressed by male elected officials. They also felt that candidates like Feinstein could not afford to be perceived only as female candidates. They believed, however, that women would be the only ones to fight for women's issues. Comments along these lines included the following:

. . . not limited to abortion rights . . . women are the poorest . . . we need child care, health care, affordable housing, education . . . these are women's issues and also central community issues. (WA)

Women are also interested in the environment . . . we live in the most polluted part of the city . . . if we do not do something about pollution our children will die. (WA)

Women are the ones who do most of the political work. (WI)

Women have the time to do a lot of the work in the community because the men are in their jobs outside the community. (WA)

General Election Results

The turnout in Boyle Heights in the 1990 election was extremely low. In an area with 98,879 residents, and 17,000 registered voters, only 6,000 votes were cast in Boyle Heights precincts, a figure representing 6 percent of the population and 35 percent of registered voters. In the three precincts in which we conducted the ethnographic research, 675

TABLE 6.3 Selected Electoral Results from the Boyle Heights Research Site

		Governor's Race		Proposition 128		140	
Precinct	Votes	Feinstein	Wilson	Yes	No	Yes	No
1902	169	104	46	80	64	58	85
1904	295	213	61	148	112	65	188
1899	211	158	39	125	68	62	128

Source: County of Los Angeles (1991).

voters went to the polls, a turnout of 37 percent of registered voters (see Table 6.3). Although the low turnout and the Democratic majority are not surprising, some aspects of the vote are worth noting.

While the Republican gubernatorial candidate, Senator Pete Wilson, won statewide by 49 percent, Boyle Heights went overwhelmingly Democratic, with 74 percent of the votes cast for Dianne Feinstein. In two of the precincts we monitored, the support for Feinstein was even greater, with 78 percent of the voters supporting Feinstein in Precinct 1904 and 80 percent supporting the Democrat in Precinct 1899.

Two points in this regard need to be highlighted. The first is the magnitude of the margin of victory for the Democrats in the barrio. Nearly three out of four voters in Boyle Heights voted Democratic. In Boyle Heights, then, the Republican party is not making the inroads into the Latino vote that may be occurring in suburban Latino districts. Second, before the election, many political analysts predicted that working-class and low-income Latinos would not vote for a woman for governor. These incorrect predictions may have been influenced by the stereotype that working-class Latinos would display "macho" attitudes. These predictions also did not take into account, as this study reveals, the prominent role of Latinas in Boyle Heights politics. Future campaigns involving female Democratic candidates in Latino areas should take this finding to heart.

Two ballot initiatives that we followed in this study, Propositions 128 and 140, met with different results. Proposition 128, the "Big Green" initiative, received almost two-thirds approval in the Boyle Heights area while going down to defeat statewide. Thus, the environmentalist issues of providing for a cleaner environment in a proactive manner were strongly supported in a community that has suffered from toxic waste and pollution and has waged battles over environmental issues.

Proposition 140, the limitation of terms for elected office-holders, was defeated by an overwhelming margin (66 percent to 34 percent) in Boyle Heights while it passed statewide by an equally surprising margin. Arguments that Latinos would benefit by having officeholders remain in elected office for only four terms were apparently offset by the recentness of Latino political gains and by the fact that local Latino elected officials, as well as Latino organizations statewide, opposed the initiative.

From these three results, Boyle Heights can be seen as one of the bastions of Democratic support, with Latino voters strongly supporting progressive environmental causes and supporting their Latino elected officials by opposing term limitations.

Explaining Electoral Participation

Despite the overall low turnout in the community, six thousand Boyle Heights voters still went to the polls. Project interviewers conducted thirty-eight exit poll interviews and elicited the following representative reasons for voting:

I always vote. I have voted for the past fifteen years.

I've been voting for many years.

It's my right.

I do my civic duty.

I vote to change the people in office.

I got tired of Republicans being governor.

I want people to listen to the Latino vote.

It's very important to give my opinion.

Three major reasons emerged for why residents voted. The first was that it was an automatic act that individuals undertook on a regular basis. Closely linked to this was a sense of obligation or civic duty, exercising one's "right" to vote. Third, some respondents linked voting to articulating community needs or to the desire to change parties or individuals in office. The small sample prevents generalizations, but it does serve to suggest that there are a range of reasons why Boyle

Heights residents voted. None of the respondents interviewed cited appeals by either individuals or organizations as the reason for casting their vote.

Two alternative perspectives in political science offer us some insights for understanding low rates of political participation. One view holds that low voting rates are common in low-income communities that are also characterized by low rates of formal education. Seen from this perspective, low participation rates are a result of a lack of knowledge about the political process (Verba and Nie 1972) or, conversely, a result of cognitive confusion brought about by the inundation of contradictory political messages by the media during a political campaign.

Another alternative perspective on low participation looks at the institutional factors that disenfranchise Americans (Piven and Cloward 1988). This perspective examines registration laws and processes. In 1976, the U.S. Census Bureau found that one-third of those adults who did not register to vote said they were unable to. Of those, about two in ten lacked transportation, found the hours or place of registration inconvenient, or did not know how or when to register. These barriers are still a problem. In addition, low-income working-class people, once registered, face other difficulties, such as lack of transportation and the inability to vote during working hours. One national survey found that more than one-third of businesses did not allow workers time off to vote. Both perspectives offer partial insights into the low electoral participation rates that characterize Boyle Heights.

The literature on voting participation reminds us that the aforementioned factors of noncitizenship (among both legal residents and the undocumented) and the high number of people below the voting age exclude significant segments of the population from political participation. Among the remaining pool of potential eligible voters, many have low levels of education and a commensurate lack of access to political information.

A contrasting explanation is offered by the literature on structural obstacles to political participation in American political life. This analysis suggests that current California voter registration procedures have a negative effect on voting. For example, by the time the 1990 campaign became visible through political advertisements in the media and political placards in the community in early October, the voter registration rolls had closed. Some Boyle Heights activists blamed historical minority dilution schemes (Davidson 1984), such as gerrymandering, for current Latino voter apathy.

These theories, however, do not fully explain low voter participation in Boyle Heights. Two structural factors that have only recently begun to be studied—the role of incumbency and the role of new campaign technologies—also appear to influence levels of participation in Boyle Heights.

The Role of Incumbency

It is now widely recognized that all elections are not of equal salience to American voters. Closely fought elections generate more interest and have correspondingly higher turnouts. Elections in which the outcomes are foregone tend not to pique the public's interest. A look at the incumbency factor in the 1990 elections shows that all offices in Boyle Heights—from school board to congressional representative— were held by Latino incumbents who faced re-election without a serious challenge. Thus, for many of the incumbents, their involvement in the election was not motivated by the possibility of losing; rather, they campaigned on behalf of a party candidate or to rally against a particular ballot initiative like Proposition 140. As a consequence, it can be strongly argued that the political organizations and political resources of these incumbents were not as fully mobilized as they would have been in a closely contested election.

Without serious challengers, the incumbents did not have to fully mobilize their own resources, such as campaign funds, volunteers, registration drives, get-out-the-vote campaigns (GOTV), and targeted mailings. For the incumbents, then, high turnout was not as critical in this election as it would have been if serious challengers had been running.

Evidence that turnout in Boyle Heights can vary dramatically was apparent in the special elections that were held for county supervisor less than three months after the general election. In these special elections, held in January and February 1991, Gloria Molina concentrated her efforts on turning out the vote throughout East Los Angeles and specifically in Boyle Heights. The results were clear. Where suburban districts experienced a substantial drop-off in voter participation for this special election (held during the beginning days of the Persian Gulf War), the drop-off in Boyle Heights was much smaller.

Thus, elections in any barrio have to be examined on the basis of what specific political offices are perceived to be at stake. High-stakes elections in Latino neighborhoods will in all likelihood generate higher voter participation than elections where the outcomes are already assured (for a historical perspective, see Quiñones 1990).

The Effect of the Parties and New
Campaign Technologies on Voter Participation

One could argue, however, that, since the general election of 1990 featured a competitive governor's race, there should have been a higher turnout in Boyle Heights. To explain why this was not the case, one needs to look at the dynamics of the gubernatorial election in the east side during the last two months of the campaign. We have already mentioned that the Democratic campaign did not open offices in the Boyle Heights area until late September and the Republican campaign never opened an office there. Democratic party resources that would have gone to GOTV drives were reallocated for media advertising to defeat Proposition 140; Republicans did not target the Boyle Heights area at all for GOTV drives. In short, although seventeen thousand votes were potentially at stake, neither party engaged in extensive, well-financed efforts to generate voter turnout for the gubernatorial election in the area.

To understand why this is so, the vote in Boyle Heights and in the east side of Los Angeles has to be seen in relation to the statewide vote. In the 1990 general election, 7,699,467 Californians voted for governor and for other statewide offices. The Boyle Heights vote represented less than 1 percent of the statewide vote. The high numbers of ineligible voters in Boyle Heights and in the east side were known to campaign strategists in both parties. This affected campaign strategies, as one elected official told the authors: "Up here in Sacramento everyone knows the math. Comparing the number of voters in the east side of Los Angeles to the voters in the west side [of Los Angeles] shows you who they [the Democrats] are going to go with. Programs and resources for statewide campaigns are allocated strictly on the basis of the numbers. Using these numbers, means we [the Latino community] always lose."

In other words, with limited resources, campaign decisions for statewide office are often made on the basis of a cost-benefit calculation. This was certainly the case in the 1990 election. Yet, limited resources also have an impact on how the campaigns are conducted in Latino barrios in California.

How modern campaign technologies affect the perception of political activity present in the barrio must be taken into account. A recurring theme among respondents was the lack of political activity on the part of campaigns. Frequent mention was made of the low number of posters and candidate visits. According to political activists in the campaign, areas in general were no longer targeted indiscriminately. Instead, voter registration lists were analyzed to determine—

by party affiliation—regular and committed, irregular, and infrequent voters.

Telephone banking and direct mail techniques were then used to contact the first-priority voters, that is, regular voters in one's own party and, if resources permitted, other voters. In all probability, few direct contacts would be made with those who had not registered or not voted in the recent past. This in turn affected how political campaigns were viewed in the community. High levels of political activity may in fact be present without the appearance of visible traditional indicators like posters and yard signs.

Yet, the tactics of the new campaign technologies, emphasizing cost-effective *direct* contacts with regular or frequent voters of their own party through mail, telephone banking techniques, or direct personal contacts by campaign workers, may have the inadvertent impact of further distancing and discouraging individuals who are not yet electoral participants.

Conclusion

Boyle Heights residents clearly recognized the importance of politics and were very involved politically in their community. Internal and external factors in the barrio, however, hindered their ability to make the link between grass-roots political involvement, on the one hand, and effective electoral behavior such as voting, on the other.

In Boyle Heights, there were two fundamental factors that affected political involvement: the nature and importance of the role of women in barrio politics and the distancing effect between statewide campaigns and communities, which could be attributed to electronically mediated campaign strategies (Elgin 1991).

The nature and importance of the political activity of women needs thorough rethinking. Most studies of Latino political participation are remarkably bereft of references to women. Women's political roles are commonly ignored or only mentioned in reference to presumed Latino domestic values and to women's support of activities in historical struggles. As this study indicates, any serious attempt to understand the dynamics of barrio politics must grapple with the effective efforts of women, who have extended the very concept of "women's sphere" to embrace the community as a whole. As ecofeminist researchers Irene Diamond and Gloria Orenstein have argued: "Women who are responsible for their children's well-being are often more mindful of the long-term costs of quick-fix solutions. Through the social experiences of caretaking and nurturing, women become attentive to the signs of distress in their communities that might threaten their households" (1990: 17). The Mothers of East Los Angeles are testimony to this dynamic.

The distancing effect of electronic campaign tactics also needs to be pondered. We do not advocate a return to more traditional methods of campaigning (i.e., door-to-door canvassing), although in some cases, this may well be desirable. Campaigns, however, must recognize the need to develop more representative and culturally sensitive approaches if they are to be successful in low-income ethnic communities.

Following a general election through ethnographic observations and focus groups allows one to see the complex set of social and political forces that impinge on electoral behavior in Latino barrios and that belie simplistic explanations and single-approach solutions. Strategies of political empowerment for the Latino community that encompass greater electoral participation will have to be, of necessity, varied and multidimensional.

Notes

1. Soon after we completed the fieldwork for this study, Los Angeles County held a special election for the first supervisorial district and elected Gloria Molina as the first Hispanic to hold this office in the twentieth century.

2. We identify focus group participants by gender and by characteristics of participants in the focus group. The codes are WA = female activist; MA = male activist; MI = male immigrant; WI = female immigrant.

References

Acuña, Rodolfo. 1984. *A Community Under Siege: A Chronicle of Chicanos East of the Los Angeles River, 1945–1976.* Los Angeles: UCLA Chicano Studies Research Publications.

Ambrecht, Biliana, and Harry P. Pachon. 1974. "Ethnic Political Mobilization in a Mexican American Community." *Western Political Quarterly* 27 (3) (September) 500–519.

County of Los Angeles. 1990. *Official Sample Ballot and Voter Information.* Commerce: Los Angeles County.

———— 1991. Official Election Returns. Los Angeles.

Davidson, Chandler, ed. 1984. *Minority Vote Dilution.* Washington, D.C.: Joint Center for Political Studies.

Diamond, Irene, and Gloria Orenstein. 1990. "Introduction." In Irene Diamond and Gloria Orenstein, eds., *Reviewing the World: The Emergence of Ecofeminism,* pp. 3–20. San Francisco: Sierra Club.

Dworkin, Anthony Gary. 1973. "A City Found, a People Lost." In Livie Isauro Durán and H. Russell Bernard, eds., *Introduction to Chicano Studies,* pp. 406–419. New York: Macmillan.

Elgin, Duane. 1991. "Conscious Democracy Through Electronic Town Meeting."
   Whole Earth Review 71 (Summer): 29–30.
League of Women Voters. 1987. *The Initiative and Referendum in California: A
   Legacy Cost.* Los Angeles: League of Women Voters.
Los Angeles City Planning Department. 1990. *Boyle Heights: May 1990, A Report
   of the Los Angeles Design Action Planning Team.* Los Angeles.
NALEO Educational Fund. 1989. *Amnesty Applicants in California Cities.* Los
   Angeles: NALEO Educational Fund.
———. 1990. *Roster of Hispanic Elected Officials.* Washington, D.C.: NALEO
   Educational Fund.
Piven, Frances Fox, and Cloward, Richard. 1988. *Why Americans Don't Vote.*
   New York: Pantheon Books.
Plotkin, Sidney. 1990. "Enclave Consciousness and Neighborhood" *Comparative
   Urban and Community Research* 3.
Quiñones, Juan Gomes. 1990. *Chicano Politics: Reality and Promise.* Albuquerque:
   University of New Mexico Press.
Romo, Ricardo. 1983. *East Los Angeles: History of a Barrio.* Austin: University of
   Texas Press.
Stewart, David W., and Prem N. Shamdasani. 1990. *Focus Groups: Theory and
   Practice.* Los Angeles: Sage Publications.
University of California at Los Angeles [UCLA]. 1965. *Hard Core Unemployment
   and Poverty in Los Angeles.* Los Angeles: UCLA, Institute of Industrial
   Relations.
U.S. Bureau of the Census. 1991a. Interview with the Division of Community
   Awareness Program Products, Los Angeles Regional Office.
———. 1991b. *The Hispanic Population in the United States: March 1990.*
   Current Population Studies Series P–20 No. 449. Washington, D.C.: U.S.
   Government Printing Office.
Verba, Sidney, and Norman Nie. 1972. *Participation in America: Political
   Democracy and Social Equality.* Chicago: University of Chicago Press.

7

Los Bravos de la Política:
Politics and Cubans in Miami

Guillermo J. Grenier, with Fabiana Invernizzi,
Linda Salup, and Jorge Schmidt

On November 6, the incumbent governor of Florida, Bob Martínez, made two stops to end his campaign for re-election. At 11 A.M., his limousine parked in front of the Smathers Center, one of the twelve elderly-care facilities in the Greater Miami area known as *comedores* for the meal services they offer to twenty-four thousand elderly Latins each day. On this day, Governor Martínez shook hands all the way from the door to the stage in the lunchroom, where he would make a final appeal for the Cuban vote. The three hundred *viejitos* (elderly) were dancing in the aisles to the accompanying drum melody that welcomed the politician.

Once on stage, the chant began. "Martínez. Martínez. *Cuatro años más* (Four more years)." With him were his wife, leaders of the Dade County Republican party, all of whom were Cubans, and two candidates for public office: Bruce Hoffman, the man vying for the state representative position from the Smathers district; and Tony Coterelo, a Cuban American running for the county clerk position. Jeb Bush was Martínez's campaign coordinator. In eloquent Spanish, featured in many commercials on Latin radio and TV for months, Jeb Bush silenced the crowd as he introduced the governor as "the first Republican governor to be re-elected in Florida with your help." Martínez spoke in tortured Spanish but echoed Bush's feeling. With the help of the Cuban community, he would be re-elected today. He ended with a plea: "So go vote, if you haven't already. And call your family members. Your sons, your daughters, your nephews, your grandchildren, tell them all to go vote for Martínez. He is one of you."

In the corner, fanning herself with a Bob Martínez cardboard fan, a grandmother turned to Grenier and said, "I don't have to call mine. They go on their own. Especially to vote for a Latino."

She undoubtedly spoke for the vast majority of people in that room. In Dade County, it is common knowledge that Cubans vote. They vote Republican and, if there is a Latin on the ballot, they will cast the ethnic ballot. Jeb Bush knew this when he scheduled this last-gasp visit to Miami. That is why, minutes after leaving the Smathers Center, Martínez stopped to drink Cuban coffee and pose at the counter of the Versailles restaurant, one of the most popular Cuban gathering places in Miami. When our researchers asked Bush why Martínez would want to visit Little Havana as his last stop on the campaign trail, he answered simply, "This is his base."

Martínez had nurtured his base. During the previous four years, he made frequent stops at the *comedores*. During an interview, the direc- tor of the service organization remarked that she had seen his Spanish improve over the years during his visits to the *viejitos*. During this campaign period he visited the Little Havana area at least three times to pitch his antitax, anticrime, and anticommunism positions. He spent hundreds of thousands of dollars in Latin media announcements and received priceless support from Cuban radio sta- tions during countless hours of talk shows and call-in programs. He did all he could to establish to the Cuban voting public in Dade County that he was their candidate, not only because he was Republican but because he was a Latin. While his commercials in English depicted his ancestry as a third-generation Spaniard, the *viejitos* and others assumed he was old Tampa Cuban.

In this election, the considerable support he received from his base was not enough. Martínez lost the election to Democrat Lawton Chiles, losing 32 percent of the Latin vote to Chiles in Dade County. His loss culminated an election cycle that strengthened the importance of the Cuban vote in Dade County and saw the emergence of some important developments in the nature of ethnic politics in the greater Miami area.

In the 1990 election, we found evidence to support the view that Cuban power is a real social, economic, and political phenomenon in Dade County and it is increasing. But this growing power is packed with tension and divisiveness. Are the Cubans taking over? Are they somewhat responsible for the apparent disenfranchisement of the African American community? It has become almost axiomatic that no candidate can win an election in Dade County without a substantial portion of the Cuban vote. Yet the significance of this growing power is unclear. During the election cycle we covered, a black candidate for a seat on the Metro Commission calculated that he could win the election by concentrating his campaign in the Cuban community, even if he conceded the votes of the black community to his black activist opponent. He was right. Yet a young Cuban American who won another seat lost the Cuban vote to the establishment incumbent, also a Cuban American, while riding to victory on the ballots of the Anglo community.

What is clear is that, during the 1990 elections, Cubans saw their importance increase across generational and ethnic boundaries as old guard Cubans lost to a new generation of Cuban Americans, and as victorious black and Anglo candidates recognized that they could not win without the Cuban vote. All ten Cuban American state legislators won re-election, as did Ileana Ros-Lehtinen, the first Cuban American member of Congress. Her election helped carry to victory the only non-Latin Republican state representative in the county, Bruce Hoffman, who won his election by 112 votes against a liberal feminist Democrat. He spoke for many of the victorious candidates when he said to our interviewer, "I owe my victory to the Cuban vote."

Methodology

This study followed the activities of a Cuban neighborhood in Little Havana during the 1990 election cycle. From August to November, a senior researcher and three assistants worked, played, interviewed, and overheard arguments and discussions in a community that feels its cultural, political, social, and economic power every day in Dade County. We interacted with neighborhood residents, interviewed its leaders, dined at its restaurants, and walked its sidewalks in a daily effort to measure stability and change, power and powerlessness. One of our researchers, Fabiana Invernizzi, worked as a volunteer in the neighborhood elderly-care facility, part of the Little Havana Activities Center and the same facility visited by the governor on election day. There she observed the activities of one of the best-run Cuban organizations in Dade County. The two other researchers worked as volunteers for the two political parties vying for power in the neighborhoods. Linda Salup volunteered her time to the Hoffman campaign, working closely with the campaign manager to organize the daily community strategy and often holding the office together during times of crisis. Jorge Schmidt volunteered for Democratic candidates, working particularly closely with the candidate for governor, Lawton Chiles, and Hoffman's opponent, Fran Bohnsack. Because of their diligent research efforts, we were able to monitor the pulse of the Latino community and the political efforts to influence its voting behavior.

We conducted 11 formal interviews with community and political leaders, 35 informal interviews with neighborhood residents, as well as 200 exit polls during each of the three election cycles. When possible, we tape-recorded the formal interviews and maintained detailed field notes on the formal and informal interviews. We also developed a questionnaire for the exit poll interviews for the two primaries.

In the research process, we compiled evidence to suggest that the Cuban community is in a state of transition, one that is metamorphosing the Cuban agenda from an exile agenda focused on a return to the homeland to an immigrant agenda concerned about domestic issues.

To put the election into its proper historical and social context, we will begin our analysis by presenting an overview of Miami and the significance of the Cuban influx into its greater metropolitan area. Then we will discuss the characteristics of the neighborhood studied, after which we will describe each of the election cycles of importance to that neighborhood. Each of the cycles—the primaries, the runoffs, and the general election—had its own dynamics and significance to the Little Havana area. Finally, we discuss some of the principal issues of the campaign as established through interviews and participant observation. We conclude with some observations on the transition of the Cuban agenda from an exile program to an immigrant one.

The City

Miami is the most Latin of any major U.S. city.[1] It is the southernmost metropolis in the continental United States, lying almost due east of Mexico City; it is much closer to Havana, Cuba, and San Juan, Puerto Rico, than it is to any other major U.S. city. At the very beginning of the creation of the city of Miami, at the end of the nineteenth century, Miami's primary concern was to the south, as it served as a training and disembarkation point for U.S. soldiers on their way to fight in the Spanish-American War in Cuba.

Today, Miami is the capital of the Caribbean (Garreau 1981). Levine (1985) goes further. He argues that Miami is the capital of all of Latin America. It has more foreign-born residents, most of whom are Latin, than any other major U.S. city. Elites from throughout the Caribbean maintain houses and bank accounts in Miami. Its community college has more foreign students, again primarily Latin, than any other college or university in the nation. In 1990, its mayor, city manager, county manager, and one of its representatives in the U.S. House of Representatives were foreign-born Latins. One of the two Spanish-language local newscasts has more viewers than do any of the local English-language television stations. The top radio station in the entire region is WAQI, Radio Mambi, a Cuban radio station that sings its top rating to a mambo beat:

> *El survey de Arbitron dice así*
> *Radio Mambi es la primera.*
> *En todo el sur de la Florida*
> *por ser Cubana y más sincera*
> *porque te informa la verdad*
> *Radio Mambi es la primera.*[2]

In a very real sense, the transformation of Miami can be traced to the arrival on its shores of Cubans fleeing the 1959 revolution. Prior to 1960, Miami was a thoroughly American city, a southern American city firmly focused northward.[3] Its original population of southern whites and Bahamian and southern U.S. blacks was supplemented, beginning in the 1920s, by a large transient population of tourists and retirees from the Northeast and the Midwest. It subsisted primarily by providing services to those who came from the north.

Cubans began arriving in significant numbers in the 1960s, following the failure of the Bay of Pigs invasion and peaking with the Mariel boatlift of 1980, which brought 125,000 Cubans to the United States. The flow has been largely one-way. Once Cubans come to Miami, few return. By 1980, Miami had the highest proportion of foreign-born residents of any U.S. city, proportionally 50 percent more than either Los Angeles or New York.

By 1990, there were nearly one million Latins in the area, just over 49 percent of the entire metropolitan population (see Table 7.1). Latins outnumber all other groups in both the city of Miami and in Greater Miami. In all likelihood, Latins have already established an absolute demographic majority in Dade County since the census count.

Among the Latins, Cubans predominate. In 1989, Cubans constituted over 70 percent of Miami's Latin population. During the 1980s, over one hundred thousand Nicaraguans and other Central Americans fled the violence and economic difficulties of their homelands for Miami, thus diminishing the relative proportion of Cubans. Nevertheless, the latter still make up nearly two-thirds of the area's Latins.

By every measure, Cubans are the most economically successful of U.S. Latino groups (Díaz 1980; Jorge and Moncarz 1980; Rogg and Cooney 1980; Borjas 1982; Pérez 1985 and 1986; Portes and Bach 1985; Massud-Piloto 1988).[4] Their success is largely rooted in three forms of capital they either brought with them or had bestowed on them once they arrived in the United States: economic, social, and political.

TABLE 7.1   Dade County Population and Ethnicity, 1950–1990

Year	Anglo	Population Black	Latin
1950	410,000	65,000	20,000
1955	579,000	101,000	35,000
1960	748,000	137,000	50,000
1965	765,000	163,000	173,000
1970	782,000	189,000	297,000
1975	754,000	226,000	467,000
1980	776,000	280,000	581,000
1985	661,000	367,000	768,000
1990	585,000	397,100	953,000

The first wave of Cubans has been labeled the "Golden Exiles," the top of Cuban society who were most immediately threatened by a socialist revolution. Many had already established a foothold in the United States and when the revolution came they simply abandoned one of their residences for another across the straits of Florida. For example, before the revolution a Cuban shoe manufacturer produced footwear for a major U.S. retail chain. He obtained his working capital from New York financial houses. After the revolution, the only change was that the manufacturing was done in Miami, instead of Havana. The dynamics of the Revolution thus upwardly biased the socioeconomic profile of Miami's Cuban population in a way that has not occurred in the Mexican American or Puerto Rican populations. Even if the Cubans could not transfer their investments, their human capital—their knowledge and experience—came with them.[5]

Perhaps the best-documented aspect of the Cuban experience in Miami has been the extent to which the Cubans contributed to the economic transformation of the county from a tourist to a service and finance center. Cubans played a pivotal role in this economic transformation. They frequently headed the import and export companies, the banks that financed the transactions, and the smaller transportation and service companies that allowed goods and services to migrate. Between 1970 and 1980, the number of Spanish-origin professionals in Miami more than doubled, and Spanish-origin executives nearly quadrupled. While Miami has only 5 percent of the U.S. Hispanic population, it has close to half of the forty largest Hispanic-owned industrial and commercial firms in the country. There are also over twenty-five thousand Hispanic businesses in Dade County. There is no doubt that Cubans in Miami have established significant wealth and local power, exercised through the increasing number of elected officials and such organizations as the Cuban American National Foundation, the Latin Builders Association, the Hispanic Builders Association, and the Latin Chamber of Commerce.[6]

There is equally no doubt that not all Miami Cubans are rich and powerful businesspeople. Even the fact of business ownership is somewhat misleading. Of the nearly twenty-five thousand Latino-owned and -operated businesses in 1982, only 12 percent had paid employees and together they generated only 18,199 paid jobs (Díaz-Briquets 1984), a number only slightly higher than the number of Latins in Dade County who belonged to unions (Grenier 1990).

Indeed, Hispanics in Miami are primarily working class, over-represented in manual occupations, and working as laborers, craftspeople, and service workers. By the end of the 1980s, Cubans in Miami were heavily represented in unions, especially in industry and manufacturing. Two of the most significant sectors for Cuban workers are the apparel and the construction industries. Their evolution is indicative of the general transformation of the Miami economy. Both industries boomed after the arrival of the Cubans and both are now dominated by them.

In terms of social capital, Cuban households have a number of social characteristics that became economic advantages in the United States. Compared to other Hispanic groups, a smaller proportion of Cuban families have young children, a higher proportion have older adults (such as grandparents) living in the household who can provide child care, and a higher proportion of married women work. This higher rate of women's labor force participation produces a median income of married Cuban couples that is about one-third higher than that of other U.S. Latins. Cuban households have a relatively large number of workers, high rates of female employment, and high levels of schooling and enrollment (Pérez 1985).

Refugee communities also frequently garner political capital, since the very status of refugee reflects a political decision by the receiving state. In the United States, groups designated as refugees are offered special governmental assistance when they arrive that is not available to other immigrants. Such was the case with the Cubans. The first wave of Cubans came in the midst of the cold war, when the United States welcomed immigrants in general and especially those fleeing communism. The Cubans' arrival also coincided with the construction of Great Society programs that provided extensive benefits to minority populations, including special programs for Cuban refugees. At the same time, the public sector promoted affirmative action to ensure ethnic and minority participation in employment.

The U.S. government created for the arriving Cubans an unprece-
dented direct and indirect assistance program. The Cuban Refugee
Program spent nearly one billion dollars between 1965 and 1976
(Pedraza-Bailey 1985). The federal government provided transportation costs from Cuba, financial assistance to needy refugees and to state
and local public agencies providing services to refugees, and employment and professional training courses for refugees. Even with programs not especially designed for them, Cubans seemed to benefit.
From 1968 to 1980, Latinos (almost all Cubans) received 46.9 percent of
all Small Business Administration loans in Dade County (Porter and
Dunn 1984).

The indirect assistance was even more important. Through the
1960s, the University of Miami had the largest CIA station in the
world, outside of the organization's headquarters in Virginia. With
perhaps as many as twelve thousand Cubans in Miami on the payroll
at one point in the early 1960s, the intelligence agency was one of the
largest employers in the state of Florida. It supported what was described as the third-largest navy in the world and over fifty front
businesses: CIA boat shops, CIA gun shops, CIA travel agencies,
CIA detective agencies, and CIA real estate agencies (Rich 1974;
Didion 1987; Rieff 1987). This investment served far more to boost the
Cubans economically in Miami than it did to destabilize the Castro
regime.

This favorable reception by the U.S. government translated not only
into millions of dollars of resettlement assistance, but also into a
"direct line" from Cuban exile leaders to the centers of political power
in Washington. Unlike other immigrant and ethnic minorities, who
must struggle painfully for years or even generations to gain access to
the corridors of power, this was available to Cuban leaders almost
from the start.

The state of Florida also passed laws that made it easier for Cuban
professionals, especially medical doctors, to recertify themselves to
practice in the United States. At the county level, in the late 1970s
and the early 1980s, 53 percent of minority contracts for Dade County's
rapid transit system went to Latin firms. Dade County schools led the
nation in introducing bilingual education for the first wave of Cuban
refugees in 1960. The Dade County Commission also designated the
county officially bilingual in the mid-1970s.

Cubans in Miami had available especially for them language
classes, vocational training, business education, and varied adult education programs. The University of Miami trained thousands of Cuban
physicians, nurses, lawyers, pharmacists, dentists, accountants, archi-
tects, engineers, veterinarians, and teachers (Mohl 1990: 49).

In sum, the total benefits available to the Cuban community appear to have surpassed those available to any other U.S. minority group. About 75 percent of Cuban arrivals before 1974 received some kind of direct state-provided benefit (Pedraza-Bailey 1985: 40, based on Clark 1975: 116). The Cuban Refugee Program was especially generous, but, on top of that, state and local governments granted special favors. Further, Cubans qualified for minority status in affirmative action programs. The presence of entrepreneurs and professionals in the Cuban refugee community provided a trained and experienced core who knew how to gain access to and use these privileges. Cuban family structure further encouraged the maximum exploitation of these new resources, as there were older family members to attend to children and domestic matters, relatively fewer children to attend to, and high numbers of workers per household, especially women. All of these combined to produce high family income and a stratified economic profile.

For all these attributes, Miami Cubans have been perceived as model immigrants. Popular press articles and the Cubans themselves tend to depict a community that is composed virtually exclusively of successful entrepreneurs who have prospered solely by dint of intense labor. While there is some truth to this image, most Miami Cubans are working class. The success that they enjoy is a result of structural factors as much as individual initiative.

The Neighborhood

If you start walking where Calle Ocho begins, in the high-rise glitz of Brickell Avenue made famous by "Miami Vice," and head west, you will travel through the history of Cuban settlement in Miami. Initially, you'll see the now-rundown tenements of East Little Havana, where the first wave of Cubans settled in the 1960s. Although Cubans consider Little Havana theirs, this eastern portion has received a succession of Latinos, and in the process has become a major entry point for Central American immigrants and refugees, who know it as a place with available work, where few questions are asked, and where English is not necessary. Continuing under the freeway, you will pass more than the usual number of boarded-up stores, the relics of the first phase of the Cuban success story, an area now described as "crime-ridden" and decayed.

East Little Havana runs westward until it crosses Twelfth Avenue, known as Ronald Reagan Boulevard. At this corner the heart of Little Havana begins. Salup reports in her notes after a walk through this area of the city:

There seems to be a little market on every other corner, either alone or surrounded by a coin laundry, auto parts and other little shops . . . for the most part, there is a lot of local color . . . adjacent to almost every market is a small cafeteria . . . a little hole in the wall with a window for service and a small counter for maybe two patrons to lean on and sip their expresso coffee . . . every cafeteria has a *guarapo* machine [a sugarcane drink].

For the next ten blocks, the sidewalk is wide and covered with red brick, the result of an urban development project directed by the Latin Quarter Incorporated, an urban redevelopment group sponsored by the City of Miami. Embedded in the brick, from here to Seventeenth Avenue, are stars representing Latin entertainers, also the work of the Latin Quarter organization. In this Latin walk of fame lies a star dedicated to Julio Iglesias, Rafael, and Celia Cruz, among other artists. According to the president of the group, the office received a threatening call one day in 1990 warning that if any more non-Cuban celebrities were honored, their stars would be ripped up.

The red brick widens at a point to encompass the monument commemorating the 2506 Brigade, which led the assault during the Bay of Pigs invasion. Down the block from the eternal flame that characterizes this monument is the living monument of Domino Park (Parque Máximo Gómez). Here each day groups of domino players, mostly retired or unemployed men sporting *guayaberas*, congregate and talk about returning to Cuba or about life "en el exilio" (in exile).

At noon daily, businesspeople walk along this sidewalk to lunch at El Pub, some stopping for a shoeshine in front of this important Cuban watering hole. One day in October, Grenier struck up a conversation with the shoeshine man and his customer. Not surprisingly, they were both Cubans and proud of it—so proud, in fact, that the conversation soon flowed to the previous night's City of Miami commissioners meeting. There, a roomful of two hundred Cubans armed with Cuban flags had objected furiously to the proposed name change of a portion of Little Havana to the Latin Quarter. He had not been there, but the man with the freshly shined shoes became angry talking about the proposal: "They want to erase the Cubans from this area. They want to de-Cubanize the whole thing. All this around you is here because of the Cubans. When we got here thirty years ago there were three streets here. Three streets! What Latin Quarter? If they change the name to anything it should be to Little Cuba. We made this place."

Continuing the walk down Calle Ocho does nothing to contradict this notion. Business after business is a tribute to Cuban entrepreneurship. Barber shops, beauty salons, bookstores, gas stations, pharmacies, groceries, insurance agencies, computer stores, flower shops, and

the ever-present Cuban restaurants with the sidewalk windows perpetually crowded with standing customers sipping Cuban coffee and
eating *pastelitos*. All are owned and managed by Cubans and serve a
largely Cuban clientele. Data from the 1980 census indicate that,
while Cuban businesses are numerous, with 20,795 in the Greater
Miami area, only 2,643 have paid employees (U.S. Bureau of the
Census [hereafter Census] 1986).

But wealth is not what Little Havana is about. It is about *la
Cubanía*—about being Cuban. The November 1990 issue of *El Condado
News*, headlined with *La Pequeña Habana*, wrote:

> To say the name "Little Havana" puts in the mouths of Cubans a taste of
> the motherland. This part of Miami is linked, very directly, to our history
> and our traditions, to Cuba, the island, and to this other Cuba that the
> tyranny forced us to build on foreign land. . . . Where, in spite of adversity
> we constructed the body and soul of our healthy, happy and carefree peo-
> ple. Cubans were grateful to and changed Miami.

At the western edge of Little Havana, on each side of Calle Ocho,
lie two residential precincts representative of much of *la Cubanía* of
Miami. These served as the focus of our study. On the north of Calle
Ocho is Precinct 562. It is a working-class Cuban neighborhood with 30
percent voter registration and an aging population. According to the
1990 census, this precinct and Precinct 575, south of Calle Ocho, averaged 92 percent Hispanic population, setting them among the most
densely Latin areas of the Miami metropolitan area.

Lincoln Díaz-Balart, the state senator who represents the district
that includes Precinct 562, is certain that ethnic succession is moving
westward from East Little Havana: "Cubans are moving out and
Nicaraguans are moving in. You can tell by the school enrollments. . . .
Most of the students in certain areas of Little Havana are
Nicaraguans. Cubans are moving further west, to Westchester, Coral
Gables, and Kendall."

While ethnic succession is occurring throughout Little Havana, we
found that it had little impact on our neighborhood. The high voter
registration figures reported in this election suggest that the area is
heavily populated by Cubans. Other demographic factors are expected to change. The population is older and therefore more female.
Voter registration is still high and it is quite possible, as we will
detail later, that this aging has brought with it a more organized
electorate, given the growing importance of the gray lobby within the
Cuban community.

In addition to this residential area, we focused our attention on

Calle Ocho from 37th Avenue to 12th Avenue. Representing all that it means to be Cuban in Miami, Calle Ocho is where the now-expanding Cuban community began its idyllic growth and dominance. In Calle Ocho you can be a complete Cuban, in control and among your own. You do not need to speak English to work, shop, or be a power broker. In fact, if you live anywhere near Calle Ocho, you can go to a Cuban doctor and fill your prescription at the local *botica* (drugstore), eat Cuban food at a Cuban restaurant, run a Hispanic Five Hundred business, buy groceries at a Cuban market, and get your hair done by a Cuban beautician next to where a Cuban mechanic is fixing your Japanese or German car. You can even be buried in a cemetery filled with Cubans within walking distance of a Cuban president's grave. Calle Ocho is, as Senator Díaz-Balart commented, "the cultural heart of the Cuban community" in Dade County and, indeed, the United States.

An Overview of the Campaigns and the Candidates

In the course of this investigation, we followed seven campaigns in Precincts 562 and 575 through three election cycles—the primary elections, held on September 2; the runoffs on October 2; and the general election held on November 2. The candidates vied for seats at all levels of government—with a congressional district, the governor's mansion, three county commission seats, and two state legislative races up for grabs. The Latino community in Miami, most notably, the Cubans, gave the added push that propelled most of their candidates to victory while offering too little support too late in the campaigns of others.

In this project, we closely followed twelve candidates running for seven offices at four levels of government (governor, member of Congress, three candidates for the Dade County Commission, and two for the Florida House of Representatives) (see Table 7.2). As we will indicate, the level of competition varied from campaign to campaign. We report on the most competitive races. In the first primary, we report on the state legislative races in Districts 113 and 114 and three Dade County Commission races (Districts One, Two, and Three). In the October primary runoff, we report on the county commission races in Districts One and Two. In the general election, we return to state legislative District 114 and report on the Florida gubernatorial race.

The Outcomes of the Races

The congressional race was noncompetitive and we only touch on it briefly. Ileana Ros-Lehtinen, the favorite daughter of the Cuban community and further proof that the *exiliados* have done well for

TABLE 7.2 Electoral Results from Precincts 562 and 575 in the 1990 Florida General Elections

	Primary		Runoff		General	
	Precinct 562	Precinct 575	Precinct 562	Precinct 575	Precinct 562	Precinct 575
Race and Candidate	%	%	%	%	%	%
Governor						
John Davis (R)	3.58	2.83				
Warren H. Folks (R)	1.19	1.30				
Marlene Howard (R)	3.34	1.52				
Anthony Martin (R)	4.06	4.79				
Bob Martínez (R)	87.80	89.59			71.62	69.68
*Lawton Chiles (D)	79.36	73.60			28.37	30.31
Bill Nelson (D)	20.63	26.38				
Congressional District 18						
*Ileana Ros-Lehtinen (R)					90.24	88.11
Bernard Anscher (D)					9.75	11.88
Dade County Commission District One						
*Mary Collins	57.14	56.68	87.83	88.82		
Betty Ferguson	16.30	19.78	12.56	11.71		
Murray Sisselman	26.63	23.53				
Dade County Commission District Two						
*Alex Penelas	27.96	27.76	38.39	33.95		
Jorge Valdés	44.07	46.67	61.60	66.04		
Raymundo Barrios	9.81	8.51				
Severino Kennedy	5.00	6.13				
Margaret Pulles	13.15	10.90				
Dade County Commission District Three						
Barbara Carey	27.09	32.29				
*Arthur Teele	72.90	67.76				
State Representative District 113						
Estanislao Carballo (R)	16.74					
William Chávez (R)	14.18					
*Luis Morse (R)	69.06					
State Representative District 114						
Tomás Borell (R)		20.95				
Alejandro Díaz (R)		30.66				
*Bruce Hoffman (R)		48.38				81.16
Fran Bohnsack (D)		55.64				18.83
Mark J. Wolff (D)		44.35				
*Winner						

Source: Authors' compilations.

themselves, handily won her re-election bid. She represents the 18th congressional district, once the stronghold of the late Claude Pepper. Affectionately referred to as "Ileanita," this darling of the Cuban media was constantly pictured conducting official Washington business or with family in tow. There was no question at the polls or in the Cuban community about whom their loyalties rested with. As one researcher observed at the Smathers Center after a Ros-Lehtinen rally:

> After distributing the [Ros-Lehtinen] leaflets, the people left and Luz, the director of the center, went to the microphone and talked to them about Ileana. She told them that Ileana was very good. "We all love her a lot and we're going to give all our support. Isn't that true?" To this, everyone clapped and I heard several of them saying: "Yes. We love her a lot." "She is very good." "She is Cuban, we have to help her." After this I went to talk to Luz. . . . I asked her if being Cuban influenced that opinion and she told me: "Of course, she is one of us."

Candidate after candidate tried to capture some of this enthusiasm, but this gushing approval was not always forthcoming. Then-governor Bob Martínez tried to cash in on his distant Latino ties, but even his whirlwind sweep through South Florida and Calle Ocho did little to breathe life into his ailing campaign. As a Cuban man in his sixties said at the polls, "I am Cuban but I voted for Chiles—Martínez is a good-for-nothing."

Mary Collins, who won the seat for county commission District One, relied heavily on the Cuban community, appearing at all the well-known Cuban restaurants and cafeterias, receiving backing from prominent Cuban politicians. Arthur Teele, who won county commission District Three, also worked the Cuban community to his advantage. His strategy succeeded. In a paradox that can only happen in a place like Miami, Cubans voted for this non-Cuban black while blacks failed to throw their support to him.

Bruce Hoffman, who won re-election for state legislative District 114, and Luis Morse, who won for legislative District 113, used their ties and enthusiastic support at the Smathers Center to assure their places in the "Cuban Caucus" in Tallahassee.

Finally, one of the most hard-fought battles occurred between Alex Penelas and Jorge Valdés, two Cubans pitted against each other for the county commission District Two seat. In all the other races that we followed, the candidates exploited some kind of obvious ethnic or political advantage to win the Cuban vote. In contrast, this race featured a generational angle: Penelas was the young blood challenging the old guard Valdés. This campaign contrasted the exile politics of the old with the domestic agenda of the new Cuban Americans, who were to stay. The race that ensued was quite telling not only of the candidates but of the changing nature of the Cuban community, as we will describe.

The First Primary

Statehouse District 113

The northern portion of the neighborhood, Precinct 562, was represented in the state senate by Lincoln Díaz-Balart (District 34) and in the statehouse by Luis Morse (District 113). Both of these men were born in Cuba and were two of the ten Cuban American state legislators from Dade County. Both readily admitted that they would not be in office were it not for the ethnic solidarity of the Cuban vote. Díaz-Balart was a Democrat until 1985, when he recognized that, to represent District 34, he had to be a Republican.

Estanislao Carballo and Willy Chávez, two Cubans, challenged Morse in the Republican primary. At the polls, a woman declared to one researcher, "I, as a Cuban, vote for Cubans. Everyone in my building is going to vote for Morse because he is the best."

The *Miami Herald* reported the day after the primaries that "[other Cuban American candidates] and Luis Morse of Little Havana all had comfortable leads in their primaries. None has opponents in the general elections in November" (September 5, 1990: 1B). On the same day, *El Nuevo Herald* quoted Morse thanking his Little Havana constituency: "I am very thankful to the Little Havana voters. I've worked hard for them and this is the result. I haven't promised them the moon, only what I've achieved, and the voters supported that" (September 5, 1990: 7A).

In a later interview, Morse said to our investigator: "I live here. I don't live in Westchester and come into my office. I can walk here from my house. I eat lunch in the area and people are always talking to me. Telling me their problems. I know what concerns them and I try to help."

Morse's opponents, Carballo and Chávez, directed their message to the Cuban community, but it was hard for them to pose a threat to last year's chairman of the Cuban Caucus. Campaign posters for the two of them abounded in the neighborhood and all along Calle Ocho. Each sent mailings to the Cuban community and each made the obligatory appearance at the Cuban radio stations. During one of our visits to a neighborhood restaurant, a political discussion between patrons concluded with one saying, "I hope that Chávez wins. He is the best candidate, but really, I don't think he has a chance." Morse received 70 percent of the vote in District 113 (*Miami Herald* [September 5, 1990: 2B]). In Precinct 562, he received 69 percent of the vote. He faced no Democratic opposition in the November general elections.

Statehouse District 114

The primary election cycle also generated activity in the southern portion of our neighborhood. Precinct 575 formed part of District 114, which Bruce Hoffman represented in the statehouse. Hoffman was the only non-Latin Republican in the Dade County delegation. In the primaries, he faced opposition from two Cuban Americans: Alex Díaz and Tomás Borell. Of the two, Díaz proved to be the stronger challenger. As a young Cuban American, he felt prepared to represent both Cubans and Anglos in the district and went directly to both constituencies. We found his campaign signs in public places and on numerous lawns and storefronts.

Hoffman, as the incumbent, had gained a reputation with the elderly in the Cuban community as a "good Republican." They saw him as someone who cared for them, and he made frequent appearances in the Little Havana area. His mailouts in Spanish differed from those in English. While the English-language brochures showed a map of District 114, the Spanish version pictured him with popular political figures Ileana Ros-Lehtinen and Mario Díaz-Balart (brother of state senator Lincoln Díaz-Balart, and himself a state representative), and listed the endorsements of members of the Dade County Republican delegation. In addition, he scheduled nightly door-to-door walks throughout the Cuban-dominated precinct. His Cuban campaign assistant accompanied him during these walks, which he considered the best way to reach his constituents.

Hoffman's approach did not go unrewarded. He won 48.48 percent of the votes cast in Precinct 575 while Alex Díaz obtained 30.66 percent and Tomás Borell 20.99 percent. Hoffman advanced to the general election with 52.91 percent of the Republican vote in his district.

Dade County Commission

The countywide election for metropolitan Dade County's Commission emphasized the strength of a unified Cuban voting bloc. As a general rule, candidates who captured a large majority of the Cuban vote won the election, especially if they also enjoyed support from other ethnic groups. Those who chose to ignore the Cubans, the Cubans overlooked at the polls. Thanks to such calculations, a black candidate who wooed the Cuban vote unseated a black incumbent who received much support from the black community.

All three races deepened the racial rift among Dade County's communities as they pitted Cuban against Cuban and black against black. The *Miami Herald* called it "a dizzying cacophony of claims and counterclaims orchestrated by media gurus whose battle cries resemble a cheerleader's: Attack, attack, attack. Deny, deny, deny" (September 2, 1990: 1B). A server at a local cafeteria expressed her dismay at the candidates: "I'm disillusioned, sick and tired . . . [the contenders] attack each other like dogs."

The three primary races our project followed featured negative campaign tactics. Candidates for the county commission seemingly went to any extreme to discredit their opponent. In an article entitled "Candidates Go for Jugular with Ads," the *Miami Herald* (September 2, 1990: 1B) described one such ad:

> He's a shadowy figure, racing across unnamed streets and into anonymous buildings clutching a briefcase in one hand, a portable phone in the other, gold bracelet gleaming from his wrist.
>   This, the television announcer warns us, is the true Arthur Teele, candidate for the Metro Commission. This is the carpetbagger, the big-business pawn, the lobbyist, tax deadbeat, financial trickster—in sum, "The Great Pretender."

County Commission District Three. Barbara Carey, the eleven-year veteran of the county commission and holder of Dade's Third District seat, the traditionally "black" seat, was trying to hold fast to her base. "During 11 years as Dade's only countywide black elected official, Barbara Carey considered herself a champion for the disadvantaged, a tireless advocate for blacks, a voice for everyone from immigrants to inner-city children" (*Miami Herald* [September 6, 1990: 1B]).

The black community considered her opponent, Arthur Teele, an outsider. Teele, a black Republican, had led the U.S. Urban Mass Transportation Administration in Washington and was a partner in one of Coconut Grove's blue-chip law firms. He did not qualify as a spokesperson in the eyes of the Miami black community. As Teele said, "[W]e felt that the only place we could not beat Commissioner Carey was in the black community. She put most of her resources in one place and I didn't" (*Miami Herald* [September 6, 1990: 1B/4B]).

Speaking often at *comedores*, Teele devoted much of his campaign to offsetting the 2-1 lead that, according to the *Miami Herald*, Carey enjoyed early in the race. Luz Rodríguez, director of the Smathers

Center, said that Teele had "them [*los viejitos*—the elderly] in the palm of his hand." She went on to say that his was one of the two campaigns that she could remember where Cubans turned out en masse for a non-Cuban. "He made the effort. He recognized the importance of the Cubans and that went over real well with our people." The *Miami Herald* (September 6, 1990: 4B) described Teele's efforts in this way:

> Teele pumped more than $55,000 into Spanish-language advertisements, much of it accusing Carey of misusing her position to save her business. . . . [Miriam] Alonso [an outspoken Miami Commissioner] carried Teele's message to Spanish-language radio shows and heralded him to her anti-Communist constituents as a decorated war veteran. "He was projected as a friend of the Cuban community," Alonso said. "Many of the things he believed in were important to us. I think he is perceived as a person who could build bridges. She [Carey] gave the impression of an incumbent who had lost control of what she was doing."

Teele won two of every three Cuban votes while losing four out of every five votes from the black community. In Precincts 562 and 575, Teele received 72.90 percent and 67.76 percent, respectively, while Carey received only 27.09 percent in Precinct 562 and 32.29 percent of Precinct 575. Unlike the candidates in the two other county commission races, Teele won an outright majority countywide and did not face a runoff.

County Commission District One. The race for the First District seat again showcased the value of Cuban electoral power. Mary Collins, a non-Latin white, pursued the Cuban vote even more aggressively than did Teele. She made frequent appearances at Cuban radio stations and tried to speak Spanish; the Radio Mambi moderator repeatedly described her as a "good Republican." She displayed her signs prominently throughout the Calle Ocho area and she did little to disguise her affiliation to the Republican party, even though the elections were nonpartisan. Collins received 57.14 percent of Precinct 562 and 56.68 percent of Precinct 575's votes, which helped her advance to the runoffs.

Betty Ferguson, a black Democrat, entered the contest for the First District as the front-runner, thanks to support from her party, community groups, and a narrow loss in 1986 to the retiring commissioner. She made no direct appeal to the Cuban community during the primaries, and claims made on Cuban radio that she was a supporter and "personal friend" of Jesse Jackson hurt her electoral standing. She won 16.30 percent of Precinct 562 and 19.78 percent of Precinct 575's votes.

The third candidate, Murray Sisselman, limited his presence in the

Cuban community to signs that read, "Vote por Sisselman Sí. . . Sí . . . Sí", yet he made a better showing than Ferguson in Precincts 562 and 575, winning 26.63 percent and 23.53 percent, respectively. Even though Sisselman got more votes than Ferguson in the Little Havana area, Ferguson advanced to the runoffs spurred on by her wins in other parts of the district.

County Commission District Two. The top contenders in the race for Metro-Dade's District Two commission seat, Alex Penelas and Jorge "George" Valdés, both belonged to Miami's Cuban community. Valdés, fifty, had been the first Cuban American to sit on the county commission. Appointed to fill a vacancy in 1981, a year later he won the open election for the District Two seat. Penelas, a clean-cut twenty-eight-year-old graduate of the University of Miami School of Law, was a practicing lawyer who had recently won re-election to the city commission of the fourth-largest city in Florida, Hialeah. Two Cuban-born candidates, Severino Kennedy and Raymundo Barrios, and Margaret Pulles, a non-Latin white, also joined the race but received little support.

More than any other race, this one emphasized the *Cubanía* of each of the contenders and reinforced the notion of the "Cuban" seat on the commission. At the polling stations, the voters had a few things to say about both Valdés and Penelas, along with the primaries in general. One man wearing a *guayabera* plastered with Morse stickers told a researcher not to vote for Valdés because he was "a crook. He has two houses in Miami Beach and a yacht, too! I know. I know him." Another voter supported Valdés, after a fashion, because "at least we know him, having been there nine years. Better a known bad than an unknown good."

Penelas won 27.96 percent of Precinct 562 and 27.76 percent of Precinct 575's votes, but received overwhelming support from the Anglo community and finished first overall. Powered by the Cuban vote, Valdés entered the runoff in second place, winning 44.07 percent of Precinct 562 and 46.67 percent of Precinct 575's votes. The runoff forced these two candidates into a head-to-head competition.

First Primary Exit Polls

While our exit polls showed support for the candidates based on their ethnic origins, community interactions revealed an ambivalence toward what one individual characterized as "unimportant elections." The field notes of one of our researchers capture the complex feelings that community members expressed about the elections.

"We have to put in Latino kids. They're good kids, honest," said a heavy-set Cuban man who greeted and was greeted in return by several people during our conversation. He had been living in the United States for 30 years, 18 of them in the neighborhood.

Today I went to the voting Precinct 575 . . . Coral Gate Park . . . There were not many people coming to vote. I got the feeling that there was not much interest, although the fact that I was there at midday could account for that. Out of the 15 people that I managed to interview, 12 were . . . at least over 65. A van from the Little Havana Activities and Nutrition Center came, bringing 4 people to vote (all women). "Tom" Borell appeared for a few minutes and left and Alex Díaz came too, but stayed longer so I had a chance to talk to him and observe the way he introduced himself to voters: "Alejandro Díaz, *Republicano, Cubano.*" . . . A lot of the people that I interviewed did not seem to be very aware of the candidates' positions on certain issues; for example, when asked why they voted for a certain person . . . "because he/she is Latin."

October Runoff Elections

County Commission District Two

In the primaries, both Valdés and Penelas had served the Cuban community an appetizer spiced with allegations of corruption, lying, and cheating. Our interviews suggest that the Cuban community resented that these candidates had waged a dirty campaign. One exit poll interviewee expressed dissatisfaction with how the campaigns had been run: "Politics have gotten very bad here, too aggressive. They shouldn't be able to take contributions . . . the millions spent to insult each other."

For the runoffs, both candidates seemed to understand that the Cubans would not stomach a rerun of similar strategies. Penelas announced days after his victory that he would soften his attacks on Valdés's integrity and voting record before the October 2 runoff election. For his part, Valdés pledged a "very positive" campaign, still spotlighting Penelas's record but no longer branding him a liar or hypocrite (*Miami Herald* [September 7, 1990]).

Valdés depended on the Cuban vote in the runoff to carry him back to the county commission, since his prodevelopment votes had made him unpalatable to the Anglo voters. Valdés was also assured of receiving the black support, and Penelas assumed he would be the favorite of the Anglos. Yet, both directed the bulk of their strategies toward Cuban voters.

Valdés attacked early by continuing to question the "Cubanness" of

Penelas. In radio spots he linked Penelas to Anglo and anti-Cuban interests:

> In 1988, the controversial Charles Dusseau grabbed the post that Miriam Alonso was winning in the county commission. Now Dusseau wants to grab the post of our commissioner Jorge Valdés, the only Cuban on the county commission, and impose on us the candidate of the *Miami Herald*, Alexander Penelas. We should go out to defend the only Cuban commissioner that has represented us in the county since 1981: Jorge Valdés. Vote. Participate. Decide. Defend Jorge Valdés with your vote.

The *Miami Herald* (September 27, 1990: 1B) ran the following story about the new radio ads: "Little Havana's radio airwaves began spitting venom this week . . . It's a street fight only Spanish-speakers can witness. That's the way the two candidates want it—Valdés to pump up Hispanic turnout next Tuesday, Penelas to contain the damage."

Valdés's ads attempted to brand Penelas a *"Cubano arrepentido,"* a Cuban who rejects his heritage. In numerous radio appearances he proposed that, in Miami, no "real" Cuban would go anywhere near the *Miami Herald* (which endorsed Penelas), Charles Dusseau (a county commissioner who defeated a popular Cuban candidate), or Gerald Richman (who lost the race for U.S. representative to Ros-Lehtinen in 1989). Even when he was not making the accusations, other radio commentators presented his "more Cuban than thou" attacks on Penelas: "Penelas has been embraced by the *Miami Herald* just like Richman and Gordon . . . [he] has started with commercials to prove that he is Cuban—[he] appears eating rice and beans and roast beef . . . how ridiculous."

Penelas's ad depicting him and members of his family sharing a traditional Cuban meal were aired in Spanish and were designed "to neutralize Valdés-fed doubts about his loyalty to traditional Cuban values . . . 'The purpose here was to make sure the voters understand Alex Penelas has very Cuban roots'" (*Miami Herald* [September 22, 1990: 1B]). In no other city in the United States would such a statement make sense but in Miami. Valdés was born in Cuba, but Penelas was born in the United States; thus, the burden of proof that Penelas was worthy of the Cuban vote was on him. In one of her many appearances on Cuban radio, Penelas's mother reprimanded Valdés for disputing her son's *Cubanía* by saying, "It is not his fault that he was born in this country."

It made electoral sense for Valdés to question Penelas's *Cubanía* because it turned attention away from his own record, which might have been unpalatable to the Cuban community. The September 27

Miami Herald editorial endorsing Penelas said that "Mr. Valdés has two opponents: Mr. Penelas and his own voting record. He's cast approval votes on countless requests from business interests and developers with which he was involved. He was also, until just this year, one of the commission's most consistent pro-development votes."

Penelas spoke to the audience at the Smathers Center on September 24. During his brief presentation, he emphasized the two issues that always play well in the elderly Cuban community: transportation and taxes. The report of one of our researchers at the site conveys the message of his brief presentation:

> Alex Penelas, running for Dade County Commission, district two, was supposed to arrive at 11 A.M., but he got there half an hour late. A man followed him around giving out brochures with some facts about the candidate. Alex soon took the microphone and spoke to all the old people in a Spanish that was not as bad as I had expected. He said he was 28 years old, graduated U.M. [University of Miami] law school and emphasized that his parents were Cuban which got a good response.

> He said that he stood for more food, more living, and more hospital service for them. "I'm going to fight for you!" he bellowed and went on to say, "Some may think that I am too young, but I will adopt you as my grandparents and I want you all to adopt me as your grandchild!" He also said, "I am very proud of my Cuban roots," and he finished off by reminding them to vote October 2nd county wide and to tell their friends and family to vote for their "grandchild". . . quite a few people got up to shake his hand. He also got a huge round of applause.

Immediately after his speech, another researcher talked to five people in the audience, all of whom liked the fact that Penelas came to talk to them. Three of them (two men and one woman) were skeptical of his youth. They preferred Valdés and thought Penelas was too young and inexperienced.

The last days of campaigning were nasty and ethnically divisive. Both candidates misled the Cubans in emotional radio spots that the *Miami Herald* called "a panoply of dirty tricks that would have made Richard Nixon blush" (October 2, 1990).

On election day, each candidate spent a large portion of the day airing last-minute appeals over Cuban radio. The beseeching tone of this Penelas message was common: "Everyone go out to vote . . . There are four hours left and we can make the difference. Other communities are going out massively and maybe our candidates and our philosophy will be defeated. May God bless you all and please, go out to vote," (WAQI, Radio Mambi [October 2, 1990]).

During our exit polling, we found that the voters in our

neighborhood had listened to the campaign and faithfully justified their votes using the words of their candidates. Those who voted for Penelas spoke generally of Valdés's lack of activity during his tenure as commissioner and of the desire to inject new blood into the system. Some also mentioned the hypocritical approach Valdés used to attack the *Cubanía* of Penelas: "Valdés remembers that he's Cuban every four years. When he had to support the Cuban [Suárez] for the mayoral race, he supported the foreigner [Ferre]."

Valdés supporters were equally as supportive of their candidate. One thirty-year-old man offered a typical response about his support for Valdés: "Jorge Valdés's record of service seems to me to be very good and aside from my thinking that he should be much more in contact with the public, which is what has been missing . . . [he] should go more often to the radio, etc., etc., I think he's done a pretty good job. [He] is a good person that has helped the Cubans."

During our election night exit poll, Valdés and Penelas split the votes of the forty people interviewed. Countywide, however, Penelas was the victor, but he did not win the majority of the Cuban vote. He managed to attract only 38 percent of the Latin vote while Valdés garnered 62 percent. Penelas did not even win in Hialeah, where he sat on the city commission. He won on the strength of the Anglo vote, of which he received a significant 85 percent. "He [Valdés] tried to wrap himself in a Cuban flag and run an emotional campaign," said a volunteer for Penelas at his victory party, "and it backfired."

County Commission District One

Mary Collins defeated Betty Ferguson for the other position on the Metro Dade Commission. Collins continued her pursuit of the Cuban vote through radio and by increasing her visibility in the Cuban community. We often saw her at the Versailles restaurant talking to customers and shaking hands. In fact, on the night before the runoff, both she and Penelas sat surrounded by supporters at different corners of the restaurant. The Collins table was unique because of the multiethnic Latinos who surrounded her. Several white Latins as well as mulattoes and blacks, men and women, were engaged in light conversation while Collins talked on her portable phone.

The campaign for county commission District One did not reach the fever pitch of the Penelas/Valdés contest within the Cuban community. Ferguson's base was the African American and liberal Anglo communities and she did very little to convince the Cuban community to vote for her. We saw only one of her campaign posters in our neighborhood, and she was the only candidate who did not direct an appeal to the Cuban radio audience, even through an interpreter. When mentioned, she was negatively compared to Collins, who was often endorsed as a "good Republican." On one occasion, she was disparaged on the radio and in the newspaper as a supporter and friend of Jesse Jackson.

Collins continued her aggressive campaigning in the Cuban community, at least once standing on a Little Havana street corner with her campaign supporters and banners, and carried her Republican credentials and her Cuban supporters to the Cuban radio stations. On election night, when it became obvious that she would be the winner, she called Radio Mambi to thank the station for its support ("You all have been wonderful") and to reiterate her support for the Cuban community: "One of the first things I am going to do is to do all that I can to expand the affirmative action contracting policies of the County to include Hispanics, not just blacks. So that Hispanics can benefit from equal employment in this way."

She clearly understood the value of nurturing the Cuban vote. As a result, she won 88 percent of the Latin vote in the runoffs, the largest Hispanic bloc received by any of the candidates during this election period. Ferguson received 13 percent.

General Election

Statehouse District 114

After the dust cleared from the runoff election cycle, Hoffman and Bohnsack increased their activities in the race for state representative. Both waged aggressive campaigns to attract the Anglo voters of the South Miami area by conducting weekend walks, posting signs, and sending mailings with antitax (Hoffman) or antigun (Bohnsack) messages. Neither paid much attention to the Cuban community. Hoffman felt certain that he would win the Cuban, mostly Republican, vote. The nightly walks he had held in the Little Havana neighborhood during the primaries were shifted to the Anglo portion of the district. He continued to nurture his Smathers Center group by taking them a turkey at Thanksgiving and dropping in at other times to say hello. His two steadiest campaign volunteers, who spoke no English, were residents of the Smathers Center and he hosted a coffee at the home of the director of the organization that ran the *comedores*. With passable Spanish he attacked his opponent on Cuban radio, emphasizing his interpretation of her view on taxes and abortion. While he did send out Spanish direct mail campaign literature during the primaries, he did not do so for the general elections.

The Hoffman strategy, as interpreted by the Bohnsack headquarters, was heavily dependent on capturing the Cuban vote. And Bohnsack did not challenge him on Cuban turf. Instead, she concentrated on the non-Cuban community. "The battleground isn't the Cubans, but the independents, the non-Hispanic Republicans and Democrats who would change party lines according to issues," said Bohnsack's campaign manager in an interview with us. Ironically, the Bohnsack campaign also did not spend much time nurturing the black vote, although for a different reason. As the campaign manager stated, "[We] didn't do [much] in the black area, they are solid too."

While Bohnsack's campaign manager emphasized that media coverage was important to the campaign, the campaign targeted "swing voters" in campaign advertisements. They concentrated on WIOD, an English all-news radio station, WTMI, and a classical music station, the stations swing voters were most likely to listen to, according to Arbitron ratings. The campaign had no strategy to target the "Spanish media" (Spanish, not Cuban).

Bohnsack lost the election by 112 votes. In victory, Bruce Hoffman considered the Cuban vote critical. He was emphatic during our interview with him the day after the election: "Look at the numbers. If the Cubans had not supported me, I would not be here." He received 81 percent of the Cuban vote in our precinct. Hoffman also benefited from his district's falling within the larger 18th Congressional District, represented by Ileana Ros-Lehtinen. Her landslide victory surprised no one, and neither did her last-minute appeals on Cuban radio directed at turning out the Cuban vote for Cuban candidates.

Gubernatorial Race

One race that did not turn out as many Cubans wished was for governor. Preliminary results indicated that, not only did Martínez lose the statehouse, he also lost 32 percent of the Latin vote in Dade County. While this result still shows a great deal of support for the Republican agenda, it marks a significant decline from the 1986 elections, when Martínez lost only 17 percent of the Latin vote in Dade County. Even in the same election cycle, popular Cuban Republicans received considerably more support from the Latin population. Ros-Lehtinen, for example, garnered 90 percent in Precinct 562, 88 percent in Precinct 575, and 60 percent countywide.

As Jeb Bush stated to our researchers, the Little Havana area was considered to be the base of the support for the incumbent. In 1986, he received 83 percent of the Cuban (Latin) vote in Dade County, but his record had been spotty. In spite of frequent trips to South Florida, with noticeable improvement in his Spanish-speaking abilities and the support of Republican leaders in the Cuban community, the Martínez bandwagon was considerably less euphoric during these elections.

Martínez had sinned in various ways. He introduced a new service tax that was eventually withdrawn because of massive opposition, but he fiddled enough with other taxing mechanisms to make the attacks on his high-tax agenda credible. He also instituted a lottery that had many Little Havana businesspeople upset. Financial problems during his administration also prompted the disbanding of the Governor's Hispanic Affairs Committee, a move that was not well received in the Cuban community in South Florida. Martínez did not have overwhelming support from the Cuban legislators and, in fact, one of them candidly claimed to have worked secretly for Bill Nelson during the Democratic primaries.

The discontent reached the streets. Prominent Cubans, Republicans and Democrats alike, openly supported Chiles against Martínez. An organization called Republicans for Chiles sent a car with amplifiers down Calle Ocho daily decrying Martinez's poor record and encouraging the mostly Republican audiences to vote for the "best man, not the party." The Little Havana business association hosted an antilottery/anti-Martínez meeting at an Eighth Street banquet hall to complain about how the lottery was damaging the Little Havana community. Alberto Gutman, the state representative from the East Little Havana area, spoke at the event and introduced his plan to restructure the profit distribution of the system. Lawton Chiles was also there, taking advantage of the opportunity to direct his campaign at the Little Havana business community.

On the radio, the same kind of opposition was heard, followed by claims that, if something was not done, "[y]ou're going to see a lot of businesses close in the coming months." This fear of closing businesses posed a direct threat to the Cuban enclave economy of Little Havana and resonated throughout the community.

The support of Cuban radio announcers, who still claimed that, despite his faults, Martínez was a Latin and a Republican who deserved the support of the Cuban community, counterbalanced the grass-roots disenchantment with Martínez. He had paid attention to Cuban Miami, claimed one popular announcer, while Chiles had not even "shown his face" in Little Havana: "I think . . . that the Chiles campaign, until now, has not made any effort to reach the Cuban community. Have they thought that the Cuban vote is unimportant? . . . For example, Martínez has come to Radio Mambí on various occasions. Chiles has not come."

Chiles *did* recognize the importance of the Cuban vote. He developed a generic Cuban message that he and his supporters delivered at the antilottery event and at other events organized by Cuban Americans for Chiles, a campaign organization active in the community during the last two weeks before the election. An excerpt from this message follows:

> Lawton Chiles has been a friend of this community for many years. As a state senator, he defended the right of Cuban professionals to work, helping remove the bureaucratic obstacles that hindered their professional certification. Thanks to his efforts, many of our doctors, lawyers and pharmacists were able to practice their professions with great success. In those times, it was not considered fashionable among politicians to court the Cuban vote. Nevertheless, in the words of Chiles, obtaining the certifications "was the right thing to do."

Issues

Politicians addressed the issues in the Cuban community that they could exploit to mobilize voters, obtain endorsements, and gather votes. Topics that concerned the business owners, such as the lottery and a bond issue, got attention. The elderly voiced concerns about transportation, which received lip service. Crime, drugs, and homosexuality were staple issues, as was the fear of "de-Cubanization." One researcher described her experience while exit polling:

> On the whole, though, most of the voters were not well-informed either about the immediate issues up for a vote or about the candidates. More than half of the people I spoke to voted for the candidates in their party, even if they were not familiar with the names. The sense that "If they are Republican, they must be good" was echoed over and over again. There were only two people that I spoke with that were Democrats, but even they did not favor the tax increase. One woman declared, "As a Cuban, I vote for Cubans!"

Lottery

The restructuring of the lottery was a theme that interested a portion of the community and eventually found an echo in campaigns, especially within the Cuban business community, one of the major intermediary organizations between Cubans and politicians. Calle Ocho business leaders opposed the lottery. Posters depicting a flamingo inside a red circle and crossed out with a red line dotted Calle Ocho business fronts. Chiles, in his campaign for governor, and Gutman, another Cuban representative of Little Havana, picked up the businesses' distaste on this issue and used it to their advantage. The following passage reveals the passion this issue elicited:

> The Lotto keeps functioning as a vacuum or a many-headed monster, that takes the money from the pockets of the people, and that is why the people don't have money to purchase the bare necessities. Just in Dade alone, in 1989, Lotto sold exactly $365,111,715 (that is, almost four hundred million dollars) that left Dade, in CASH . . . If there is no money, there is no consumption; without consumption, there is no production; if there is no production, there will be too many employees, in other words, unemployment increases and with that, robberies, crime, and corruption. (*Trinchera Hispanoamericana* [November 5, 1990])

Campaign promises about the lottery closely paralleled the community's concerns and entailed restructuring the amount allotted in prizes as well as allowing vendors to make higher profits from ticket sales.

Taxes

Similarly, the theme of taxes reverberated throughout many campaigns. Morse, Hoffman, and Díaz-Balart considered taxes and associated budgetary issues of prime importance to their Cuban constituents. One exit poll interviewer expressed in her notes that

> the topics on everyone's minds [at the Koubek Center polls] were taxes, drugs, and crime. Taxes were mentioned because a bond issue was being voted on that was opposed by many residents [of Little Havana]. One disgruntled voter said that he worked for the city and knew that the taxes weren't really needed. He said that too much money was being wasted on salaries that were undeserved. Another voter felt there were already enough taxes . . . an overwhelming number of the voters I spoke to were Republican, with very few Democrats. I found it interesting though, that many of these staunch Republicans mentioned the need for increased government or city funding for education and social projects for seniors or the poor.

Politicians remained silent on the issue of a sales tax increase from 6 to 7 percent to be invested in transportation. Some supporters claimed that the tax would free up money for other government functions in dire need of funding, such as Jackson Memorial Hospital's Trauma Center, police protection, transportation for the disabled, drug rehabilitation, and parks and museums. The Cuban radio media voiced vehement opposition to the tax primarily by questioning the trustworthiness of elected officials to use the tax for its intended purpose. Some politicians even spoke against all taxes, as did Estanislao Carballo in an ad that read "Voting friend: My first law as representative will be: no new taxes for retirees that have no income other than their limited retirement. Paying new taxes is equivalent to destroying their budgets." In the end, the Cuban community voted 70-30 against the penny increase.

Transportation

While most candidates mentioned the importance of transportation problems, none expressed the type of concern voiced by some of the community residents. The Smathers patrons, particularly, considered transportation the most important problem for politicians to address. An excerpt from our field notes conveys this sentiment:

> Luis [a volunteer at the Hoffman campaign] said that the worst problem in the community was transportation. He went on to say, "I heard that we're going to get rid of the 'mini-buses.' This takes away jobs from the people [the drivers]. That's their life! Who is going to employ them—the city? Luis was really upset about the transportation situation and went on "The bus system is terrible. I know many people and many elders that use the buses."

Crime and Drugs

Crime and drugs, often articulated as one problem in the Calle Ocho area, was recognized by Lincoln Díaz-Balart as an important issue, although he did not believe that the Little Havana area suffered more than other sections of town from criminal behavior. "The perception," he noted, "is that it is a problem but in reality, I am sure that it is no more of a problem, or even less of one, than in other sections of town."

De-Cubanization and the Miami Herald

A hidden issue throughout all of the campaigns was that of anti-Cuban forces within the community working against the interests of the Cuban population. This fear of anti-Cuban sentiments or de-Cubanization could be seen in the Penelas/Valdés campaign and was consistently manifested in the Cuban media's attitude toward the *Miami Herald*. The *Herald* is a consistent target of criticism within the Cuban community; it is perceived to be too politically liberal and anti-Cuban, dedicated to undermining the hard-won political gains of the Cuban community and in particular of officeholders who are Cuban or sympathize with the Cuban "cause." From a public discussion at the Miami City Commission comes this description of the *Herald*: "That newspaper factory that generates hatred among our community

(Applause, Shouting) putting [*sic*] blacks against Cubans, Jewish against Cubans, because they are using that cynical slogan 'divide and conquer' . . . to squash this working community that has made out of Miami a central point of the United States."

Fueling the criticism, the *Herald* ran articles on corruption and conflict of interest allegations that indicted state representative Al Gutman, Hialeah mayor Raúl Martínez, and acting Hialeah mayor Julio Martínez, to mention a few. Further, the newspaper's editorial board switched its endorsement from Mary Collins to Betty Ferguson after the primaries, giving ammunition to the sectors that accused the *Herald* of threatening the interests of the Cuban community.

The Latin Quarter

The Latin Quarter, a city program designed to redevelop forty blocks of the four hundred-block Little Havana area, began to receive much attention in the Cuban radio and newspapers during the electoral campaigns, although it was not an issue in any campaign. The project resurrected the fear of de-Cubanizing the Little Havana area and led to a very heated discussion in the Miami City Commission meeting of October 18, a discussion that was echoed in the streets of Little Havana for days afterwards.

Alberto González, the polemic producer of "La Mogolla" (The Mess), a satirical Cuban radio show, led the way in this fight. According to an article in the *Miami Herald*, "González explained that the use of the name Latin Quarter is graver than what some might suppose because, `Cuban nationality is being injured.' So grave, he emphasized, that it can reach the point of having 'deaths.'" Others echoed González's sentiments at the City of Miami Hall on the night of October 18, 1990. A researcher present at the meeting wrote the following:

> I arrived at 7 P.M. and a capacity crowd was already inside the Commission chambers. The overflow crowd was outside, and they were a mob scene unto themselves. . . . The debate was being broadcast over loud-speakers . . . there were police everywhere.
>
> Everyone was wearing a "La Mogolla" pin. . . . There were lots of riled-up old people everywhere, waving Cuban flags frantically.
>
> As I pushed my way into the chambers, people were standing and chanting, yelling and raising their fists. There were makeshift protest signs all over the place.
>
> I ran into two men, Pedro and Angel, [who were] holding signs right at the

door. . . . The signs read "We belong to the *La Mogolla* club and we're here because they want to change the name of Little Havana." This was the impression everyone was under. . . [as they would break] into chants of "Latin Quarter, No Va, No Va y No Va."

While the fear of de-Cubanization was a real one among the people in the street, we found that the Latin Quarter issue was a flash point that had little heat. Representative Morse considered it "extremely overblown" and with little true community significance. According to the president of the Latin Quarter organization, who was Cuban, businesspeople supported the development potential of the project. Yet, some non-businesspeople continued to doubt the intentions of the project. As one opponent said, "if the *Miami Herald* defends the Latin Quarter, it is because the Latin Quarter is not good for this community."

Poverty: The Hidden Issue

Abortion, taxes, crime, drugs, the lottery, and the ever-increasing anxiety of de-Cubanization were all issues that stirred the Cuban community. Issues that were actually addressed by politicians are another story. One issue that is seldom reported but that promises to have far-reaching effects is the increasing poverty of Latinos in Miami. On the radio show "La Antena de la Calle Ocho" for September 26, 1990, at 9:00 A.M., the commentator blared, "The commissioners approved spending sixteen million dollars in . . . housing for the poor? No. For a tennis stadium!"

At the organizational level, leaders of community service organizations voiced some concerns that contributed to our understanding of the community. The Little Havana Community Center serves low-income people and its organizational viability depends on state and federal support. Of particular concern to the center is the increasing poverty of Latinos in Miami. This is a problem that is not commonly associated with Cubans, says the director of the organization, but that is a significant one nevertheless: "There is poverty and even homelessness among Cubans too, but the extended family networks hide the problem. . . . Also, the Cubans are the least likely to come to the shelters for help. I don't know if it is *orgullo* [pride] or what."

When a researcher first approached the director to find out more about this issue,

She then said, matter-of-factly, "Oh you're doing it on the homeless?" Since this was not something we had discussed as a problem in the community, I was caught a bit off guard. If there is a homeless problem, this community has done a great job of keeping it quiet . . . the community has a wide range of services, among them: help with utility payments, giving out food, giving out clothes, resettling of refugees, skills training twice a week, thrift shop and filling out of forms for aid.

Another researcher's notes from an interview with the director reveal the following: "She told me 90 percent of the people that [use the organization] are Latin, many of whom are women who have many children and no husband to support them." She predicted that the issue would increase in importance as more immigrants came into the Little Havana area. At that point, she said, "people will be surprised at the number of Cubans that need help too." During one of our visits to the Center, she was attempting to place seventeen homeless Cubans who had been sent back to Miami from their work assignments cutting sugarcane in Belle Glades.

The director of the Little Havana Activities Center, the organization that directs the *comedores*, was also concerned about social service dollars available to serve her twenty-four thousand constituents. Her concerns, however, had a peculiar twist. Most of her constituents were active Republicans, some of whom lived in the districts of Democrats who were strong supporters of her program. She told us: "Sometimes it's a problem. It is hard to explain that the folks from the other party are the ones that support their meal services just as much or more than Republicans. Of course it helps that here the Republicans are Cubans and they always support us."

She turned this potentially problematic situation to the advantage of the organization by turning her *viejitos* into the most potent political machine in the Little Havana area. She made sure that her constituents were politically aware of the candidates who supported the agency. During this campaign she held a reception for Bruce Hoffman and was present when Governor Martínez visited her Smathers Center on election day. Yet, Democrats considered her one of them. It was hard to detect the humor in the voice of those who referred to her as the "Empress of Little Havana."

Conclusion

There remains little doubt that, in the 1990 election cycle, the Cuban American voter played a key role in the victories and defeats of the candidates. Those politicians lucky enough to be Cuban American relied heavily on the ethnic vote; for their part, the non-Cubans in the running had to develop a Cuban strategy to ensure success.

The role of both the Republican and the Democratic parties remains unclear as we explore the political behavior of Cuban Americans. While most Cubans are Republicans, some Cuban American politicians claim that the Republican party has not done much for them. The Democratic Party simultaneously recognizes the need to foster a presence in the Cuban American community but has been unable to take advantage of grass-roots dissatisfaction with the Republican party.

At the state and local levels, the Republican party has benefited from Cuban Republican registration, established on the basis of the foreign policy position of Republican presidents. This has helped secure a position of parity in state politics. As one Cuban American state representative said "The Democrats might not be doing much for the Cubans but let me tell you, neither are the Republicans. They do not support us as much as we think they should. They don't like the idea of Cubans running the party down here and they resent our independence." This independence is reflected in the liberal voting patterns of a large portion of the Cuban delegation as well as in the bipartisan coalitions established by the "Cuban Caucus."

One measure of a liberal voting pattern is the tendency of the Cuban American politicians to favor labor issues. In 1989, members of the Cuban Caucus voted for labor-supported legislation over 81 percent of the time. This represents a record 5 percent better than Democrats statewide and 21 percent better than Republicans.

In the 1990 election period, Cuban American voters articulated a series of issues that reflected the growing importance of domestic issues to the Cuban community. Taxes, abortion, and homelessness were examples of the emerging immigrant voice of the exile community. While Cubans are often considered to be antagonistic to African American agendas in county politics, this election cycle also saw Cubans responding favorably to an African American candidate and propelling him to victory. Teele, the winner, was a conservative Republican who made it known to the Cuban community that his efforts and money would go toward campaigning in the Cuban community.

Another point in the continuum of transition is the split Cuban vote between Penelas and Valdés. Valdés, as the old guard Cuban politician, emphasized *Cubanía* as a necessary qualification to represent the Cuban community and managed to win the majority of the Cuban vote but did not win enough to be re-elected. Penelas, for his part, was the "crossover" candidate and sustained a sizable portion of the Cuban vote while appealing to the non-Latin white voters as well.

A future focus of analysis for the Cuban American experience in Dade County will be to chart the shift from an exile or refugee agenda to an immigrant agenda. Research by Grenier (1992) on the rise of the Cuban American labor movement in Dade County highlights the development of an immigrant agenda among the Cuban American working class. The continued incorporation of Cuban Americans into the political, economic, and social structure of the United States will establish the parameters of the Cuban American immigrant agenda.

Notes

1. The term "Miami" can have a number of referents. Most narrowly, it means the city of Miami. It can also refer to the broader urban area encompassed by Dade County or the Miami SMSA. In some cases, it even loosely refers to all of South Florida, including Fort Lauderdale and farther up Florida's east coast. In this chapter, we use Miami to refer to the contiguous urban area in Dade County.

2. Arbitron says it's so/Radio Mambi is number one/In all South Florida/Because it's Cuban and sincere/Because it tells you the truth/Radio Mambi is number one.

3. Literature on Miami is increasing rapidly. Banfield (1965) discusses Miami as it was in the 1950s and the early 1960s. Mohl, in a number of insightful articles, focuses on ethnic relations (1983, 1985, 1986, 1987*a* and *b*, 1988, 1989, 1990). Warren, Stack and Corbett (1986) and Stack and Warren (1986) discuss contemporary ethnic politics, while Porter and Dunn (1984) examine racial tensions, as does the U.S. Commission on Civil Rights (1982). Wilbanks (1984) addresses one of Miami's most headline-gathering issues, homicide. In 1987, three popular books also appeared: Allman, Didion, and Rieff. Grenier and Stepick (1992) contains a collection of articles on Cubans, Haitians, African Americans, politics, language, and organized labor.

4. Cuban success has been attributed to different factors, including cultural and psychological variables, human capital, state support, and the peculiar nature of Miami's Cuban economic community, that is, the ethnic enclave. Our own interpretation does not necessarily contradict these others, but we do de-emphasize cultural and psychological variables.

5. See Peterson and Maidique (1986). Although they ostensibly argue that Cubans have a peculiarly entrepreneurial mentality, their data are equally if not more consistent with our hypothesis that structural factors and human capital are the crucial variables in creating successful Cuban American business leaders.

6. Incidentally, the Cuban American members of Miami's power structure appear to have similar class, economic, and even sectorial interests as the local non-Cubans and elites in other cities. They are substantial business leaders or executives, especially in real estate and development (see Stepick et al. 1990).

References

Allman, T. D. 1987. *Miami, City of the Future*. New York: Atlantic Monthly Press.
Banfield, Edward C. 1965. *Big City Politics*. New York: Random House.

Borjas, G. J. 1982. "The Earnings of Male Hispanic Immigrants in the United States." *Industrial and Labor Relations Review* 35: 343–353.

Clark, Juan. 1975. "The Exodus from Revolutionary Cuba (1959–1974): A Sociological Analysis." Ph.D. dissertation, University of Florida.

Díaz, G. M., ed. 1980. *Evaluation and Identification of Policy Issues in the Cuban Community*. Miami: Cuban National Planning Council.

Díaz-Briquets, Sergio. 1984. "Cuban-Owned Businesses in the United States." *Cuban Studies* 14 (2) (Summer): 57–68.

Didion, Joan. 1987. *Miami*. New York: Simon and Schuster.

Garreau, Joel. 1981. *The Nine Nations of North America*. New York: Houghton Mifflin.

Grenier, Guillermo J. 1990. "Ethnic Solidarity and the Cuban American Labor Movement in Dade County." *Cuban Studies* 20: 29–48.

———. 1992. "The Cuban-American Labor Movement in Dade County: An Emerging Immigrant Working Class." In Guillermo Grenier and Alex Stepick III, eds., *Miami Now! Immigration, Ethnicity, and Social Change*, pp. 133–159. Gainesville: University Presses of Florida.

Grenier, Guillermo, and Alex Stepick III, eds. 1992. *Miami Now! Immigration, Ethnicity, and Social Change*. Gainesville: University Presses of Florida.

Jorge, Antonio, and Raúl Moncarz. 1980. "The Cuban Entrepreneur and the Economic Development of the Miami SMSA." Unpublished, Department of Economics, Florida International University.

Levine, Barry B. 1985. "The Capital of Latin America." *Wilson Quarterly* (Winter): 46–73.

Luytjes, Jan. 1983. *International Banking in South Florida: Analysis and Trends*. Miami: Bureau of Business Research, Florida International University. April.

Massud-Piloto, Félix Roberto. 1988. *With Open Arms: Cuban Migration to the United States*. Totowa, N.J.: Roman and Littlefield.

Mohl, Raymond. 1983. "Miami: The Ethnic Cauldron." In R. M. Bernard and B. R. Rice, eds., *Sunbelt Cities: Politics and Growth since World War II*, pp. 67–72. Austin: University of Texas Press.

———. 1985. "The Origins of Miami's Liberty City." *Florida Environmental and Urban Issues* 4: 9–12.

———. 1986. "The Politics of Ethnicity in Contemporary Miami." *Migration World* 14 (3).

———. 1987a. "Ethnic Politics in Miami, 1960–86." In Randall M. Miller and George E. Pozzetta, eds., *Ethnicity in the Urban South*. Westport, Conn.: Greenwood Press.

———. 1987b. "Trouble in Paradise: Race and Housing in Miami during the New Deal Era." *Prologue: Journal of the National Archives* 19 (Spring): 7–21.

———. 1988. "Immigration through the Port of Miami." In M. Mark Stolarik, ed., *Forgotten Doors: The Other Ports of Entry to the United States*, pp. 81–98. Philadelphia: Balch Institute Press.

———. 1989. "Shadows in the Sunshine: Race and Ethnicity in Miami." *Tequesta: Journal of the Historical Association of Southern Florida* 49: 39–40.

————. 1990. "On the Edge: Blacks and Hispanics in Metropolitan Miami since 1959." *Florida Historical Quarterly* (July): 37–56.

Pedraza-Bailey, Silvia. 1985. *Political and Economic Migrants in America: Cubans and Mexicans.* Austin: University of Texas Press.

Pérez, Lisandro. 1985. "The Cuban Population of the United States: The Results of the 1980 U.S. Census of Population." *Cuban Studies* 15 (2) (Summer): 1–18.

————. 1986. "Immigrant Economic Adjustment and Family Organization: The Cuban Success Story Reexamined." *International Migration Review* 20 (1): 4–20.

Peterson, Mark F., and Modesto A. Maidique. 1986. "Success Patterns of the Leading Cuban-American Enterprises." WP 86–104, Research Report Series, Innovation and Entrepreneurship Institute, School of Business Administration, University of Miami.

Porter, Bruce, and Marvin Dunn. 1984. *The Miami Riot of 1980: Crossing the Bounds.* Lexington: Lexington Books.

Portes, Alejandro, and Robert Bach. 1985. *Latin Journey.* Berkeley and Los Angeles: University of California Press.

Rich, Cynthia Jo. 1974. "Pondering the Future: Miami's Cubans after 15 Years." *Race Relations Reporter* (November 5).

Rieff, David. 1987. *Going to Miami: Exiles, Tourists, and Refugees in the New America.* Boston: Little Brown.

Rogg, E. M., and R. S. Cooney. 1980. *Adaptation and Adjustment of Cubans: West New York, New Jersey.* New York: Hispanic Research Center.

Stack, John F., and Christopher L. Warren. 1986. "Ethnic Conflict and the Internationalization of Miami." In Carlos Alvarez, ed., *Migration and Ethnicity: A Global Perspective.* Westport, Conn.: Greenwood Press.

Stepick, Alex; Max Castro; Marvin Dunn; and Guillermo Grenier. 1990. "Changing Relations among Newcomers and Established Residents: The Case of Miami, Final Report." Miami: Center for Labor Research and Studies, Florida International University. February.

U.S. Bureau of the Census. 1986. *Census of Minority Business Enterprises.* Washington, D.C.: U.S. Government Printing Office.

U.S. Commission on Civil Rights. 1982. "Confronting Racial Isolation in Miami." Washington, D.C.: U.S. Government Printing Office.

Warren, Christopher L.; John F. Stack; and John G. Corbett. 1986. "Minority Mobilization in an International City: Rivalry and Conflict in Miami." *PS: Political Science and Politics* 19 (3) (Summer): 626–634.

Wilbanks, William. 1984. *Murder in Miami.* Lanham, Md.: University Press of America.

About the Contributors

Rodolfo O. de la Garza is Mike Hogg Professor of Community Affairs and professor of government at the University of Texas at Austin. In addition to serving as principal investigator of the five-city study of Latinos and the 1990 elections, he has directed several other projects on Latino political participation. Most important among these is the Latino National Political Survey.

Martha Menchaca is an assistant professor of anthropology at the University of Texas at Austin. Her research focuses on Mexican Americans in the Southwest and ethnographic methods.

Louis DeSipio is a doctoral candidate in the Department of Government at the University of Texas at Austin. His research focuses on ethnic politics and immigrant incorporation. During the 1993–1994 school year, he will serve as a visiting assistant professor at Wellesley College.

New York Research Site

Anneris Goris is a member of the faculty of the Puerto Rican and Black Studies Program at Hunter College. She is a founder of the City University Dominican Research Center.

Pedro Pedraza is director of the Language and Education Task Force at the Centro de Estudios Puertorriqueños at Hunter College, with which he has been affiliated for the past twenty years. His research interests include ethnographic studies of the Puerto Rican community and of language use.

Houston Research Site

Néstor P. Rodríguez is an associate professor of sociology at the University of Houston. He specializes in research on immigration and community development.

Noelia Elizondo, David Mena, Ricardo Rojas, Adolfo Vásquez, and *Frank Yeverino* assisted Dr. Rodríguez with the project research.

Chicago Research Site

John Valadez is an assistant professor in the Department of Race and Ethnic Studies at the University of Wisconsin-Whitewater. His scholarly interests include ethnic politics and Chicago politics.

Los Angeles Research Site

Harry Pachon is Kenan Professor of Politics at Pitzer College and national director of the National Association of Latino Elected Officials (NALEO) Educational Fund. He is coauthor of *Latinos in the United States* (with Joan Moore) and has performed extensive analysis of the impact of noncitizenship on Latino political empowerment.

Lourdes Argüelles is an associate professor of sociology and women's studies at Pitzer College.

Rafael González managed the Boyle Heights project and coordinated the student interns.

Miami Research Site

Guillermo J. Grenier is chair of the Department of Sociology and Anthropology and director of the Florida Center for Labor Research and Studies at Florida International University. His research interests focus on labor issues. His most recent book is *Miami Now! Immigration, Ethnicity, and Social Change*.

Fabiana Invernizzi, Linda Salup, and *Jorge Schmidt* assisted Dr. Grenier with the project research.

Index